On Taking Offence

T0355197

Studies in Feminist Philosophy is designed to showcase cutting-edge monographs and collections that display the full range of feminist approaches to philosophy, that push feminist thought in important new directions, and that display the outstanding quality of feminist philosophical thought.

STUDIES IN FEMINIST PHILOSOPHY

Published in the Series:

Ecological Thinking: The Politics of Epistemic Location
Lorraine Code

Self Transformations: Foucault, Ethics, and Normalized Bodies
Cressida J. Heyes

Family Bonds: Genealogies of Race and Gender
Ellen K. Feder

Moral Understandings: A Feminist Study in Ethics, Second Edition
Margaret Urban Walker

The Moral Skeptic
Anita M. Superson

"You've Changed": Sex Reassignment and Personal Identity
Edited by Laurie J. Shrage

Dancing with Iris: The Philosophy of Iris Marion Young
Edited by Ann Ferguson and Mechthild Nagel

Philosophy of Science after Feminism
Janet A. Kourany

Shifting Ground: Knowledge and Reality, Transgression and Trustworthiness
Naomi Scheman

The Metaphysics of Gender
Charlotte Witt

Unpopular Privacy: What Must We Hide?
Anita L. Allen

Adaptive Preferences and Women's Empowerment
Serene Khader ,

Minimizing Marriage: Marriage, Morality, and the Law
Elizabeth Brake

Out from the Shadows: Analytic Feminist Contributions to Traditional Philosophy
Edited by Sharon L. Crasnow and Anita M. Superson

The Epistemology of Resistance: Gender and Racial Oppression, Epistemic Injustice, and Resistant Imaginations
José Medina

Simone de Beauvoir and the Politics of Ambiguity
Sonia Kruks

Identities and Freedom: Feminist Theory between Power and Connection
Allison Weir

Vulnerability: New Essays in Ethics and Feminist Philosophy
Edited by Catriona Mackenzie, Wendy Rogers, and Susan Dodds

Sovereign Masculinity: Gender Lessons from the War on Terror
Bonnie Mann

Autonomy, Oppression, and Gender
Edited by Andrea Veltman and Mark Piper

Our Faithfulness to the Past: Essays on the Ethics and Politics of Memory
Sue Campbell
Edited by Christine M. Koggel and Rockney Jacobsen

The Physiology of Sexist and Racist Oppression
Shannon Sullivan

Disorientation and Moral Life
Ami Harbin

The Wrong of Injustice: Dehumanization and Its Role in Feminist Philosophy
Mari Mikkola

Beyond Speech: Pornography and Analytic Feminist Philosophy
Mari Mikkola

Differences: Between Beauvoir and Irigaray
Edited by Emily Anne Parker and Anne van Leeuwen

Categories We Live By
Ásta

Equal Citizenship and Public Reason
Christie Hartley and Lori Watson

Decolonizing Universalism: A Transnational Feminist Ethic
Serene J. Khader

Women's Activism, Feminism, and Social Justice
Margaret A. McLaren

Being Born: Birth and Philosophy
Alison Stone

Theories of the Flesh: Latinx and Latin American Feminisms, Transformation, and Resistance
Edited by Andrea J. Pitts, Mariana Ortega, and José Medina

Elemental Difference and the Climate of the Body
Emily Anne Parker

Racial Climates, Ecological Indifference: An Ecointersectional Approach
Nancy Tuana

On Taking Offence
Emily McTernan

On Taking Offence

EMILY McTERNAN

OXFORD
UNIVERSITY PRESS

OXFORD
UNIVERSITY PRESS

Oxford University Press is a department of the University of Oxford. It furthers the University's objective of excellence in research, scholarship, and education by publishing worldwide. Oxford is a registered trade mark of Oxford University Press in the UK and certain other countries.

Published in the United States of America by Oxford University Press 198 Madison Avenue, New York, NY 10016, United States of America.

© Oxford University Press 2023

Library of Congress Cataloging-in-Publication Data
Names: McTernan, Emily, author.
Title: On taking offence / Emily McTernan.
Description: New York, NY, United States of America : Oxford University Press, [2023] | Includes bibliographical references and index.
Identifiers: LCCN 2022054525 (print) | LCCN 2022054526 (ebook) | ISBN 9780197613108 (paperback) | ISBN 9780197613092 (hardback) | ISBN 9780197613122 (epub)
Subjects: LCSH: Bullying. | Harassment. | Courtesy. | Offenses against the person.
Classification: LCC BF637 .B85 M384 2023 (print) | LCC BF637 .B85 (ebook) | DDC 177—dc23/eng/20230301
LC record available at https://lccn.loc.gov/2022054525
LC ebook record available at https://lccn.loc.gov/2022054526

DOI: 10.1093/oso/9780197613092.001.0001

Paperback printed by Marquis Book Printing, Canada
Hardback printed by Bridgeport National Bindery, Inc., United States of America

For C, F & I

Contents

Acknowledgements   ix

Introduction: The defence of offence   1

1. Taking offence: An emotion reconsidered   9
    1.1. Philosophers on taking offence   10
    1.2. An analysis of taking offence   12
    1.3. Distinguishing offence   20
    1.4. Rethinking offence: Domestic, not catastrophic   25
    1.5. The limits to taking offence   27
    1.6. Towards a defence: From victimhood to social standing   32

2. What taking offence does   36
    2.1. Social standing and the role of social norms   37
    2.2. Taking offence and reinforcing norms   42
    2.3. Taking offence and renegotiating norms   46
    2.4. In defence of negotiating social norms   53
    2.5. On negotiating through offence   55

3. Do sweat the small stuff: On the nature and significance
    of social standing   62
    3.1. Between excess and deficiency   63
    3.2. Social standing as an equal, part I: Why the 'small stuff' matters   66
    3.3. Social standing as an equal, part II: The power to set the terms   74
    3.4. Defending the significance of affronts   79
    3.5. Resisting by taking offence   83

4. The limits of justified offence: On anger, intent, and uptake   86
    4.1. Anger, offence, and the act   87
    4.2. Contesting offence   93
    4.3. "But I didn't mean it": On intention and blame   95
    4.4. "But *that's* not offensive": Disagreement and the offensive   100
    4.5. When offence lacks uptake   108

5. Only joking!: On the offensiveness of humour   114
    5.1. Theories of humour and the offensive   117
    5.2. Some linguistics of jokes   123
    5.3. How offensive jokes function   126
    5.4. The riskiness of humour   129

6. A corrective civic virtue: Weighing the costs and benefits of offence   132
  6.1. Offence as a civic virtue: Arguments from equality and civility   134
  6.2. The costs of offence to the offending party   140
  6.3. Justifying the costs of offence   146
  6.4. Burdens on the offended   153

7. A social approach, our lives online, and the social emotions   158
  7.1. A regulatory turn   160
  7.2. Taking offence online   165
  7.3. The social emotions beyond offence   171

Bibliography   175
Index   189

Acknowledgements

I am deeply grateful to the participants in a wonderfully constructive book manuscript workshop: Hallvard Lillehammer, Simon Caney, Simon Kirchin, Chris Mills, David Axelsen, Jennifer Page, and especially to Katy Wells for organising the event. I am also very grateful to Jennifer Page and two anonymous referees for OUP for their insightful and helpful comments on the full manuscript. I am grateful for insightful comments from many others, including Cheshire Calhoun, Jeffrey Howard, Stephen John, Christopher Nathan, Christian Schemmel, Fabian Schuppert, Philip Seargeant, Robert Simpson, Kai Spiekermann, Manuel Vargas, Joey Whitfield, and audiences at LSE, UCL, UCSD, and the Universities of Bayreuth, Cardiff, Copenhagen, Duke, Durham, Leeds, Manchester, Northumbria, Oxford, Pompeu Fabra, Reading, York, Wake Forest, Warwick, and Zurich.

A Leverhulme Research Fellowship provided the time to write up this book and funding from a Templeton Religion Trust grant, "The Beacon Project," gave me the space to first form its ideas. I am grateful to both funders. Chapter 1 has been published as "Taking Offense: An emotion reconsidered", *Philosophy & Public Affairs,* 49(2) (2021), 179–208, with the exception of the brief discussion of blame which appears in Chapter 4. I am grateful to the associate editors for helping me to improve the piece.

Above all, thanks are owed to my partner for doing more than his fair share during the start of our pandemic-era childcare fiasco, without which the book would have ground to a halt. Thanks also to the University of Warwick, my partner's employer, for the excellent family friendly policies which made that possible.

Introduction

The defence of offence

The subject of this book is an emotion that philosophers have largely overlooked and yet one that is the target of intense public debate: taking offence. This is an everyday emotion, often taken at small and ordinary slights of daily life. However, especially in an era of public criticism of those deemed too easily offended, it is easy to overlook offence's significance and social value. This book aims to rehabilitate taking offence.

Rather than addressing the question familiar from jurisprudence of whether the state ought to regulate offensive behaviour, I ask the philosophically neglected questions of whether we ought to take offence, when, and within what limits.[1] My focus is the offended, and not those who cause offence. Against the widespread popular perception of offence as a civic vice, this book defends taking offence as often morally appropriate and socially important.[2] Within societies marred by hierarchies of unequal social standing, and when taken by those who face systematic attributions of lower social standing, an inclination to take offence at the right things and to the right degree is a civic virtue.

This is a defence not of public shaming, which I argue has little connection to taking offence properly understood, but of the often small in scale offence that ought to be recognisable from our ordinary social interactions. I do not adopt Joel Feinberg's influential account of offence in jurisprudence, on which any disliked state resented and wrongfully caused in us counts, from disgust to annoyance.[3] Instead, this book examines an everyday but

---

[1] The question of regulation is a familiar one in legal and political philosophy following Feinberg, *Offense to Others*; recently extending to university regulations in Sher, "Taking Offense"; Waldron, "Taking Offense: A Reply". One exception, but one criticising those who take offence, is Barrow, "On the duty of not taking offence".

[2] As examples of this popular view see Campbell & Manning, *The Rise of Victimhood Culture*; Collini, *That's Offensive!*; Lukianoff & Haidt, *The Coddling of the American Mind*; Fox, "Generation Snowflake", *'I Find That Offensive!'*.

[3] Feinberg, *Offense to Others*, ch. 1. Nor his notion of 'profound offense', ch. 9.

On Taking Offence. Emily McTernan, Oxford University Press. © Oxford University Press 2023. DOI: 10.1093/oso/9780197613092.003.0001

distinctive emotion of offence, the same as that studied by linguists and sociologists; the emotion that you might experience, to varying degrees, when someone pushes in front of you in a queue, puts you down in front of your boss, ignores your outstretched hand rather than shaking it, or makes a sexist joke.[4] That is, the offence we take when someone offers an affront to our social standing as we perceive it. While sometimes offence pushes us to break off relations with the offending party, often our resulting estrangement is expressed through acts as small and temporary as a raised eyebrow or pointedly not laughing at a joke.

What this book defends, as morally and politically significant, is the way in which taking offence negotiates social standing in everyday contexts. A central idea is that to take offence is to *resist* another's affront to one's standing and, in so doing, to stand up for one's social standing and, often, that of one's group. By taking offence, one marks another's act as ignoring, diminishing, or attacking one's standing. Where one's offence is visible, one also communicates one's rejection of the affront to others. Further, to take offence can be a way to negotiate the background social norms that enable us to express and shape social standing.[5] Sometimes, taking offence sanctions those who transgress against shared norms: to offend others is often socially costly. At other times, taking offence makes a bid to change the shared norms around respectful treatment, either by contesting the social meaning of the norm, say, as expressing disrespect where it had been seen as respectful treatment, or by proposing a new norm, through acting as if there is a different norm in play that another transgresses against. As a result, the book argues that taking offence can be an act of direct insubordination against a social hierarchy.[6] When taken by those deemed to have less social standing within that hierarchy, and especially when taken at a familiar affront to standing, to be offended is to resist the ordinary patterning of socially unequal relations.

---

[4] For linguistics studies on impoliteness and causing offence see, for instance, Brown & Levison, *Politeness*; Culpepper, *Impoliteness*. The same emphasis on studying causing offence, rather than taking it as is found in philosophy has been noted: for instance, in Haugh, "Impoliteness and taking offence in initial interactions"; Tayebi, "Why do people take offence". Exceptions include these articles and Tagg et al., *Taking Offence on Social Media*.

[5] Here, I draw on Buss, "Appearing respectful" and Calhoun, "The virtue of civility". See Chapter 2 for a discussion.

[6] Bell characterises one feminist defence of negative emotions as being on the grounds that they are 'emotional insubordination', in "A woman's scorn", p.81. Taking offence, I will argue, is a particularly direct act of insubordination, directly disputing the ranking, rather than, say, revealing that one ranks oneself as equal enough to others to be angry at them: see, for instance, Spelman, "Anger and insubordination".

This book's defence has been written against a background of widespread popular criticism of the inclination to take offence, prompted by a perception of a rise of a so-called culture of taking offence. Along with social commentators, a handful of psychologists and sociologists have entered the fray, offering criticisms of the social function of offence and depictions of the resulting harms to individuals and society. These harms range from undermining people's mental health to the suppression of free speech and of open debate where people fear to incur the wrath of the easily offended.[7] Commonly, these criticisms also characterise the inclination to take offence as a weakness; for instance, as a product of oversensitivity or as a retreat into 'victimhood'.[8]

However, offence is an emotion ripe for reappraisal. It is not offence-taking in general that provokes such critiques: the concern is not with, say, the way men react in the bar when someone bumps into them and spills their drink, nor with the British custom of tutting at queue jumpers. Rather, the critiques target challenges to the inequalities and injustices of everyday interactions. For instance, some target campaigns against microaggressions; those every day and apparently innocuous "degradations, and put-downs" that are experienced by members of oppressed or systematically disadvantaged groups.[9] Others tackle protests against offensive jokes and codes of conduct that seek to limit which jokes are acceptable.[10] Still others consider revisions to dating norms in the light of the 'MeToo' movement begun by Tarana Burke.[11] Yet there is something familiar about these criticisms to social justice movements: they bring to mind the charge of 'political correctness' that was prevalent in the 1990s.[12] The charge of oversensitivity, of paying too much attention to the *details* of social interactions, is not novel; rather, it recurs in the reception of claims to greater social equality.

---

[7] Largely in popular writings, with examples in note 2, but also in some academic journals; see, for instance, Campbell & Manning, "Microaggressions and moral cultures"; Haidt, "The unwisest idea on campus".

[8] On victimhood, see Campbell & Manning, "Microaggressions and moral cultures" and "The new millennial 'morality'"; Fox, "Generation snowflake" and "*I Find That Offensive!*".

[9] This is Chester Pierce's characterisation, who coined the term, see, for instance, "Stress analogs of racism and sexism", at p.281. For examples of critiques with this focus see Haidt, "The unwisest idea on campus"; Lukianoff & Haidt, *The Coddling of the American Mind*; Campbell & Manning, "Microaggressions and moral cultures".

[10] See Campbell & Manning, "Microaggressions and moral cultures", which discusses 'ethnic jokes', at p. 707; Lukianoff & Haidt, "The coddling of the American Mind".

[11] Collective, "Nous défendons une liberté".

[12] A parallel also noted in Aly & Simpson, "Political correctness gone viral".

This book, then, offers a re-characterisation of offence, both from the broad disliked states of legal philosophy and from the popular view of offence as hurt feelings or playing the victim. Instead, to take offence is to defend one's standing.[13] Mine is a normative not empirical project: I argue not that offence is taken in any particular social movements but, rather, that under the right conditions to take offence would be a fitting, morally justified, and even desirable way to resist injustice. In offering this argument, I aim to undermine the force of one objection to movements for social justice; namely, that they involve 'mere' offence-taking. Sometimes, these criticisms mischaracterise anger and other motivations *as* offence. At other times, however, these criticisms wrongly dismiss offence, rather than seeing it as one way to resist injustice.

This defence has also been written in the context of increasing interest in the emotions within moral and political philosophy. A range of emotions have been the subjects of moral appraisal and, especially within feminist philosophy, defences of their significance in contexts of injustice, including anger, bitterness, forgiveness, and resentment.[14] I am proposing that we add offence to that list. Yet one might resist the inclusion of offence amongst the emotions deemed morally and politically significant. The others are moral emotions, in being fundamentally concerned with moral issues, or invoking moral concepts like blame.[15] By contrast, on my analysis offence is an emotion fundamentally concerned with features of our social interactions and assessments of our social standing. One might think that this renders a moral defence of taking offence inapt.[16] The small-scale features of social

---

[13] By discussing offence in terms of standing, it might seem that I align offence with honour. There is some connection between honour and the book's focus on affronts to one's standing as a social equal, in that taking offence at an affront to one's standing as an equal sometimes concerns what it is to be an honourable or upstanding member of a group. Being treated as less than a social equal is sometimes expressed through challenges to one's standing as an honourable or upstanding member of a society, and failing to be treated as an upstanding member of some particular group can, at times, be a manifestation of one's general lack of equal social standing. But there is more to our standing, and so more to taking offence, than these issues of honour. This book tackles the connections between offence, honour, and pride only in passing.

[14] As examples, see, on anger, Frye, *The Politics of Reality;* Lorde, "The uses of anger"; Bell, "Anger, virtue, and oppression"; Cherry, "The errors and limitations of our "anger-evaluating" ways"; against anger, see Nussbaum, *Anger and Forgiveness.* On accusations of bitterness to silence the oppressed and angry, see Campbell, "Being dismissed". On forgiveness and resentment, Murphy, "Forgiveness and resentment"; Walker, *Moral Repair,* ch.4.

[15] For definitions of moral emotions see, for the former, psychologists for whom the category of moral emotion is marked out in terms of what an emotion does within a society, e.g. Haidt, "The moral emotions"; for the latter, see D'Arms and Jacobsen, who state, 'Guilt and anger have been called "moral emotions" precisely because they present their objects in the light of such moral concepts as desert, fault, and responsibility', in "The moralistic fallacy", p. 87.

[16] For instance, Macalester Bell observes that contemporary ethics has paid little attention to questions of status and esteem, in her analysis of another emotion fundamentally concerned with

interactions at which we take offence, from another's failing to shake our hand to inappropriate jokes, may appear to have particularly little moral or political relevance.

Against this, I argue that the details of ordinary social interactions make up the fabric of a life lived as a social equal or unequal. In so doing, I seek to broaden the current debate over emotions with its focus on anger to include a wider range of emotions with moral and political significance. I also answer an abiding challenge to relational egalitarians: namely, that they tell us too little about what it is to live as social equals, especially regarding relations amongst citizens rather than relations between state and citizen.[17] The book defends the normative significance of patterns of everyday behaviour as constituting a distinctively social dimension of equality. As a result, my defence of offence will be of that taken at precisely the apparently trivial and small-scale details of social interactions, and so the very form that its opponents find most objectionable.

The book proceeds as follows. In Chapter 1, I offer an analysis of a distinctive emotion of offence, in contrast both to Joel Feinberg's disunified account, where any disliked state resented and wrongfully caused in us counts, and to the abstract account in the philosophy of language on slurs, which gives us little sense of what it is like to feel offended. On my account, offence is taken at affronts to social standing, involves feeling estranged from the person(s) who offers the affront, and results in a tendency towards acts that express one's withdrawal from the offender. I contrast offence to nearby emotions— of anger, pride, disgust, and contempt—to outline its unusual place as both an other-condemning emotion and an emotion of self-assessment. This analysis has implications not only for how we conceptualise offence but also for what we think about those who take it. Offence tends to be a smaller-scale and a more everyday emotion than those who make claims about its threat to society suppose, and one that is ripe for moral reassessment.

In Chapter 2, I analyse the social function of taking offence: when I take offence at an affront to my standing, what can this emotion do? Against popular opinion, which regards those prone to offence as embracing victimhood

standing: contempt. In *Hard Feelings*, p. 99. Or take Nussbaum's criticism of anger concerned with status injury, *Anger and Forgiveness*.

[17] Jonathan Wolff labels this vagueness an 'abiding problem' in his "Social equality and social inequality", pp. 213-5. See also Fourie, "What is social equality", p. 109; Lippert- Rasmussen, *Relational Egalitarianism*; Schuppert, "Non-domination, non-alienation and social equality", p. 444.

or displaying emotional fragility, I argue that those who take offence defend their standing. Expanding on Cheshire Calhoun and Sarah Buss's defences of the moral and political significance of manners and civility, I first examine how the social norms that let us convey our respect and equal regard to others are also one way in which social hierarchies are constructed through the pattern of our social interactions. Second, I defend taking offence on the grounds that it is an appropriate way to stand up for one's social standing and that of one's group through negotiating social norms. My task in this chapter is a normative, not a descriptive one. It is to demonstrate that *were* one to take offence as a route to challenging these social norms, then one would have the right target—those social norms—and one would impose the right kinds of costs on those who cause offence; namely, those that usually follow from our transgressing social norms. Third, I justify such a negotiation of social norms against both those sceptical of the role of social norms in our lives and those who would object to the role of offence in particular as a tactic in that negotiation.

However, this account of the social role of offence does not by itself suffice to defend taking offence. For that, one would need to hold that social standing has the kind of significance that justifies taking offence when others ignore, attack, or mistake one's social standing, especially when they do so in small and everyday ways. Chapter 3 defends both the significance of social standing and the desirability of taking offence at affronts to it against a background of social inequality. To do so, I first answer that persistent challenge to relational or social egalitarians that they tell us too little about what it is to live as social equals. I offer an account of the social dimension of the ideal of social equality in terms of five features of the patterns of social interactions between groups, along with the power to negotiate the terms of our interactions. Drawing on feminist defences of the emotions of anger, bitterness, and contempt, I then argue that taking offence is a valuable and distinct way to resist and protest inequality, one justifiable even where it fails to bring about norm change. Where members of one group are commonly attributed less social standing than members of another, taking offence is not only a way to resist that patterning of social relations but also an act of insubordination against a social hierarchy, of value even where it fails to revise the underlying social norms.

The second half of the book explores the scope and strength of this defence of offence. I begin in Chapter 4 by examining the potential limits on when taking offence can be justified in a particular interaction. First, in the face of a common focus on anger as the apt response to injustice, the chapter carves out a space for offence as one way to directly resist to a particular form of injustice. Second, I consider the relation between offence, intent, and blame. One may think that whether taking offence is justified depends on whether an agent intended to offend, or is otherwise culpable for the offending act, but I argue that blame and offence are separate, if sometimes overlapping, social practices. Third, I explore the claim that disagreement over the offensiveness of an act undermines the justification of taking offence but argue that mistakes the social role of taking offence. Finally, I address failures of uptake, considering whether offence could be no longer justified, all things considered, where it is widely mistaken for emotional oversensitivity, or otherwise produces a backlash.

In Chapter 5, I use the book's framework for justifying offence to analyse the relationship between offence and humour. Often, people often take offence at jokes or other forms of humour. Yet the fact that a remark or act was intended as a joke or as humorous is often offered as a reason *not* to take offence. So, the next time that you cause offence, would "but I was joking" be a good response to offer—and be a reason for others to take less offence? Conversely, is there something that explains why humour so often appears offensive? The chapter resolves this tension, exploring the role of humour in sustaining unequal social standing. Jokes and other humorous remarks often do present more serious affronts to standing than would equivalent but non-humorous utterances, on all three of the main theories of humour. But I argue that taking offence can be an effective way to resist the impact of an offensive joke: it can be to dispute that 'we' around here agree with the humour's underlying derogatory propositions, or to protest the discounting of the importance of the norms protecting a group's standing on which the humour of an offensive joke might rely.

Chapter 6 asks whether one might be not only morally justified in taking offence but obligated to do so. I defend a disposition to take offence as a civic virtue, against a background of social hierarchies and at least for those who are subjected to systemic social inequality. First, I offer two arguments for offence as a civic virtue, on the grounds of equality and as a derivative virtue of civility. Second, to make the case for offence as a civic virtue requires defusing a central challenge to any defence of offence: namely, that the costs imposed on the offending parties are excessive or otherwise indefensible. Third, I argue that a disposition to take offence would not be excessively burdensome for the person who cultivates it.

In Chapter 7, I turn to a contemporary issue, of offence taken online and, especially, on social media. First, I contrast the move towards regulation of offensive content to the potentially greater advantages of leaving the dynamics of offence and repair to play out in cases that fall short of hate speech. Second, I argue that while the difference between our online and offline lives is often exaggerated, our practices of offence-taking may translate poorly in online interactions that are publicly visible and that occur between fleetingly connected strangers. The way in which offence might then spiral also reveals the importance of the background of continuing relations and social norms that ordinarily constrain our expressions of offence. Closing, the book points towards the wider significance of social emotions beyond offence within moral and political philosophy.

1

Taking offence

An emotion reconsidered

A stranger in the pub bumps into you spilling your drink and then doesn't apologise, or someone pushes past you to grab a seat on the train. A colleague makes a dismissive remark about your work in front of your boss. A man cat-calls a woman on the street, or wears a T-shirt declaring, 'keep calm, watch lesbians'. One reaction to affronts like these is to take offence. Philosophers have said a great deal about *causing* offence, especially whether we should punish or prevent it, but very little about what is to *take* offence, let alone whether we should.[1] Hitherto the focus of moral and legal philosophy has tended to be the offender, not the offended. Meanwhile, taking offence has captured popular attention, with a multitude of books and opinion pieces condemning 'oversensitive millennials' and 'generation snowflake'.[2] There being offended tends to be characterised, I argue mistakenly, as a kind of emotional upset, borne of oversensitivity or emotional fragility, or as a re-treat into victimhood.[3]

In this chapter, I offer an analysis of what it is to take offence and what doing so is like. On this analysis, a more nuanced and positive appraisal of this emotion becomes possible as compared to its popular reputation. First, I survey the shortfalls of the limited amount that philosophers have said about taking

---

[1] With thanks to Jeremy Waldron for noting this contrast. See, to illustrate, legal philosophy following Feinberg, *Offense to Others*; recently extending to university regulations in Sher, "Taking Offense"; Waldron, "Taking Offense: A Reply". See also philosophical work on slurs, e.g., Anderson & Lepore, "Slurring words"; Popa-Wyatt & Wyatt, "Slurs, roles, and power". The same emphasis on studying causing offence, rather than taking offence, is noted in linguistics, e.g., Haugh, "Impoliteness and taking offence in initial interactions"; Tayebi, "Why do people take offence"; for examinations of politeness, impoliteness and causing offence, see Brown & Levison, *Politeness*; Culpepper, *Impoliteness*.

[2] For instance, Campbell & Manning, "Microaggression and moral cultures" and *The Rise of Victimhood Culture*; Lukianoff & Haidt, *The Coddling of the American Mind*; Fox, "Generation Snowflake".

[3] In particular, see the opening chapter of Fox, *'I Find That Offensive!*. See also the depictions in Campbell & Manning, "Microaggression and moral cultures" and *The Rise of Victimhood Culture*. Within philosophy see Sher's characterisation of offence as hurt feelings, "Taking Offense".

On Taking Offence. Emily McTernan, Oxford University Press. © Oxford University Press 2023.
DOI: 10.1093/oso/9780197613092.003.0002

offence before proposing an alternative analysis. Second, I distinguish offence from nearby emotions, like anger, disgust, and pride. Third, I turn to the
implications for not only for how we conceptualise offence but how we regard
those who take it. On my account, offence tends to be a smaller-scale and more
everyday emotion than those who make claims about its threats to society
may have supposed, and one ripe for a moral reassessment. While offence may
appear excessive, that is most likely only in limited cases: namely, those that
require symbolic withdrawal or proxy forms of estrangement. Further, that appearance of excess may be illusory: at times, grander gestures of offence can be
defended given the distance between the offended and offending parties.

The rest of this book then offers a defence of the value of this emotion,
detailing when it is, and isn't, morally appropriate and socially desirable.
Many of the cases of offence I address below are not ones that I later defend
as valuable. This chapter's central topic is what makes an instance of taking
offence fitting, rather than morally appropriate, or intelligible not defensible,
although I draw out some implications for our moral assessment of those
who take offence.[4]

1.1. Philosophers on taking offence

Taking offence has received relatively little attention from philosophers.
When analysing slurs, philosophers of language consider the pattern in our
offence-taking, such as how it varies when differently situated individuals use
one and the same slur; when the slur is mentioned rather than used; or when
presented with the negation of a slurring sentence.[5] However, their interest is
in conceptualising slurs and not analysing offence, and the resulting notion
of offence is very thin. To illustrate, on one representative account offence is
defined as the 'achieved effect on audience members' of a slur, 'determined in
part by their beliefs and values'.[6] Such depictions tell us little about what it is
like to be offended.

---

[4] For a defence of a sharp distinction between an emotion as fitting, in that it "accurately presents
its object as having certain evaluative features" and as morally appropriate, in that it is the right way to
feel, see D'Arms & Jacobson, "The moralistic fallacy", e.g., p. 65.

[5] E.g., Popa-Wyatt & Wyatt, "Slurs, roles, and power"; Anderson & Lepore, "Slurring words",
pp. 632–635. The pattern of our offence taking is also considered within the philosophy of humour, especially concerning offensive jokes and whether these are, by virtue of being offensive, less
amusing. Chapter 5 examines the relation between offence and humour.

[6] Popa-Wyatt & Wyatt, "Slurs, roles, and power", p. 2881, who state that this account is adapted
from Hom, "Pejoratives", at p. 397.

Likely the most influential account of offence is that offered by Joel Feinberg. On what he terms a strict and narrow sense, offence is any disliked state that I attribute to another's 'wrongful conduct' and for which I resent them.[7] This definition incorporates a wide range of disliked states like disgust, affronts to one's senses, shame, and annoyance.[8] To illustrate, take the breadth of the central examples of Feinberg's discussion: a series of untoward experiences you might have while travelling on a bus, such as someone masturbating next to you; eating a disgusting picnic; or running their fingernails down a slate tablet.[9] On a plausible reading of Feinberg, his 'offence' is taken at nuisances a person cannot easily ignore.[10] However, his is not a depiction of any discrete emotion and nor does it describe what it is like to be offended; rather, any disliked state counts. Given the aim of Feinberg's account that breadth ought not be surprising; he examines what conduct a state might regulate beyond that which causes harm. Yet there is a distinct way that to be offended feels as compared to being annoyed or disgusted. That distinct notion of offence, which I seek to capture in §1.2, is one that should be familiar both from our ordinary experience in navigating social relations and from the popular discussion of a 'culture of taking offence'.

Continuing with those who fail to see offence as distinct, some conflate it with anger.[11] However, one task of this chapter and of this book is to show that would be misleading; indeed, in important respects offence is closer to contempt and pride. Another conflation sometimes found in popular discussion, often more implicitly than explicitly, is to regard being offended as a form of harm, in terms of being an injury to feeling or doing damage to someone's self-esteem.[12] However, while offensive conduct might cause such harm, that

---

[7] Feinberg, *Offense to Others*, p. 2.

[8] *Offense to Others*, ch. 1, especially pp. 1–2; 10–14. Feinberg also offers an account of 'profound offense' that looks to be mostly a mix of moral outrage and disgust at sanctity violations; again, then, one that is disunified and diverse, ch. 9.

[9] *Offense to Others*, pp. 10–14.

[10] Consider Robert Simpson's characterisation of Feinberg's offence as "all subharmful mental states in which the agent's attention is frustratingly 'captured'", in his "Regulating offense, nurturing offense", p. 237.

[11] For example, see Rini, "How to take offense", which, despite its title, discusses anger. Martha Nussbaum's notion of 'status-focused anger' that takes the 'road of status' may appear akin to offence if stripped of the desire for payback, *Anger and Forgiveness*, ch. 2. I discuss this in §1.3.

[12] To illustrate, see some analyses of microaggressions and 'generation snowflake', especially those that focus on 'victimhood', in footnotes 3 and 4, particularly the opening description of school events in Fox, *'I Find That Offensive!'* While legal philosophers often define offence in contrast to being harmed, possible exceptions within the philosophical literature are John Shand, who defines

does not suffice as an account of what offence is. For a start, it fails to capture all the relevant instances. I am not harmed when someone fails to shake my outstretched hand or makes a mildly sexist joke, yet I could be offended.[13] Indeed, I think it is possible that sometimes taking offence, when others back you up on the rightness of your offence, can even be pleasant: feeling like an affirmation of one's standing, rather than constituting a harm.

1.2. An analysis of taking offence

What, then, is it to like to take offence? I start by offering three sets of cases that are likely to provoke offence. What they all share, despite their varying levels of seriousness, is that they are affronts to social standing: the standing we deem ourselves due, that we expect to be respected, recognised, or expressed, through our social interactions.[14]

As paradigm cases of the first set, where our social standing is disregarded, consider a stranger who queue jumps right in front of you, who pushes past you to grab the last seat on the train, or who spills your drink without apologising. Or take a colleague who repeatedly fails to remember your name. In these cases, someone disregards some ordinary token of respect or consideration that we deem ourselves due. Often, such instances cause offence by virtue of violating a widely held social norm of what counts as respectful, polite, or appropriate behaviour, expected from all.[15]

For the second set of cases of direct attacks on one's social standing, consider the man who wears a T-shirt declaring, 'keep calm and watch lesbians!', who waves a banner declaring 'iron my shirt' at a rally for a female politician, burns an American flag, or defaces a bible.[16] Alternatively, suppose a

'personal offence' as "feeling justifiably hurt", "Taking offence", p. 704; and Sher's characterisation of offence as hurt feelings, "Taking offense".

[13] Feinberg also notes the separation of harm and offence, as 'a different sort of thing', *Offense to Others*, at p. 3; and regards his bus cases as not instances of harm, at p. 14.

[14] This is distinct from moral standing, in the sense of being a member of the moral community, and political standing, such as being able to vote, as Chapter 3 defends.

[15] For an account of how socially established rules or norms let us communicate respect, tolerance and consideration, or their absence, see Calhoun, "The virtue of civility"; on the moral importance of manners, Buss, "Appearing respectful".

[16] "Iron my shirts" was a sign held up against Hillary Clinton; for a discussion, see Carlin & Winfrey, "Have you come a long way, baby?" Some of these Feinberg would label profound offences, including flag burning and, perhaps, bible defacing, see his *Offense to Others*, ch. 9. However, I characterise these acts not as felt as 'impersonal', as Feinberg proposes, but personal both in the sense that only

colleague reveals an embarrassing detail about your personal life in front of your boss.

The third set is cases where someone dismisses another or mistakes her social standing in a downwards direction: where person A assumes that person B has less standing than B takes herself to have, or less than B's situation would usually entail that B be attributed, were it not for some confounding feature. To illustrate, suppose that an estate agent talks only to the male companion of his female customer, even though she is the one selling the house. As another instance, take Rebecca Solnit's case of the woman having her own book explained—'mansplained'—to her at a party.[17] A further case would be when academics or doctors who aren't white and/or aren't male often find that their title isn't used, where it is for their white male colleagues.[18] Given the nature of the mistakes made, these instances often amount to indirect attacks on a person's standing.[19] Sometimes, these may be unintentional: the offending party might not mean to target the offended individual; indeed, they may not intend to affront anyone.

Where instances like these do cause offence, that emotion has three defining properties. First, the person who takes offence believes, judges, or perceives that her social standing has been affronted, whether being ignored, diminished, or attacked by the act at which she takes offence. Here, I remain neutral amongst competing conceptions of emotions, for instance, as involving beliefs, judgements or perceptions, as far as is possible given that offence is a complex emotion. The affront is the intentional object of the emotion: that at which the emotion is taken.[20] What counts for whether an individual takes offence is her own perception of her standing and how that standing ought to be manifested in the ways in which others treat and regard her within social interactions of particular kinds, within particular contexts.

those individuals who identify strongly with the nationality or religion in question could take offence and that the act is then experienced as a strike against oneself and one's group. I return to this shortly.

[17] Solnit, *Men Explain Things to Me*, ch. 1. Epistemic injustices are often affronts of this kind, see Fricker, *Epistemic Injustice*.

[18] For a study of this phenomenon amongst doctors, see Files et al., "Speaker introductions", which found that when the introducer was female and the speaker male, titles were used in 95 per cent of cases, but with a male introducer and female speaker, titles were used in only 49.2 per cent of cases.

[19] Microaggressions, like the titles case, are paradigmatic examples of this type. Chester Pierce coined this term, e.g., "Stress analogs of racism and sexism". On their relation to social standing, see McTernan, "Microaggressions, equality, and social practices"; and, on racial microaggressions being 'used to keep those at the racial margins in their place', see Pérez Huber and Solorzano, "Racial microaggressions", p. 302.

[20] To borrow Peter Goldie's example, an emotion's intentional object may not be its cause: I might feel irritated *at* my partner, but because I drank too much coffee, "Emotion", p. 930.

To illustrate, I might think that my standing is such that in a professional context people ought to greet me by shaking my hand rather than patting my head, yet amongst friends I might find a handshake unduly formal and even unfriendly. When I do not get the expected greeting, I may take offence. For most of us, our sense of our social standing, and so the behaviours we expect from others, is heavily shaped by the socially salient groups to which we belong or are taken to belong and the social roles that we occupy. For example, a doctor expects deference from a patient, or a middle-class white woman expects the police to treat her with courtesy. Some also incorporate other attachments into their conception of their social standing, say, a national identity, religion, or their long-supported sports team, such that an affront to it can be experienced as an affront to them.

Sometimes, political philosophers appear to take social standing to be some settled 'amount' or constant rank that a person holds across a life.[21] But, instead, in formulating this first property of offence, by a person's perception of her own standing I have in mind something closer to the sociological and sociolinguistic notion of 'face'; namely, that image or persona that we present to others, that is constructed through and negotiated during particular interpersonal interactions. I include within that one's sense of identity and social position, as one presents it in some setting. On Erving Goffman's classic account, face is defined as

> the positive social value a person effectively claims for himself by the line others assume he has taken during a particular contact. Face is an image of self delineated in terms of approved social attributes.[22]

Miriam Locher offers a helpful analogy to a 'mask' that the person puts on in a particular interaction although the success of that presentation depends upon those with whom one interacts.[23] When we take offence, what we are doing is reacting to some affront to—and so threat to—our social standing, as we are conceiving, constructing, and presenting it in an interaction.[24]

---

[21] An instructive example is Lippert-Rasmussen, *Relational Egalitarianism*, but it is also found in relational egalitarian's talk of 'equal respect', to which I return in Chapter 3.

[22] Goffman, *Interaction Ritual*, at p. 5. For a discussion of the origins of Goffman's idea, see Qi, 'Face'.

[23] Locher, "Situated Impoliteness", p. 188.

[24] Conception and not just presentation counts. For instance, sometimes we may conceal aspects of our identities and nonetheless be offended by remarks about groups to which we take ourselves to belong, even where we are not presenting as such in a particular context. With thanks to Jennifer Page

Informed by the notion of face, when I discuss social standing there are two differences from a settled rank view. One is that standing is dynamic, not static. It is up for negotiation and can vary across interactions with different people or in different settings: at work, for instance, one may present a different self-image to that one would convey in the park with other mothers, where the relevant socially valued traits differ. Admittedly, that variation is constrained by the social rules in play as to what kinds of 'moves' can be successfully made and have uptake from others.[25] As one such constraint, explored in Chapter 3, socially salient identities will tend to shape standing across interactions.

The other difference is in what one's sense of one's standing encompasses. Our sense of ourselves will be informed by various aspects of our identity, social position, and social roles.[26] However, while social standing in my sense has a comparative element, in that it is something we construct with and contrast to others, it need not include a ranking against others. Further, as noted above, our self-image can incorporate various attachments, such as one's moral commitments or religion, if one takes these to be valuable or socially important attributes. If I attack, dismiss or fail to recognise some aspect of yourself that you take to have value, that is a threat to the way in which you wish to present yourself. As a result, my act may be a fitting thing at which to take offence.

As the second property of taking offence, the offended person, regarding her standing to have been affronted, will feel estranged from the offending party. That estrangement comes in varying degrees: she might feel alienated from the other person, or simply taken aback by what they did, a phrase that gives us a sense of how this is a small, temporary moment of estrangement. Alternatively, she might feel bored by the interaction, or even amused at the person and what they have done. Repeated cases of being offended in the

---

for noting this kind of case. Note, too, that failures of recognition can thus count as affronts: these can be failures to see the other as they wish to be seen.

[25] The emphasis in sociology and linguistics is on the co-construction of standing in each encounter: see Goffman, *Interaction Ritual*, on the line that one takes in a particular interaction, or Locher and Watt's depiction of face as "socially attributed in each individual interaction", declaring "any individual may be attributed a potentially infinite number of faces", comparing these to 'masks' that are "on loan to us for the duration of different kinds of performance", "Politeness theory", p. 12. However, constraints from social position are often referenced; for instance, Locher and Watts continue their description with someone who "performs in the role of a Prime Minister, a mother, a wife, a gardener", a person, then, occupying a particular set of social positions, "Politeness theory", p. 13.

[26] Standing is not therefore reducible to identity: it concerns the self-image I project and construct in this setting, not 'who I am'.

very same way are particularly liable to be characterised by amusement, as are notably egregious instances of commonly experienced phenomena, such as in Solnit's case of a woman having her own book 'mansplained' to her.[27] The woman is not laughing *with* the man explaining her own book to her, but *at* the situation and perhaps the offender too: at the absurdity of such slights still happening, and the absurdity of the person committing them. What unites these varying feelings as ones of estrangement is that all distance the offended from the offender.

Third, the person who is offended will tend towards actions that express her estrangement: actions of withdrawal. At first glance, the behaviours associated with taking offence look highly varied.[28] For example, at one end of the scale a person who is offended may raise an eyebrow, turn away from the person making an inappropriate remark, pointedly refrain from laughing at a joke, or leave slightly too long a silence before responding. At the other, they might refrain from any future relationships with the offender, whether in their personal or professional life, or call for the imposition of further costs of broader withdrawal on that person, say the loss of a job or honorary position.[29] However, what unites these is they all are ways of withdrawing from the other in our social relations, of pushing the other away, or out. A pointed silence can be a very effective, if temporary, way to express our estrangement from another. While we may not always act on our offence, say, if we fear another will retaliate, the tendency towards withdrawal is a relatively strong one: usually there is a reason where do not, such that the default is that we would express our emotion. Sometimes, we even communicate our estrangement unintentionally, say, by being silent for just a moment too long.

This account of offence makes it a particular and unified emotion, unlike Feinberg's cluster of disunified states. What it is like to have this emotion is to take it that one's standing has been attacked, dismissed or ignored, to feel estranged from the person who commits the offensive act, and to tend towards acts of withdrawal. At least to those of us not too deeply steeped in Feinberg's way of thinking, this emotion ought to appear familiar. It is an everyday emotion that you might feel when a colleague makes a sexist joke, someone pushes in front of you in a queue, or your partner is condescending. It is also

---

[27] Solnit, *Men Explain Things to Me.*

[28] I borrow the idea of an action tendency from the psychology of emotion; on its use there, see Haidt, "The Moral Emotions", p. 853. An emotion motivates or disposes one towards particular types of action.

[29] For descriptions of this sort of consequence, see the cases described in Ronson, *So You've Been Publicly Shamed.*

one that we may feel to varying degrees: sometimes, being taken aback for only a moment; other times, being so offended that we break off relations for good.[30]

The analysis accords, too, with the way in which sociolinguists and social psychologists regard offence as an emotion concerned with affronts to one's 'face', such as the impoliteness or disrespect of others.[31] Finally, it accommodates many of Feinberg's classic cases on the public bus as ones where we might take offence in my sense, yet makes clear how some fall short of being paradigmatic or clear instances of offence.[32] To illustrate, we can reframe his cases of disgust, such as vomiting up a meal in public or engaging in public sex acts, as also instances of failing to sufficiently attend to other's comfort, and so manifesting a disregard for others that may offend. Yet in such cases disgust, not offence, would be the primary emotion.

One might object that nonetheless my analysis wrongly excludes some cases of apparent offence. First, then, we appear to use the notion of offence to describe things other than affronts to our social standing. Take the idea of an offensive smell or other affronts to the senses; or the notion that one's aesthetic sensibilities have been offended, for instance, on seeing some hideous interior décor. In such cases, we perceive no affront to our social standing. So, too, we are not necessarily estranged from anyone when something smells or looks bad. All that is shared with the standard cases above is a desire to withdraw, here, from that affront to one's sensibilities. Thus, these would not count as offence proper, as I define it—unless the interior décor is done to spite you, the smell is inflicted deliberately, or somehow otherwise manifests another's disregard of you.

However, a plausible reading of these cases is that the term 'offence' is merely being used to capture the way in which our senses are affronted, rather than our truly feeling offended. It is a dramatic use of language to describe someone's decorating attempts as offensive but odd to be genuinely offended, and the best way to characterise one's reaction to a terrible smell is as disgust. Still, all I need for this book's argument is to insist that at least in paradigmatic cases of offence all three of the properties are present.

---

[30] Sometimes, such variation is taken as evidence for the state in question being an emotion, e.g., see Sharpe, "Seven reasons", on amusement.

[31] See Culpepper, "Reflections on impoliteness"; D'Errico & Poggi, "The lexicon of feeling offended"; Goffman, *Interaction Ritual*; Locher, "Situated impoliteness"; Locher & Watts, "Politeness theory"; Poggi & D'Errico, "Feeling offended"; Tagg et al., *Taking Offence on Social Media*.

[32] I include as cases of offence instances that Feinberg's notion of 'profound' offence would not, such as mildly sexist jokes and failures to shake hands.

Furthermore, the target of current debates over offence concerns such offence at affronts to standing (despite the fact that these debates often confuse this with claiming victimhood) and not people becoming more sensitive to smells or interior décor.

Second, it appears that we can be offended even where there is no particular agent to whom we can attribute the affront; for instance, we could take offence at a sign, when we don't know who put it up, or take offence at the actions of an institution that express disrespect for people like us, even if no agent within that institution intended that outcome. To reply, clearly, some relation to agency is required. There is no affront to social standing from the mere fact that it rains, say, even where that frustrates one's interests in staying dry: there is no agent disregarding one's interests. However, in the cases of the institution and the sign, we know that agents are involved in the resulting state of affairs. On my account, no direct intent of one agent to put another down is required to take offence: given its dependency on uptake from others, our construction and projection of our image is far more vulnerable than limiting it to only such direct threats would suggest. I might be also offended, say, by another not noticing my presence, or some unintentional putdown. Hence, there is no reason to rule out the arrangements of an institution, nor a sign put up by an unknown other, from presenting an affront to our social standing. Yet nonetheless there is good reason to restrict offence to acts where there is some agent(s) involved, in that our standing is constructed through our *social* interactions.

That raises the issue of in what sense an interaction must be social in order to provoke offence. This ought not be confused with how public an affront is. Our social standing is something negotiated in particular interactions, and thus can be threatened in classically private settings, such as one's partner making a dismissive comment at home, as well as in cases with more witnesses. Still, our standing is something we construct with and for others. One may think, as a result, that restricting offence to affronts to standing still rules out too much. Suppose that I find out through reading someone's private diary that they hold a very low opinion of me. Mightn't I still be offended, even if they have never expressed their view to anyone? In general, can I be offended by the private attitudes of others, where I come to know these?

I suspect that in the particular case one's offence may be driven, or at least compounded, by the diary writer's hypocrisy in presenting a falsely pleasant public face, and so chiefly by one's interactions with the writer. To compare, if already knowing that someone thinks little of me, I read their private diary, evidence of their low opinion is unlikely to add to any offence I feel. Still, the written words themselves, and other discoveries of negative private attitudes, can indeed cause offence, given that they present some sense of a threat to one's standing. After all, our sense of our standing is constructed socially, and is influenced both by how others treat us and how they regard us. Merely knowing that someone else holds a low opinion is a challenge, of sorts, to how one wishes to present oneself and, if expressed, could undermine one's standing.[33]

A third apparent exclusion looks more troubling. Despite the earlier remarks on offence, some might doubt that offence taken at affronts to one's religion, from depictions of the prophet to people burning bibles, fits well into an analysis of offence that is centred on social standing.[34] Yet philosophers of jurisprudence in particular may take these to be paradigmatic instances of offence. Much the same might be thought about affronts to one's moral commitments. However, while religious cases may have been paradigmatic ones for the law, they are less clearly so in everyday life. Likely, most of us take more offence over the details of social interactions, such as someone snubbing us, or a colleague overlooking our contribution. Certainly, it is these sorts of social interactions that capture the attention of sociolinguists and linguists who consider offence.[35] In addition, religious and moral affronts are often mixed cases: ones that combine offence with other emotions, such as disgust at purity violations or anger at violations of moral codes.

Still, however, my analysis can capture the way that offence can be taken on the grounds of religious and moral commitments: sometimes, a transgression against these commitments is fittingly experienced as an affront to one's standing. That can happen when people incorporate religious and moral commitments into their constructions of their selves, whether in taking these to be valued attributes, say, regarding oneself as a good Christian or a committed vegan and seeing these as valuable things to be; or in taking such commitments to be part of one's identity, in ways that open one to related dismissals or attacks to standing. Then, affronts to one's religion or moral commitments become fitting candidates for offence: in attacking or dismissing these commitments you may threaten my standing as I perceive

---

[33] With thanks to a referee for raising the issue of how public an affront needs to be.

[34] With thanks to a referee and to Robert Simpson for pointing out this problem.

[35] For instance, Haugh, "Impoliteness and taking offence", examines offence at minor impoliteness and slights in conversation; Tayebi, "Why do people take offence?" at details like the effort a host puts into dinner.

it, by dismissing the value of what I take to be a good feature of myself or slighting people like me.

For offence to be fitting, however, the acts of another must be plausibly taken to be targeted at you, or those like you, a restriction I further defend later in this chapter. What I have in mind by talk of "targeting" here is that there is an affront that concerns you and yours, one pertaining to your standing—and not that the offending party intends to target the offended party. This explains why not all rejections or violations of moral or religious commitments offend: not all are to do with my standing. To illustrate, suppose that I take donating to charities to be a moral duty and meet someone who usually fails to do so. Their behaviour does not seem to provide grounds for offence. Alternatively, take the priest who has an extramarital affair in a moment of weakness of will, for which he sincerely repents. I might be deeply disappointed or disillusioned, rather than offended.

But a subset of transgressions of moral or religious commitments do look likely to provoke offence rather than, say, disgust: those where one's religious or other value commitments are attacked directly or dismissed. That happens when they are made into objects of fun, such as in the show the *Book of Mormon* with its mockery of core tenets of Mormonism as absurd, given the dismissive attitude towards one's commitments thereby expressed; or where one's commitments are deliberately or pointedly violated. These turn the violation of a code into something about you in the relevant sense to threaten standing. The vegetarian is not likely to take offence at the mere knowledge that somewhere in the world, someone is eating meat. But they may when a colleague deliberately eats meat next to them, while commenting that vegetarian food tastes bad. The latter is a deliberate provocation or challenge to what they value, where the former is not.

1.3. Distinguishing offence

With the analysis in view, the next task is distinguishing offence from nearby emotions. In particular, it might be thought that offence is simply a form of anger, although that may simply reflect anger's contemporary popularity amongst moral and political philosophers.[36] Below, I argue that not only is

---

[36] See, for instance, Bailey, "On anger, silence, and epistemic injustice"; Bell, "Anger, virtue, and oppression"; Bommarito, "Virtuous and vicious anger"; Cherry, "The errors and limitations"; Srinivasan, "The aptness of anger"; for more critical views on anger, see Pettigrove, "Meekness and

offence distinct from anger but, further, that in crucial respects both contempt and pride lie closer. Gabriele Taylor observes that there are many ways
to carve up emotions and which we choose often reflects our interests in so
doing.[37] Nonetheless, two common groupings map out the relevant terrain.
The first are emotions of self-assessment or self-conscious emotions, such as
pride, shame, and guilt. These emotions have the self as their object and, as
Taylor describes, a person feels them when she believes that she has 'deviated
from some norm' and so 'altered her standing in the world', whether posi-
tively (pride) or negatively (shame, guilt).[38] A second, contrasting set are the
other-condemning emotions, the central instances of which are anger, contempt, and disgust.[39] These negative emotions tend to have another person
or another's acts as their object.

Within this latter set, anger is an emotion of approach: of engaging with
and especially attacking or getting back at another whom we perceive variously as violating a moral norm, injuring us, or committing an injustice. As
Jonathan Haidt depicts anger, for instance, it 'generally involves a motivation
to attack, humiliate, or otherwise get back at the person who is perceived
as acting unfairly or immorally'.[40] By contrast, contempt and disgust are
emotions of withdrawal, not engagement: we tend to avoid the company of
those towards whom we feel such emotions.[41] What provokes our disgust is
a violation of some purity or contamination related norm, from which we
recoil.[42] Feeling contempt, we regard another as inferior and, as Macalester

'moral' anger"; Nussbaum, *Anger and Forgiveness*. There is a long history of work on anger, from
Aristotle to the defences of Frye, *The Politics of Reality*; and Lorde, "The uses of anger", amongst
others.

[37] Taylor, *Pride, Shame, and Guilt*, p. 1.
[38] See Taylor, *Pride, Shame, and Guilt* for a depiction of self-assessment emotions, for the quote,
p. 1; on self-conscious emotions, Lewis, "The self in self-conscious emotions".
[39] For discussions of other-condemning emotions and the 'CAD triad' of contempt, anger and disgust, see, e.g., Haidt, "The moral emotions"; Rozin et al., "The CAD triad hypothesis"; for a dispute
over how to separate anger and disgust, see Royzman et al. "CAD or MAD?"
[40] Haidt, "The moral emotions", p. 856. See also the common association of anger with injustice,
e.g., Bailey, "On anger, silence, and epistemic injustice"; Bommarito, "Virtuous and vicious anger";
Bell "Anger, virtue, and oppression".
[41] For a discussion of avoidance behaviours in disgust and contempt see Dubreuil, "Punitive
emotions". See also Haidt, who depicts disgust as including 'the motivation to avoid, expel, or otherwise break off contact', "The moral emotions", p. 858. However, Haidt regards contempt as motivating
"neither attack or withdrawal" but rather "the object of contempt will be treated with less warmth,
respect, and consideration in future interactions", "The moral emotions", p. 858. Bell discusses active
and passive contempt in her *Hard Feelings*.
[42] On the connection to contamination see Dubreuil, "Punitive emotions"; Rozin et al., "The CAD
triad hypothesis"; Royzman et al., "CAD or MAD?" On the CAD triad, disgust is associated with an
"ethic of divinity" and a broader sense of purity and impurity with notions of contamination at its
core, see Rozin et al., "The CAD triad hypothesis".

Bell depicts, have a 'dismissive and insulting attitude that manifests *disregard* for its target'.[43]

So, where does offence fit? Offence looks like a negative emotion with, at first glance, the acts of another as its object: we do not take offence at ourselves. If so characterised as amongst the other-condemning emotions, offence would rest closer to contempt and disgust than anger. Offence is an emotion of withdrawal, not approach, lacking that payback or vengeance aspect common to anger which some even treat as definitional.[44] When offended I may merely be taken aback and feel a little estranged. Or consider that offence, unlike anger, can be characterised by amusement, as a form of withdrawal: take the egregious mansplaining of one's own book. By contrast, if someone is both angry and amused, their amusement likely eats away at their anger. Offence also centrally concerns not injustice or a direct moral norm violation as anger often does but, rather, the violation of social norms, or acts of disrespect and disregard. While there is a close relation between these social acts and injustice, to be explored over the following chapters, I will also defend a distinct role for offence in responding to such acts.

That difference in its object—being a reaction to an affront to standing— also distinguishes offence from disgust, which is instead concerned with perceived contamination. As a result, the two emotions often come apart: stepping in dog poo is disgusting, but it is not offensive. Nonetheless, there is some overlap; for instance, we might find being spat on both disgusting *and* offensive. Norms of what counts as polite, respectful, or appropriate behaviour, the transgressions of which often cause offence, incorporate some norms around bodily functions and contamination. To deliberately inflict something disgusting on another, or even to negligently expose them to such, can cause offence by its being a failure to be considerate of the other and their interests.[45] Still, if I accidentally vomited on you, stricken by sudden onset of food poisoning, you would be disgusted but not offended.

Offence may sit even closer to contempt and its related emotions like disregard, disdain, aversion, and an urge towards mockery.[46] Not only is contempt characterised by an estrangement in our relations to the other,

---

[43] Bell, *Hard Feelings*, p. 8. On seeing the other as inferior, Dubreuil "Punitive emotions", p. 45.

[44] See Nussbaum, *Anger and Forgiveness*. Some have argued that anger doesn't always lead to a desire to harm or take vengeance; for instance, Bommarito observes this is the case for anger at one's father, "Virtuous and vicious anger", p. 5. One might respond that this is not 'full' anger.

[45] Calhoun observes the connection between civility and bodily functions, "The virtue of civility".

[46] Drawing on Haidt here who comments, "Contempt paints its victims as buffoons worthy of mockery or as nonpersons worthy of complete disregard"; "The moral emotions", p. 858.

variously characterised as coolness, withdrawal, or a lack of consideration or respect, but it also is centrally concerned with what some psychologists term an 'ethic of community', and so "moral violations involving disrespect and violations of duty or hierarchy".[47] As a result, contempt, like offence, concerns status. Contempt, however, is a deeper and less surmountable form of estrangement from relationships than offence: contempt would be corrosive of close relationships, say between friends or lovers, where offence is not. Further, while contempt has as its object the person, offence has as its object the act: we can be offended where we do not know which agent performed the act whereas we cannot feel contempt.[48] Most importantly, in feeling contempt we regard the other as inferior. By contrast, offence responds to a challenge to, or denial of, our social standing and we need not regard the other as inferior in order to take offence at their behaviour. Indeed, for us to take offence, we must regard the other as having sufficient standing to be capable of presenting a challenge to our social standing; we cannot perceive the other as too far beneath us or else we would not take offence. Contempt has no such lower limit.

This relevance of the other's standing to provoking offence captures a feature of our experience: sometimes people are no longer offended by acts of a kind that once they found offensive. One explanation is that an affront no longer constitutes any real threat to standing; for instance, being mistaken for a student by one's students might be offensive to the junior academic, but a decade later, as a professor of great renown, it may no longer be so. The claim here is not that we can only take offence when our standing is in fact successfully undermined but, rather, that an act must succeed in being an affront to our standing. Such success requires the other has the capacity to threaten our standing, even if they fail. However, the bar to be exceeded to constitute a threat to standing is a low one and nor must the threat be serious: our social standing in any particular interaction is up for negotiation and can be threatened through acts as small as a rude remark.[49] There is one final feature of this case to note: some might even find it flattering to be mistaken for a student as they age. That reflects, I suspect, a social hierarchy that values youth. Within an ageist society, the affront of

---

[47] For the definition of ethics of community, see Haidt, "The moral emotions", p. 858.

[48] On contempt as a whole person emotion, see Bell, *Hard Feelings*. Admittedly, we might label the act 'contemptible'.

[49] Echoing the notion of 'facework' or 'relational work' in sociolinguistics, see Locher, "Situated impoliteness"; Locher & Watts, "Politeness theory".

having one's social position mistakenly downgraded to 'student' becomes simultaneously a boost.

Despite offence's connections to contempt and disgust, some may not yet accept that offence and anger are distinct. The association of anger with "status injury" stretches back to Aristotle, as Martha Nussbaum notes. Anger, then, is often taken at acts that threaten standing.[50] So, is what I term 'offence', merely a variant of this status-anger? Suppose it were so. Still, offence would be distinct from the forms of anger that are often defended by contemporary moral and political philosophers, where we justifiably feel anger at grave injustice and evil, or at least moral violations.[51] But this distinction between anger and offence is no mere matter of terminology, of the sort best resolved by conceding that offence is one form of anger. Doing so threatens to obscure what offence is like: as described above, it is an emotion of withdrawal, not engagement, concerned with social, not moral, violations.[52] Further, as I now explore, offence, unlike anger, also fits poorly into the strict divide between emotions of self-assessment and other-directed emotions.

Offence, then, is unusual in that it could be characterised as not, or not only, an other-condemning emotion. Instead, while offence has received limited attention from social psychologists, when it is addressed it is taken to be a 'self-conscious' emotion, alongside pride, shame, and guilt.[53] To be offended is to suffer a blow to one's honour or public face, and so, perhaps, to one's self-image. Isabella Poggi and Francesca D'Errico describe it, for instance, as a 'nick' to that self-image.[54]

Nonetheless, offence does not function quite like other emotions of self-assessment. Rather than the agent doing something that alters 'her standing in the world' as she perceives it, another agent rejects, mistakes, or

---

[50] Nussbaum, *Anger and Forgiveness*.

[51] Assuming here that we are in the realm of 'status-injuries' that do not rise to straightforward moral violations, unlike many of Nussbaum's cases, such as rape. For illustrative defences of anger at injustice: see Bell, "Anger, virtue, and oppression"; Srinivasan, "The aptness of anger"; or Bommarito, "Virtuous and vicious anger", who discusses anger as manifesting a concern for justice and explicitly carves off 'personal' or 'non-moral' anger. Of course, the line between status injury and injustice is hard to draw: collectively, small scale status injuries can amount to patterns of injustice, for instance, on microaggressions, see McTernan, "Microaggressions, equality, and social practices".

[52] Although some violations of social norms transgress against moral norms, say, around dignity or respect for persons. Chapter 3 explores the moral significance of manners.

[53] See D'Errico & Poggi, "The lexicon of feeling offended" and, for this claim, Poggi & D'Errico, "Feeling offended", p. 1.

[54] "Feeling offended", p. 1.

overlooks the way in which the agent regards her own standing within some particular social world, and the agent reacts against that.[55] For instance, while in feeling shame, one adopts other's view of oneself and perceives oneself as lesser or as failing at some standard; in offence, one resists the other's view. Still, an aspect of self-assessment remains in taking offence, in that we weigh our standing anew in the light of the other's threat.[56] When someone offers an affront, often we reconsider how we are viewed in certain contexts or, at least, by that person. Our construction of our 'face' or public image is disputed and realising this is one of the defining properties of offence. But another is that in taking offence, we resist rather than accept the lowering of our standing. Indeed, sometimes, when making our assessment of our standing, we even feel confirmed in our sense of having higher standing than the offending party treats us as if we have, and so offence shades back into an other-condemning emotion. Thus, offence is distinctive in lying somewhere in between an emotion of self-assessment and an other-condemning emotion.[57]

1.4. Rethinking offence: Domestic, not catastrophic

Offence, then, is a distinct emotion that should be disentangled from other close emotions like disgust in a way in which Feinberg fails to do. With this re-characterisation in view, I turn to why it motivates a more nuanced moral appraisal of the emotion of taking offence and those who take it, as compared to the popular perception. To begin, on my account offence becomes a more domestic emotion than it is sometimes taken to be. Public discourse on offence focuses on the extreme end of the spectrum of associated behaviours: public exposure to shame and shunning. Yet often offence will not escalate to such

---

[55] Borrowing again Taylor's depiction, *Pride, Shame, and Guilt.* See also Lewis' depiction of the emergence of self-conscious emotions from "reflecting on our own appearance and thinking about others thinking about us", "The self in self-conscious emotions", at p. 119. There is clearly here a connection between pride and offence. As a first stab, one might observe that the prideful person is often offended.

[56] In support of this characterisation, on one depiction of how the subjective view of one's face and the external appraisal line up: "face is an image of self possessed by a person through their interest in how they are regarded or judged by others, and face is a social representation of a person reflecting the respect, regard or confidence others have in them", Qi, "Face", p. 287. How others then regard one, is clearly relevant to constructing this image.

[57] While contempt also involves a dimension of comparison of self to other, in that you take yourself to be superior, the self-assessment is far from as central. Contempt is primarily an emotion concerned with the assessment of another, with the assessment of oneself being derivative.

behaviours, rather, much of it is every day: involving raised eyebrows, tisk-tisking, or other minor signs of disapproval. Against popular perception, this lack of escalation is even seen in many online interactions: in a recent study of offence on a social media platform found the reactions of offence to be largely small-scale in nature.[58]

One might question why taking offence ever escalates, if we are able to express our offence and signal to others our withdrawal merely by, say, failing to laugh at a joke or turning away. There are two possible answers, the first of which may lie behind some of the fear of a (supposed) culture of offence. On that first answer, some may see offence as the kind of emotion that, once felt, tends to escalate; just as some characterise anger as involving a loss of control and provoking indiscriminate, excessive violence.[59] In this case, once I am offended then I am inclined to keep escalating my behaviour until drastic consequences result for the offending party. However, this answer does not ring true when we consider many everyday cases of offence in which no such escalation occurs, say, when your partner makes a rude remark about your cooking, or a colleague makes some inappropriately sexist joke. Nor is this a plausible way to think about emotions like offence any more than it is about anger: many emotions do not sweep away all measured responses. When someone says that they were angry at their computer freezing, so they smashed it with a hammer, our reaction is not to accept what happened as simply a normal part of feeling anger; at least, not that of an emotionally mature adult, rather than a toddler.

Further, there is a second, alternative answer for why sometimes we see an escalation in offence-taking, especially when interacting with strangers online. Sometimes the everyday, small-scale ways of expressing withdrawal aren't available to us, as I examine below, and so we may be pushed towards starker ways to display offence. However, rather than being necessarily indiscriminate or excessive, these starker ways might be the only way to express the withdrawal that characterises being offended in such settings; at the end of the chapter, I argue, further, that these grander displays can be as morally appropriate as those smaller in scale.

---

[58] A study into Facebook, reported in Tagg et al., *Taking Offence on Social Media*.

[59] For a nuanced argument on this point, focusing on anger being turned inwards within a community, see Pettigrove, "Meekness and 'moral' anger".

1.5. The limits to taking offence

To continue the case for a more nuanced appraisal of offence, I propose two limits to when taking offence is apt, based on the distance between the potentially offended party and the affront in question. That distance, I argue, can render taking offence inapt in two senses: in whether taking offence fits the situation at hand, but also in that when people take offence outside these limits, that opens them to moral criticism. Further, proposing these limits will tackle two aspects of our practices that those sceptical of offence may find especially objectionable: where others pile on in taking offence and where people search out grounds on which to take offence.

As the first limit, the analysis of offence has implications for *who* can fittingly take offence at a particular act. Just as it is intelligible for a parent to take pride in the achievements of a child as 'theirs' in some sense, often people take offence when the standing of their group is affronted. The relevant group membership or facet of identity could be one with which they identify or with which they are commonly identified by others. Given that people's construal of their own standing is often tied to such features, this should be unsurprising. As a consequence, an affront can also be shared by other members of the same group, even where these individuals were not themselves the direct or intended target of an affront. For instance, a woman might be offended when another woman in her office is called a 'girl' by their boss. That this is an affront to her standing too makes sense against a background context where there is often a lack of respect for women and one way that is manifested is through reminders of lesser standing, such as describing adult women as 'girls'—a reminder to both the woman called that, and those who witness it.

Sometimes, however, our offence-taking can be unintelligible: there are conceptual restrictions on when it is appropriate to take offence. Just as in Hume's case, where a man takes pride in a fish in the sea that has nothing to do with him, so, too, we can mistakenly take offence at slights too distant or disconnected for our offence to make sense. The affront at which one takes offence must be target something that it makes sense for me to incorporate into my sense of my own standing.[60] If, instead, I take offence at an affront to

---

[60] There is a parallel here between being offended and taking pride, which should be unsurprising given that both of these emotions relate to our standing and what we value about ourselves, see Hume, *A Dissertation on the Passions*, Book II, Part I, pp. 275–294.

the social standing of some group to which I am not a member nor otherwise closely associated with, or a slight made about an individual to whom I bear no relation to and to whom I share no facet of identity, then I am mistaken in the object of my offence.

The thought here, then, is that it is not my place to be offended, just as I cannot forgive on other's behalf or feel pride on the grounds of another's achievements, at least where those others are unrelated to me. Taking such offence would be to mistake how the world is: to think myself connected to some affront, where I am not. I would incorporate into my self-conception and presentation of self, something that is nothing to do with me. Often, it would also be a moral mistake. A wrong is done to someone whose own standing is affronted that is not done to the person who witnesses an affront targeting someone else. To take offence at an affront to another obscures that difference.[61]

Given this limit to the intelligibility of offence, there is a sharp distinction to be drawn between the claim 'that's offensive' and someone actually taking offence. We can label some act offensive without feeling offended ourselves. Further, we can label some act offensive even where the slight is too distant from us to intelligibly be offended. Thus, on my analysis, the emotion of taking offence does not include statements of the form, 'that's offensive'. Of course, we may experience unpleasant sensations when people say things that we label offensive, even where those statements do not affront our own standing. A man seeing a T-shirt with the slogan 'women, get back in the kitchen' or a straight person hearing jokes about bisexuals being greedy, might feel uncomfortable, disconcerted, embarrassed, or even disgusted. Sometimes, the third-party counterpart of offence may be indignation. At other times, we might call something offensive without any accompanying emotional response. None of these, however, are the same as feeling offended and the resulting action tendencies also differ. Thus, while being offended consistently disposes people towards a particular pattern of behaviour communicating estrangement, to label something offensive does not.

This limit on offence means that, as a result, I resist what one might term a 'social justice warrior' phenomenon: namely, the piling on with offence-taking at affronts made to unrelated or connected others. Taking offence on another's behalf and acting in ways that express offence's kind of estrangement

---

[61] With thanks to Hallvard Lillehammer for his push to clarify whether the distinction here is taxonomical or ethical.

from the offending party makes both a conceptual and a moral mistake. However, this implication is a plausible reading of our emotions: there is something different in how you feel when it is *you* that someone insults, compared to when they insult someone else. Further, we tend to find something suspicious or disingenuous about the unrelated, uninvolved person taking offence at a slight made to someone else; we think that they are making the situation all about them. Indeed, unless they are conceptually mistaken about offence, that is the best way to make sense of their really feeling offence rather than merely pretending: that they are turning the slight into an insult that affects them too. For instance, I could be offended that someone thinks *I* would put up with such affronts to others. That might turn an other-directed offensive remark into a salient issue for one's standing. Suppose, for instance, that you take yourself to be the sort of person that others ought not say such things in front of, given your professional position of neutrality, or your consistent work promoting social justice. But even if so, the offence is not taken at the affront itself, but at the other person saying such things in front of you. The affront at which offence is taken, then, is not the statement about another group, but the presumption about yourself.

Hence, when people pile in, taking offence at affronts directed to others, they are open to moral criticism. Such individuals look self-involved, in turning an affront to another into one that affects them. In addition, they obscure what is going on, rather than illuminating the injustice done to those who experience frequent affronts to social standing, which Chapter 3 returns to examine. That is not to say that outsiders ought never react but, rather, that it would be preferable to respond in another way, say through emotions such as indignation and hence, likely, with behaviours other than withdrawal. Indignation, for instance, as a species of anger, would likely provoke reactions of (negative) engagement instead.

The second limit to taking offence concerns which affronts, amongst those that target me, are apt candidates for offence. It might seem a quirk of my analysis that while the focus on the 'culture of taking offence' in the media has emphasised twitter spats and public shaming, I focus on the more everyday interactions where we take offence in pubs or on trains, and at friends, colleagues, or partners. Further, given my characterisation of the emotion of offence as one of feeling estrangement and tending us towards acts of withdrawal, a question arises as to its scope. Can one take offence at the act or speech of an unrelated, unconnected, distant stranger?[62] One can, of course, feel anger at gross slights to standing or attacks on basic moral standing, whomever performs such transgressions. However, when it comes to offence one cannot withdraw from relationships to entirely unrelated or unconnected others, i.e., from those to whom one stands in no existing relation. That may simply mean that we would be frustrated in any attempt to express our emotion. More troublingly, however, nor can one become estranged from someone with whom one shared no prior social relation or connection. What then would estrangement mean? A person can't feel more estranged from another, where the other is a stranger he will never meet and with whom he has nothing in common, no shared connections, nor previous contact.

Hence, it looks like in order to be conceptually coherent, offence must be taken at the acts of someone else to whom one bears some existing relationship or connection, sufficient for it to be possible for one to feel *more* estranged from that person. Were offence subject to such a limitation in scope, it would not be unique. Grief, for instance, also has a requirement of a prior connection to its object. However, in the case of offence, there are good reasons to be permissive about who could potentially count as close enough for their actions to provoke offence.

First, what counts for conceptual coherence is the kinds of relations from which people can feel themselves estranged. It looks like some people have a wide-ranging understanding of to whom they bear sufficient connection such that they could feel more estranged. For instance, it appears intelligible, if perhaps a tad dramatic, to state, 'I no longer recognise myself as British after Brexit'. Someone might take their citizenship to be a sufficiently significant bond feel a relationship to all their co-citizens and, further, rest that relationship on perceived shared values. But others might not.

---

[62] With thanks to Serena Olsaretti for first noticing this implication of the analysis. One might think that knowing one no longer wants contact with some random, unconnected stranger in itself counts as feeling estranged. Yet that seems a stretch beyond the permissive understanding of relationships from which one can be estranged to follow: in the absence of prior expectations of contact, the size of the global population makes it look odd to view all strangers as people we'd potentially be in contact with—unless they offend. At the least, for reasons I shortly discuss, others are likely to fail to read one's behaviour as expressing withdrawal. However, that isn't to deny the possibility of strangers that you encounter offending you: you can be estranged from someone who you didn't previously know, say when a stranger yells a slur at you in the street. The thought in this case is that the offensive act itself creates a connection of the right kind to underpin taking offence; that connection arises from being addressed directly. In these cases, one is in direct contact with the offending party, and in an interaction that concerns your presentation of self. Further, in cases where you have such direct contact with a stranger and they offer you an affront, it is easy to meaningfully convey withdrawal, say, through turning away. With thanks to an anonymous referee for pressing me on these points.

It is also possible to express a withdrawal from another both from a distance and only symbolically. Focusing on behaviours like not shaking hands, or tutting might mislead us into thinking that it is only possible to manifest offence within some ongoing, face-to-face relationship. Yet we can convey withdrawal without physical contact, such as by blocking someone on social media or declaring we no longer read their work. Sometimes we can even merely symbolically withdraw by, say, stating that we would not accept invites where that person would be present—even if we never receive any. Still, there is some limit to symbolic withdrawal: if the other never had any expectation of connection with us, then our act may have limited social meaning, or even fail to symbolise withdrawal altogether.

Second, sometimes we may take a form of 'proxy' estrangement, with accompanying tendencies to withdraw from these proxies, where we are not in contact with the one whose behaviour we take to be slighting us or ours but we are in contact with some who are associated with or connected to the person who slights us. Then, we find ourselves estranged from the associated others. Take the French woman offended by Trump's 'grab them by the pussy' remark, who feels a sense of estrangement from those who vote for Trump despite having no relation to Trump, and never living in America. Perhaps she would make statements such as, 'I can't understand people who vote for Trump', or would cease to invite Americans who vote Republican to her parties.

Thus, my account captures our practices of taking offence. We usually take offence within existing relationships like teacher-student, amongst friends, or at co-citizens. Sometimes, the connection is more distant: say, where a stranger in another country has tweeted some remark about one's group. Then we are pushed towards symbolic withdrawal or proxy forms of estrangement and withdrawal. However, that distance is what produces some of the more excessive offence reactions: symbolic or proxy forms are harder to perform with subtlety. Where I am in daily contact with someone and they are attuned to my behaviour, I do not need to do very much to convey that I am offended. This could explain why the offence we take in interpersonal relations often takes a subtle form; say of a small silence or turning away when one's partner says the wrong thing. Not much is needed to do the work. Where we are not in such close relations to another, something more dramatic is sometimes required, insofar as we wish to convey our offence.

Finally, here lies a reason why many find people taking offence at slights made by people to whom they share no obvious relation odd or objectionable. We might begin to think that sometimes people try too hard to draw a link such that they can relate to the other in a way that makes taking offence fitting. We can find people's claiming relations with very distant others absurd or think it suspect, in revealing some kind of bad faith. "What's that got to do with you" becomes a reasonable retort, and the social meaning of one's symbolic withdrawal is in doubt.

1.6. Towards a defence: From victimhood to social standing

The goal of this chapter has been to detail a distinct emotion of offence. On this account, when person A takes offence at B's doing φ, where 'φ' includes omissions, and where 'B' can be a person, group agent, or institution:

(i)   A believes, judges, or perceives that φ is an affront to her social standing as she perceives it;

(ii) and so, A feels estranged from B as a result of B's doing φ, even if only for a moment;

(iii) and, as a result, A has a tendency towards acts that express withdrawal from B.

Further, I defended two restrictions in scope. One is at which affronts we can take offence: namely, those that I can reasonably take to target my standing. The other is from whom the affronts come: we must have some kind of relation to the person who commits the affront such that we can be estranged, or where we can estrange ourselves from proxies for the person who offends.

This is an emotion ripe for moral reassessment. Even before the defence begins in the chapters to follow, already this analysis provides a partial response to those who suggest that a rise in our inclination to take offence would harm our relations to one another. For a start, I have domesticated this emotion: often, offence is small-scale and, often, it takes place within ongoing relations and without major ruptures. This is a perfectly ordinary emotion, with a role to play in our social relations regulating how we relate to one another and the ways in which we do or don't respect each other's projected sense of standing. Further, we can be, and often are, very precise in the extent of offence that we take.

There will be a limited category of cases where offence is more likely to escalate and seem excessive: those where the relationship to the person who offends is sufficiently distant that there is a need for symbolic withdrawal or proxy forms of estrangement. However, in such cases, these forms of expression may be the only way to convey offence, given that distance. That should shape our moral assessment of some of the apparent excesses in our practices of taking offence. Some grander expressions of offence might be proportionate, insofar as it is appropriate to take offence, by virtue of being the only possible ways to display it. One might object that, instead, people in such circumstances ought not take offence. While grand gestures may be the only possible ways to convey one's offence, these would still be disproportionate for the act in question: it would be to react as if the distant other had done something much worse than, in fact, they had. Yet underlying this objection is a flawed assumption, namely, that grander gestures, whether made by those near or far, are costlier to the offending party than would be smaller ones, and so disproportionate. Instead, however, a friend or your boss failing to laugh at your sexist joke in front of people you respect or are in frequent contact with likely inflicts a greater sense of having mis-stepped and may well do more significant social harm than a stranger blocking you on social media or declaring that they won't appear at an event with you. A subset of the grander acts of offence then, turns out to not be as costly as one might suppose.

An opponent might respond that even if grander acts are not costlier, simply their scale can render them disproportionate: grander acts express greater estrangement but, surely, one and the same offensive act ought to provoke the same degree of offence, regardless of whether one is near or far. However, rather, where the offending party is distant, starker acts may convey the same degree of offence or estrangement: a partner cares about a raised eyebrow, while an acquaintance would be indifferent. The estrangement expressed by two very different acts of withdrawal can be much the same, given the different starting points. The rarer, grander gestures of offence, then, are not necessarily to be dismissed as disproportionate or as evidence of excess; rather, they may be measured ways to convey offence at a distance.

I finish with the strongest reason to reassess offence, given this chapter's analysis. To be inclined to take offence is commonly regarded as a matter of victimhood, or as manifesting an oversensitivity towards harms to one's feelings. Take the widespread notion of a 'snowflake' generation in popular culture, or Campbell and Manning's rendering of the culture of taking offence as a 'culture of victimhood'.[63] Instead, on my analysis, those who take offence are attending to their standing and how others regard them. That should change our moral assessment. For a start, such attention to our standing is a pervasive feature of our social lives, rather than the novel phenomenon that some take it to be. Indeed, that offence is nothing new should be confirmed by the history of work on 'face', politeness, and offence: a history far longer than the current cultural panic over people taking offence.[64] Most of us are attuned to everyday details of how others treat us salient for determining whether we are given the level of respect we consider ourselves due, from the greetings others use, the jokes they make, where they touch us, or the attention that they pay us. People pay differing levels of attention, sometimes indefensibly: consider the person easily offended because she is hypersensitive to threats to her social standing; or the grand professor, who expects many acts of deference and is constantly affronted when those whom he deems his inferiors fail to abide by his expectations. Still, to pay some attention to our standing looks appropriate: how we are regarded by others shapes how our lives go and, often, has a bearing on how the lives of those who are like us go too, as Chapter 3 returns to detail.

What, then, if some were taking more offence these days, as the cultural critics fear? Suppose, say, that women were more easily offended now at what used to be dismissed as banter in the workplace or as acceptable flirting. What would that tell us? Then offence becomes ripe for a defence akin to that feminists offer for anger.[65] Members of marginalised or oppressed groups may sometimes take offence, and that offence may get uptake from others. In particular, others will realise that some type of behaviour offends, in being read as an affront to social standing, and they might be wary of risking the associated social costs of causing such offence. Hence, to take offence at dismissals or attacks on one's social standing sometimes looks like a way

[63] Campbell & Manning, "Microaggression and moral cultures", "The new millennial 'morality'".
[64] E.g., Goffman, *Interaction Ritual*; Brown & Levison, *Politeness*.
[65] E.g. Frye, *The Politics of Reality*; on racism, Lorde, "The uses of anger". For an analysis of a set of such defences of anger, and a parallel defence of contempt, see Bell, "A woman's scorn".

to resist being treated as less than another's equal. Thus, depending on who takes it, and at what, offence is ready for a defence that both sees the emotion as diagnostic of injustice, in highlighting where some aren't treated as equals, and as a way to resist that injustice: a defence unfolded over the following chapters. Now that we are clear about what offence is, we can begin to see what it might be able to do.

2

What taking offence does

While philosophers have largely neglected the question of whether and when taking offence can be justified, this question looks pressing in the face of popular criticism of a so-called culture of taking offence.[1] In popular critiques, to take offence is regarded as at best a useless reaction borne of emotional fragility, or a manifestation of 'victimhood'. At worst, an inclination to take offence is regarded as actively socially dis-valuable.[2] However, having clarified what taking offence is, across this chapter and the next I seek to rehabilitate offence's moral and social value.

Against popular opinion, this chapter defends taking offence on the grounds of its social function. In particular, given the role of offence in negotiating and reinforcing social norms, to take offence can be a way to stand up for one's social standing and that of one's group. The idea that taking offence stands up for standing will form the heart of the defence of offence unfolded in the following chapters. As a consequence, I argue that in a context of social inequality, and where an affront is to one's standing as a social equal, to take offence can be a morally appropriate response, including for many of the very acts that opponents to taking offence deem innocuous or unworthy of such reactions, such as microaggressions or using terms of address for others that they reject.

My defence is not a purely instrumental one, made on the grounds that taking offence is the most effective strategy, despite the fact that I defend the social value of our practices of taking offence. After all, grief need not be effective in some further end, nor produce the best overall consequences, in order to be the right emotion to feel or to be an emotion with valuable

---

[1] For popular critiques, see, for example, Lukianoff & Haidt, *The Coddling of the American Mind*; Campbell & Manning, "The new millennial 'morality'". There are a couple of exceptions in philosophy, which also criticise offence, e.g., Barrow, "On the duty of not taking offence". One might also consider Nussbaum, *Anger and Forgiveness*, on status anger; Chapter 3 examines whether the critique that she offers of such anger applies to taking offence.

[2] On victimhood, see Campbell & Manning, "Microaggression and moral cultures", "The new millennial morality"; Fox, "Generation snowflake". On social disvalue, see also Lukianoff & Haidt, *The Coddling of the American Mind*.

On Taking Offence. Emily McTernan, Oxford University Press. © Oxford University Press 2023.
DOI: 10.1093/oso/9780197613092.003.0003

social roles. I have in mind here Strawson's line on the reactive attitudes, that while these practices like resentment or guilt might be useful, we ought not "forget that these practices, and their reception . . . really are expressions of our moral attitudes and not merely devices we calculatingly employ for regulative purposes".[3] Taking offence can be useful but it is also an expression of our moral attitudes around how to live together in society: for instance, it can reveal a commitment to living together as equals, or, by contrast, and where I would not defend it, a commitment to social hierarchies. In this chapter, I defend the aptness of what offence can target, of the social norms and social meanings underpinning our acts, and examine how offence can thus resist attributions of lower social standing. In the next chapter, I justify the underlying attitudes towards one's social standing that are reflected in taking offence, where the affront at which offence is taken targets one's social standing as an equal.

Two notes on the argument to follow. First, in offering this defence, I commit neither to the claim that some new culture of offence has emerged, nor that the best way to characterise objections to, say, sexist dating norms or microaggressions is that they involve taking offence. Rather, I defend taking offence as a morally appropriate and socially valuable way to respond to such affronts to equal social standing, such that *were* people to take offence in such instances, it would be justified. Second, I do not attempt to capture the full nature of the wrong done when we, for example, commit microaggressions or perpetuate gender-based stereotypes. While I discuss unequal social standing, that is not to suggest that contributing to such inequality is the only, nor necessarily the most, significant wrong or harm done. As one example, research suggests that experiencing racial microaggressions may harm mental health.[4]

2.1. Social standing and the role of social norms

When we take offence, that reaction is usually visible to others. Where it is not, an explanation is often available for why we repress the outwards

---

[3] Strawson, *Freedom and Resentment*, p. 25. Offence might be counted as a reactive attitude: it concerns other's regard for us. Yet the relation between offence and moral responsibility is a looser one than between, say, resentment and blame, as Chapter 4 examines. If offence does lie within the family of reactive attitudes, we would do better treating the reactive attitudes separately or, at least, to not assume that all of them function as resentment does.

[4] E.g., Nadal et al., "The impact of racial microaggressions".

manifestation of our emotion. For instance, perhaps I am offended but too dependent on your whims to risk letting you know, or I could be biding my time before revealing that I am offended in order to maximise the impact of my reaction. Yet the signs that I take offence vary in both kind and degree. I might only tell you that I am offended, criticise your action, simply raise an eyebrow, or fail to laugh at your jokes. But I could also let others know about your behaviour. I may even suspend my relations towards you to varying degrees, depending on the level of offence caused; for instance, refusing invites to events where you will be present, ceasing to be your friend, or withdrawing my custom from your business. How, then, should we assess the impact of this varied set of reactions?

Here is one possible answer. Sometimes, by taking offence an individual can negotiate with another over how they ought to be treated: when someone else takes offence at my act, that gives me reason to modify my future behaviour. Especially when it comes to small details of our interactions—such as the titles or pronouns we use, pointedly holding the door open for a woman, or asking people, "But where are you from, really?"—the person who causes offence may deem it not worth experiencing, nor even risking, the same negative reactions another time and, hence, behave differently the next time round. Most of us, much of the time, seek to avoid causing offence to others.[5] Having another person withdraw from us can be costly even where the resulting estrangement is only partial. Indeed, merely the unpleasantness of another's being offended might suffice to shape future behaviour; when we offend others we might be embarrassed or have that nebulous unpleasant feeling that comes from thinking that we have somehow mis-stepped.

That taking offence generally imposes costs on those who offend may suffice to hold that taking offence is a way to stand up for yourself. In feeling offence, we take it that another ignores, attacks, or mistakes our social standing as we see it, and reject their attribution of lower standing. Now it appears that we also resist that attribution through making it unpleasant or even undesirable for the person to so act, excepting those unusual individuals who delight in upsetting others, creating unpleasant situations, or being shunned.[6]

---

[5] This is supported in work on 'face' and politeness norms, especially regarding our desire to avoid threatening face and conflict: see the central account, Brown & Levinson, *Politeness*; for a survey see, for instance, Kasper, "Linguistic politeness". Distance and power make a difference to our politeness however: for a discussion of relevant work, see Kasper, "Linguistic politeness", pp. 201–202; on impoliteness, see Culpepper, "Reflections on impoliteness", *Impoliteness*. I discuss this in Chapter 3, §3.3.

[6] Such outliers might be more common online, consider the internet 'trolls'. One explanation might be that social disapproval has less force when it comes from strangers or when at a distance.

To so resist might look like an attractive thing to do, especially where the affront to one's standing targets some shared aspect of your identity. Then, to take offence would also amount to standing up for your group. When others slight some aspect of our identity, say, declaring, "women always cry in science laboratories", the affront to standing isn't solely personal. Hence, to react to that affront is not entirely self-directed.

Conceptualising the issue solely in terms of one individual interacting with another, however, is to underestimate the way in which taking offence can intervene in our social relations. As a consequence, it tells us too little about the nature of the costs imposed to determine whether or not they are justified. Indeed, it makes the actions that tend to accompany offence more likely to look disproportionate. One might think that we should instead put up with the minor inconveniences or small-scale rudeness of others, overlooking rather than reacting to these. So, over the next two chapters, I defend taking offence as a way to negotiate hierarchies of social standing and the significance of everyday social interactions in constructing our social standing. To begin, this chapter offers an account of the functions of taking offence framed in terms of relations between groups. I do not thereby claim that taking offence is never individual, in the sense of targeting some idiosyncratic feature of an individual or in occurring between two parties with no knock-on effects or involvement of others. However, Chapter 3 exposes just how much of our offence taking concerns the relations between groups and the social norms or practices that underpin our interactions.

The account of the functions of taking offence starts with a descriptive claim, the moral and political significance of which is defended in the next chapter: respect, disrespect, and our respective social standing are often reflected and conveyed through our social norms and practices and whether we follow these when interacting with others. Sarah Buss and Cheshire Calhoun argue that in particular this holds true for those social norms that pick out appropriate or polite ways to behave or, conversely, what counts as impolite or even beyond the realms of what is decent or appropriate.[7] To illustrate, to shake someone's hand and look them in the eye shows them respect in contexts where that is regarded as a polite greeting, as does listening to their opinions. So, too, not following some widely adopted social

---

[7] Buss, "Appearing respectful"; Calhoun, "The virtue of civility"; see also Olberding, "Subclinical bias". For a broader defence of the moral importance of manners and politeness, see Olberding, "Etiquette", *The Wrong of Rudeness*.

norm can signal to others and to the person concerned that you do not regard them with respect or as having as much standing: say, pushing in front
of them in a queue; refusing to shake their hand; or constantly interrupting
their attempts to speak. These last two Amy Olberding depicts as failures to
cooperate with the way in which another wishes to interact that, where repeated, transform a person's communicating into their merely attempting to
communicate. Describing a woman whose handshake is ignored, Olberding
states, "Her gesture of social accord becomes instead a visual demonstration
of powerlessness".[8]

We are in the realm of behaviours governed by social norms in the sense
that these are behaviours we take to be the right ones for 'us' (our group),
that we expect to occur, and that are enforced through social sanctions.[9] For
Buss and Calhoun, such social norms are what enable us to show others how
we regard them, by providing a shared language by which we can convey respect, consideration, or tolerance—or their absence. As Calhoun comments,
"Social norms for what is due others make it possible to successfully deliver
an insult, a snub, a demeaning gesture. They also make it possible to offer
tokens of respect or considerateness or tolerance".[10] Buss argues that treating
people politely is the way in which we can express respect for others directly.
As she observes, it would be "rather odd" to constantly repeat, "You are
worthy of respect".[11]

However, such social norms are not only a shared way to display respect—
or its absence—but also a way in which we can either convey or highlight
differences in social standing, in more or less subtle ways.[12] Members of
privileged social groups will tend to find that their interactions more often
characterised by respect than members of other groups; indeed, the latter
may frequently face slurs or demeaning gestures that violate ordinary norms

---

[8] "Subclinical bias", for the quote, p. 290.

[9] Here I borrow from Elizabeth Anderson's definition of norms emphasising their 'normativity'
in her "Beyond homo economicus". See also Fehr & Fischbacher, who define norms as 'standards of
behaviour that are based on widely shared beliefs how individual group members ought to behave in
a given situation', "Social norms and human cooperation", p. 185. For another account, see Bichierri,
"Norms of cooperation". For an examination of the central issues with defining norms see Brennan
et al. *Explaining Norms*. This chapter attempts to be largely neutral amongst accounts of norms except
where otherwise noted.

[10] Calhoun, "The virtue of civility", p. 264. Without these, she suggests, we could not "successfully
communicate our moral attitudes toward others", p. 260. Olberding also analyses the social communication that etiquette rules enable, see for instance, "Etiquette", p. 428.

[11] Buss, "Appearing respectful", p. 802.

[12] For a stark case, see Buss' discussion of 'untouchables', "Appearing respectful", p. 810. But my
concern is with justice, such that class-sensitive rules are at issue too.

of appropriate behaviour. That is, unless one's membership of a privileged or high-status group intersects with one's membership of some socially disadvantaged group, where one may find the treatment one would ordinarily receive by virtue of the former periodically or even frequently undermined by its intersection with this other facet of one's identity.[13]

Social norms around respectful or appropriate treatment are also often themselves graded in order to express differing degrees of standing, such that even where social norms are followed they nonetheless convey a difference in social standing. For examples of the latter, you are supposed to shake hands with adults except for the Queen and the depth of a bow is supposed to vary with people's differing ranks. So, too, there are varying norms around how much eye contact to make to count as respectful, and with whom, and who gets to interrupt whom and how often; for instance, women get interrupted far more often than men, obstructing their communication.[14] Alternatively, take the norms around the correct way to address emails ranging from 'Dear (title) x' to 'Hey there'; or the 'ladies-first policies' that Calhoun depicts, from opening doors or offering seats that are taken to be the way to display respect, given our social norms, and yet manifest a background belief that women are weaker and in need of physical protection.[15] Or consider the social norm of using gendered pronouns to refer to others and to regard it acceptable to simply guess at which pronouns another uses.

Such signals through our norms in part constitute what it is to have unequal standing in the social sphere: these are ways in which the social gradient is realised and so to act in accordance with these norms is not merely expressive but, rather, structures our social worlds and their hierarchies. Buss comments that we cannot appropriately walk around saying "You are worthy of respect". But we also don't tend to walk around saying, "I respect you as a woman, a little less than I respect men", or "You are worth a little less respect than me because I'm rich"; the subtle gradations of our social norms often do that for us.[16] That, or the extent to which people tend to comply with the

---

[13] With thanks to Manuel Vargas for pressing this point with the example of Obama's experiences as the first African American US president.

[14] Again analysed in Olberding, "Subclinical bias"; see also Olberding, "The moral gravity of mere trifles". For one study, see Anderson & Leaper, "Meta-analyses of gender effects".

[15] Calhoun, "The virtue of civility", p. 262–3; Buss also discusses such norms, questioning whether sexism is an 'essential part of the message of the behavior', "Appearing respectful", p. 811–2. For a stronger interpretation of how these norms reflect unequal standing, see Frye, *The Politics of Reality*, pp. 5–6.

[16] This may conflict with Calhoun's understanding of the door opening case where what is civil and thus a display of respect, tolerance, or consideration is to follow the relevant norm, even if it is gendered. Discussing cases like door opening, for instance, she argues "men often have to choose

relevant social norms about politeness, recognition, and respect in the first place in their interactions with certain groups of people. To illustrate, Amy Olberding characterises her different experiences when interacting with others when working as a maid, where many failed to follow norms of politeness, as compared to the respect she receives now she is a professor.[17] Or, take the comments we make to women about their appearance or parenting skills that we wouldn't make to men, deeming them improper. We are often careless, or inattentive, when it comes to interacting with those whom we regard as 'lesser'.[18]

2.2. Taking offence and reinforcing norms

The above accounts of the moral significance of manners and politeness say little about how we keep these norms going, nor about how to reshape such norms.[19] The latter is especially pressing because these accounts say little about cases where what is respectful treatment divides along group lines. So, what role can offence play in mediating such social norms? To be justifiable, offence must play the right kind of role in social interactions, in this case, targeting the right social phenomena. Still, this is no narrowly consequentialist account: target, not outcome, is what counts.

First, then, social norms are not like laws.[20] Social norms require social reinforcement and social negotiation: they do not exist outside of people

between a comprehensible *display* of a respectful attitude and *treating* women as they ought to be treated were our society a gender egalitarian one", "The virtue of civility", p. 263 (italics original). The suggestion here is that the attitude displayed is of respect, but of *unequal* respect; more in the manner of Frye's analysis of the case, where what we see is a disregard of what women, in fact, need, *The Politics of Reality*, pp. 5–6.

[17] Olberding, *The Wrong of Rudeness*, p. 47.
[18] Ibid. This will not be a phenomenon confined to interactions between members of different groups; for instance, one can see the same inattentiveness where women interact with other women, as compared to men.
[19] Buss, "Appearing respectful", offers a moral assessment of manners and discusses what would count as a bad system of manners but does not address how to change the system nor sustain it. Closer to my interest, Calhoun analyses a conflict between what displays respect and what in fact would be treating the other respectfully and suggests that it is a collective achievement when we come to have less unjust shared understandings, without discussing how we get there, see "The virtue of civility", pp. 262–265. Olberding considers some mechanisms that might produce behaviour that follows social rules, mentioning both the possibility to inculcating habits in children and as adult along with the kind of emotional contagion that might cause our mannerly behaviour to influence others, see "Etiquette", pp. 430–431, p. 442. This chapter frames the social practices and norms as a collective, not individual, achievement.
[20] That is not to deny the complex interaction between laws and social norms, see, for instance, around tax law, e.g., Lederman, "The interplay between norms and enforcement". Instead, I want to

believing that they are in place; expecting that others will follow the norm; acting as if those norms are in place; and being willing, sometimes, to penalise those who step outside of the norm. A social norm just is a combination of an expected social practice or pattern of behaviour and a set of normative attitudes around that behaviour; namely, that we ourselves ought to do φ, that others in our group ought to do φ, that those who don't do φ manifest some failing, and some willingness to enforce these norms exists in the group.[21]

There may be outliers: cases of social norms that fail to meet all these conditions. For instance, Geoffrey Brennan and his co-authors consider the social norm that one ought not urinate in swimming pools. They ask us to suppose that in some society, this might be a social norm in that people believe one ought not to urinate in pools, presume that others are not doing so, and would be disapproving if someone did, and yet, nonetheless, in that society, many people urinate in pools.[22] However, the social norms that we do not tend to follow are unstable: the fact that we expect others will also act in accordance with a norm is often essential to our willingness to abide by that norm.[23]

Second, emotions play a central role in reinforcing social norms.[24] The usual list includes guilt, disgust, contempt, anger and embarrassment and, above all, shame. These emotions both motivate us to comply with norms and to punish violators. Sometimes, the emotion itself is 'punitive'.[25] I propose that offence be added to this list for enforcing the norms surrounding social standing, especially those regarding politeness and impoliteness, and what counts as a gesture of respect or regard. That role ought to be supported by reflecting on ordinary practice: often we take offence when precisely these

contrast what it is to think about norms from the ways in which political philosophers have tended to think about laws—and law givers. Another way to regard the difference is in terms of formal versus informal or non-formal norms, see Brennan et al., *Explaining Norms*, ch. 3.

[21] Again, following Anderson, "Beyond homo economicus"; see also Brennan et al., *Explaining Norms*.
[22] Brennan et al. *Explaining Norms*, pp. 20–21, the case of the 'Moldovans'.
[23] See Bicchieri & Xiao, "Do the right thing", for a defence of the importance of what people think others are doing.
[24] For a survey, see Dubreuil, "Punitive emotions". As one example, Fehr & Fischbacher note their role in cooperation and punishment, "Social norms and human cooperation", p. 189; as another, Walker examines resentment as a form of anger responding to "perceived threats to expectations based on norms", *Moral Repair*, p. 114. For a study on the role emotions play, and especially the importance of 'social' emotions and not just anger, see Hopfensitz & Reuben, "The importance of emotions".
[25] Dubreuil, "Punitive emotions", esp. p. 36.

norms are violated, as at the queue jumper or the person who makes a rude remark or snubs your greeting. Indeed, this connection is taken as a given within the linguistic and sociological work on face and politeness, where what is rude, disrespectful, or inappropriate is taken to cause offence.[26]

Some of the emotions involved in norm enforcement are self-directed, such as embarrassment and shame, being emotions that we might feel when we violate what we take to be a norm, or that others may try to create in us on the basis that we have violated some norm. Others are outwards-directed, such as anger and contempt, in that the witness or victim of a norm viola-tion feels these towards the norm violator. In this sense, offence would fall into the outwards-directed category, despite the fact that being offended also encourages a self-assessment of our standing when considering if an-other affronts us. Within this category, taking offence is particularly apt for violations of norms around standing because it acts within that system of norms that communicate respect, consideration and the like. When offence is taken against transgressions against such norms, it demonstrates that the person who takes offence endorses these norms, valuing them to the point that she is willing to support these through imposing social sanctions.[27] That applies even when those sanctions go no further than simply the effects of her taking offence on the offending party.

To manifest contempt for another, by contrast, is a break with the norms of respect and consideration for others: we deem them not worth respecting.[28] While disgust can also be a response to violations of norms related to po-liteness, the relevant norms for disgust, as the last chapter elaborated, are not always centred on standing; rather, they are norms about what bodily functions ought to be private, what bodily fluids are deemed unclean, and other contamination-related norms.[29] Disgust would often appear

[26] For a discussion, see Haugh, "Impoliteness and taking offence", p. 36; see also Tagg et al., *Taking Offence on Social Media*; or Culpepper's work on politeness, e.g., *Impoliteness*.

[27] There are some similarities here to the signalling account of blame, see, for instance, Shoemaker & Vargas, "Moral torch fishing". With thanks to Manuel Vargas for noting this connection. Offence may be one of what they term the 'blame-like interpersonal practices', which also have signalling functions. But it would be worth taking its 'signals' separately, partly as a result of the distinction from anger pressed throughout this book. For now, note that offence's signal is a particular one con-cerning social standing, and might be a better signal of one's social 'tribe', than of the 'moral tribe' that they suggest for blame, "Moral torch fishing", p. 7. So, too, offence is not necessarily an especially costly signal, depending on the context in which offence is taken: to be offended at something widely deemed unacceptable may be of little cost and can be signalled without much effort, for instance, with a raised eyebrow.

[28] Haidt comments that "the object of contempt will be treated with less warmth, respect, and con-sideration in future interactions", "The moral emotions", p. 858.

[29] See Calhoun's observation on the very physical nature of civility in earlier times, "The virtue of civility", pp. 253–254 & p. 257.

inappropriate as a response to offensive affronts, such as, say, rudely refusing to shake someone's hand. So, too, anger in these cases, especially where the transgressions are minor or where the meanings of acts are disputed, risks appearing disproportionate, at the least when it is not a generally shared view that such an affront is a moral violation or injustice.[30]

When framed in terms of individual interactions, taking offence imposes costs on the person who offends, thus changing the balance of reasons that a particular person has to act in the way deemed offensive in the future. That influence on future behaviour might, perhaps, spread to others who witness the offence taking too when they interact with the particular person who has taken offence. But, framed against a background of social norms, when I take offence then often I impose a social sanction on the one who transgresses against the norm, unless my offence is very well-disguised, given that people tend to be highly sensitive to such social cues. As a result, offence has a broader role to play in shaping behaviour.

To illustrate, take the norm of queuing in a line. Suppose that one takes offence at a norm violator who pushes to the front, perhaps tisking or pointing them out to others in the queue, or making a pointed comment, like "some people!". The social sanction just is a person or people being offended at what the person does and the resulting social consequences, including the unpleasantness of experiencing this emotion as directed towards one; the costs it imposes on relations together through any resulting withdrawal or estrangement; and the fact that others may see too that one has transgressed, along, perhaps, with resulting feelings of embarrassment or shame at the misstep or transgression. When I take such offence, I contribute to the impression that this is indeed a norm that our group follows, with which we are willing to act in accordance.

When we take offence at the violation of a social norm, sometimes we thus contribute to reinforcing and so sustaining that norm, not only for the norm violator but for ourselves and others who witness the interaction. Exactly what this form of enforcement looks like and what communicates to others

---

[30] Note that the claim here is about what appears disproportionate. The contrast here between moral and social norms should not be interpreted too strongly. I am not claiming there are no moral reasons to abide by politeness norms; indeed, the insight that Buss in "Appearing respectful" gives us is that there are such moral reasons; so, too, Calhoun, "The virtue of civility". Nor am I denying claims about the significant injustice that can be done, cumulatively, through choice of language, minor details of social interactions, and so on, which I explore in the next chapter. Rather, the relation between moral violations and such social norms is indirect and occurs through the cumulative effects against background conditions, which in part explains why anger can *appear* less apt, at least at first. Chapter 4 returns to the relation between offence and anger.

that we are offended, varies with context. So, too, does the degree of subtlety that taking offence can admit: a raised eyebrow might not always be noticed but, when it is, it is sometimes sufficient. The moral or political value—or dis-value—of this depends, of course, on the norm that is being reinforced or underpinned. Sometimes, following social norms enables communications of respect and expresses an underlying attitude that another is one's social equal. At other times, social norms contribute to social inequality and other injustices.

2.3. Taking offence and renegotiating norms

Enforcement is not the only role that taking offence may play. When we take offence, sometimes we reinforce existing norms but, at other times, we instead renegotiate the norms in play. Sometimes, then, social norms are contested. Some set of social norms, understood a certain way, is widely adopted within a society. A subgroup within that society proposes or adopts new or adapted norms; for instance, regarding how to structure conversations, address one another, or over which questions are acceptable and which are demeaning, overly intrusive, or otherwise inappropriate. Alternatively, they propose extensions of existing norms to people who have not tended to be included within that norm's scope. This group then attempts to spread the new or adapted norms beyond their group to the rest of society. Below, I suggest routes by which taking offence *could* contribute towards that spread. I'm not claiming that offence *is* taken, which would be a sociological and empirical claim but, rather, suggesting that taking offence could be morally justified and, later in the book, that it should be taken.

I begin with some examples. One set of claims come from the so-called 'culture of taking offence'. Take the campaign against 'everyday sexism' or alternatively, the microaggressions project, with its attempt to publicise the unacceptability of saying things like, 'but where are you really from?' or 'how can two women have sex?'[31] Alternatively, take the shifting rules of behaviour and contestation over what is appropriate in workplaces and dating culture

---

[31] On the first, see Bates, *Everyday Sexism*. On microaggressions, Chester Pierce first coined this term for racial, and to a lesser extent gendered, affronts, e.g., see his "Stress analogs of racism and sexism". That term is now used to cover a range of everyday slights facing members of disadvantaged groups, e.g., Nadal et al., "Sexual orientation microaggressions"; Sue, *Microaggressions in Everyday Life*.

in general, prompted by the expansion of the 'Me Too' campaign.[32] The other set are claims that were once accused of exemplifying a culture of 'political correctness gone mad'.[33] Take objections to taking 'he' to be gender neutral; the proposal that one use the title 'Ms' rather than insisting on using terms that reveal a woman's marital status; or arguments against treating Christmas as a universal celebration when many do not celebrate it.

In part, these examples concern norms about social standing within society, contesting and seeking to redefine the social norms through which we express respect, tolerance, and consideration; for instance, addressing what questions we tend to ask, or which festivals are usually celebrated in workplaces or schools. The campaigns for such changes bear the hallmarks of being about norms in addressing what 'we' ought to do: the commonly accepted standards of behaviour within a society. The objections target acts widely regarded as acceptable, like taking Christmas to be celebrated by all or making mildly sexist jokes in one's workplace. In addition, the objections are made public, supporting the claim that the aim is a shift in shared norms. For instance, there are projects that collect together stories of those who have experienced everyday sexism and microaggressions, and use these to try to shift our understanding of their acceptability.[34] So, too, often the goal of these campaigns is often not to change the law, say, through legally enforcing the absence of microaggressions, or at least not to only change the law, but, rather, to shift our conventions and general expectations over the correct way to behave: our social norms.[35]

The reason for the shift is that the commonly accepted behaviours are taken to contribute towards injustice: to social inequality through undermining people's standing; to discrimination; and even to promoting attitudes that promote violence and harassment.[36] To illustrate, take the characterisation

[32] For a critique of such extensions of 'Me Too' see the *LeMonde* letter, Collective, "Nous défendons une liberté".

[33] For a discussion of political correctness that links it to the 'culture of taking offence', see Aly & Simpson, "Political correctness gone viral".

[34] For the projects, see "The microaggressions project" at http://www.microaggressions.com; https://everydaysexism.com.

[35] On conventions, expectations, and their relation to norms, see Bichierri, "Norms of cooperation", Brennan et al., *Explaining Norms*. Laws against sexual harassment are an exception.

[36] See, for instance, from the microaggressions project's description: "this project is a response to 'it's not a big deal'—'it' is a big deal. 'it' is in the everyday. 'it' is shoved in your face when you are least expecting it. 'it' happens when you expect it the most. 'it' is a reminder of your difference. 'it' enforces difference . . . 'it' can silence people. 'it' reminds us of the ways in which we and people like us continue to be excluded and oppressed. 'it' matters because these relate to a bigger 'it': a society where social difference has systematic consequences for the 'others'." At https://www.microaggressions.com/about/.

of microaggressions as "putdowns or degradations" in Chester Pierce's original coining of the term. So, too, consider that 'mansplaining' is taken to reveal a view that women have lesser epistemic standing, or the unequal status
of women that is implied by men treating female subordinates at work as
potential dates.[37] Alternatively, take treating Christmas as universal which
suggests that Christianity is the 'standard', with the beliefs of others deemed
'other' and of lesser social significance.

Relating campaigns like the above to norms of appropriate behaviour or
respect might seem an objectionable characterisation, one missing the significance of the injustice done. However, my goal here is not to describe what
is most wrong with the particular acts objected to: that is a different project
and one that would require deep engagement with the history and empirical
details of particular forms of oppression.[38] Rather, it is to observe that the
social meanings of our behaviour are often conveyed through a background
of norms that set out what ordinary interactions look like in ways that are
both uneven for members of different social groups and that facilitate clear
infractions of direct affronts. The patterning of social interactions puts people
in 'their place' within the social hierarchies that mar our society.[39] Norms
around what counts as respectful, impolite, or beyond the pale, pattern our
everyday behaviours in ways that express people's different social standing;
indeed, they in part constitute what it is to have unequal standing, as the next
chapter elaborates. This is most visible in examples like bowing rather than
shaking hands but it can also be seen in more ordinary interactions. For instance, to continue the theme of greetings, take the fact that men shake one
another's hands but often opt for alternative ways to greet women (a kiss, a
hug), or, alternatively, consider norms around who gets to speak first or who
it is (and isn't) rude to interrupt.

The above leaves unaddressed whether those involved in the campaigns
in fact do take offence. Again, I do not make any claims that a new culture
of taking offence is emerging, nor that social justice movements are well-
characterised as motivated by offence.[40] Rather, I suspect that taking offence

---

[37] On microaggressions, Pierce, "Stress analogs of racism and sexism"; on mansplaining, Solnit,
Men Explain Things to Me. The next chapter examines epistemic injustice in more detail.

[38] As one illustration of the kind of work in question for microaggressions, see Pérez Huber &
Solorzano, "Visualizing everyday racism".

[39] Pérez Huber and Solorzano depict racial microaggressions in precisely this way, as "a form
of systemic, everyday racism used to keep those at the racial margins in their place", "Racial
microaggressions", p. 302.

[40] For one such claim, Campbell & Manning, "Microaggression and moral cultures".

is a prevalent part of our everyday social interactions and by no means restricted to, nor even most prevalent amongst, members of disadvantaged or
oppressed groups, although that is an empirical question.[41] But my task is
a normative, not a descriptive one: to demonstrate that *were* one to take offence as a route to challenging the social norms, that would have the right
target (these social norms) and impose the right kinds of costs on those who
offend (those that usually follow from transgressing social norms).[42]

In particular, first, taking offence can be a way to express a new or altered
social norm and a strategy to propose that we adopt it. So, when I take offence sometimes I act *as if* there is some norm in place, say, regarding acceptable terms of address, that you have just transgressed. If you or others go
along with my censure, that helps to give the sense that this is now the social
norm that we follow. Indeed, people tend to be very sensitive to social norm
enforcement: there are strong social norms around enforcing social norms.[43]
Where you try to enforce a norm that others do not think is the social norm
in play, then people may protest. As a result, conversely, when I seek to act as
if there is some new norm and no one corrects me, where social norms are
being contested that is a good way to get others to think 'we'—the relevant
group—have this new norm in place.

Again, this is a place where offence might be a more appropriate-seeming
emotion than other norm enforcement related emotions like anger or contempt. These other emotions may be more likely to trigger resistance at
a seemingly inappropriate way to enforce a norm. That may sound like a
context-specific empirical claim, where which emotion functions best will
simply depend on how things go in a particular case. But there are good
reasons to think that how appropriate these emotions seem is likely to differ
across cases. To feel contempt for someone is a more serious break in relations

---

[41] Take Calhoun's observation that members of these groups have tended to have to content themselves with less consideration, respect and tolerance than that members of more advantaged groups
receive, "The virtue of civility".

[42] And sometimes those opposing the social practices and norms do appear to take offence, say,
refusing to laugh along with the sexist joke, pointing out that the assumption Christmas is universal is exclusionary, or withdrawing from further contact with someone who makes racist
remarks. Importantly, these acts are often on a much smaller scale than the public shaming that has
preoccupied philosophers and the media, see to illustrate Billingham & Parr, "Online shaming" and
"Enforcing social norms"; Tosi & Warmke, "Moral grandstanding". Regardless, the point here is to
suggest that to take offence could be a good way to target social norms—whether or not it is so used.

[43] For a discussion of the willingness of third parties to punish norm violation, even at cost to
oneself and without receiving any benefits, see Fehr & Fischbacher, "Third-party punishment". On
the general effectiveness of social norms, see McTernan, "How to make citizens behave" and "Moral
character".

with another than is merely feeling offended and, indeed, contempt offers a more serious challenge to another's social standing: we regard them with contempt. To feel anger is often regarded as condemning another for falling short of some shared moral standard, as Chapter 1 described, where one has done an injury, harm or grievous wrong. But campaigns for altered norms around the differential treatment of social groups often face resistance from others who see no issue with the old norms, casting doubt on there being a shared standard of what it is right to do at least for some of these cases. Under conditions of such disagreement, as Chapter 4 returns to discuss, offence might be used to negotiate. Note that here I do not address the respective moral justifications for taking offence and anger: anger may yet be a justified reaction to small details of social interactions. Nor do I intend to downplay the seriousness of such details: the next chapter explores the relation between acts like microaggressions and sexist jokes on the one hand, and injustice on the other. Rather, I address how the emotions are 'read', or the social assessment of the emotion; a separate question from which reactions are morally appropriate.

Second, a particular group taking offence can change the social meaning of following a certain social norm. Here, I adopt a thicker sociological or social psychological understanding of how social norms function: one which includes a consideration of the social meanings of norms, such that these norms exist against and contribute to a background social context, with a set of shared understandings or interpretations of behaviour.[44] A whole set of behaviours that might have appeared to meet existing norms around how to treat others—say, that culturally insensitive fancy dress is acceptable, or that toilets should be divided into male and female—shift in their meanings to be statements of a set of political beliefs, respectively, against 'political correctness' or against rights for people who are transgender.[45] As a consequence, the identity that one might be assuming in behaving in certain ways changes from, for instance, following norms amongst college students about what makes excellent fancy dress, to being the kind of person who deliberately offends particular groups, or being someone who adopts a particular political affiliation. Once these meanings take root, we might sometimes expect anger as a response to violations, where their message is now one of injustice, discrimination, or prejudice and we expect the other to know this. The

[44] See for instance Lessig, "Social meaning and social norms".
[45] See, for instance, the "a culture not a costume" campaign, at www.ohio.edu/orgs/stars/Poster_C ampaign.html.

person who deliberately seeks to inflict on others what others deem harmful may then appear an appropriate target of anger.

Third, taking offence penalises people who fail to comply with the new norms because, as suggested earlier, it is costly to have others be offended at you. Imposing such costs can increase compliance to a new norm or reduce compliance to an old norm.[46] Now, however, there is more to say about what those costs are beyond feeling shame, being shunned, or having an unpleasant experience. Social norms are often tied to our sense of belonging to, or identifying with, some group or society.[47] Thus, there are associated costs when we fall short of following some social norms of feeling like an outsider or not belonging, heightened by the resulting behaviour of the offended party withdrawing from the offender. Consider failing to buy a round in the pub at the right moment, or, depending on the location, being a man who orders a half pint rather than full pint of beer. Further, owing to their varying social meanings, following some social norms and not others conveys something about what kind of person we are, or how we want others to perceive of us. If I want to think of myself as a progressive, say, then I better follow what other progressives think is the thing that people like us should do.[48]

Taking offence, then, can be used both to reinforce norms and to renegotiate them. Yet there is no inconsistency between these claims but, rather, two different social functions of one and the same emotion. Indeed, sometimes taking offence can appear in both roles with regards to one and the same behaviour: one group may take offence at a violation of norm A, while another takes offence at others still following norm A as they deem it disrespectful.

With this account of the roles that offence can play in view, I make some observations. Sometimes, groups that lack power might (and do) manage to change social norms. To take offence to shift norms is a collective, not individual, endeavour. And to take offence, even where it challenges a particular

---

[46] For one discussion of norms breaking down where norm adherence gets costly, via game theoretic experiments, see Fehr & Fischbacher, "Social norms and human cooperation", at p. 189.

[47] For one discussion of social identity theories/self-categorisation theories and the importance of group norms in people conceptualising their group membership, including how this improves modelling of the influence of norms on behaviour, see Terry & Hogg, "Group norms", for the theoretical framework, see especially pp. 779–780. They state, "People do not only enact social norms for social approval, because others have told them to, or because others are watching. On the contrary, norms can be enacted in private—a particular group membership just needs to be the contextual basis for self-definition", p. 780.

[48] Sunstein makes a similar comment that what we choose to do can be a result of how we want to think of ourselves and have others think of us, against a background of norms, "Social norms and social roles", p. 916.

social norm, is a way to negotiate *within* the system of social norms. Taking offence ought not to be interpreted as a break in civility but, rather, part of the construction and maintenance of such a system and its piecemeal improvement. Generally, when we intend to show respect, toleration or consideration for another, we seek to do what they will understand as conveying such respect. Yet we do not live within social worlds where there are always universally shared social understandings, even within a single society. Given this variation, we need some tactic by which to negotiate. To take offence indicates to another that they fail to act in a way that you read as respectful or appropriate. That variation is not always related to the fact that societies are marred by relations of inequality, although often it is, given that the dominant social norms likely reflect the interests of the socially dominant group.

Consider, for instance, the shifting range of greetings that might appear fitting from handshakes to hugs, reflecting the appropriate (neither excessive, nor insufficient) degree of familiarity and acknowledgement. These vary with cultural backgrounds. But they may also vary owing to changes in background conditions: for instance, in an era following a pandemic, such norms could be in flux, with what was deemed an ordinary social gesture, of a hug, seeming a far more intimate gesture or one that communicates that a person has a relaxed attitude towards risk. Clearly, in the cases above, I discuss norms of far greater normative significance, being ones that structure socially unequal societies, as the next chapter elaborates.

Thus, to take offence informs others about what counts as respectful to us and hence is a move within a culture of civility or respect. Incorporating offence into the system of civility stands in contrast to a popular perception that a culture of taking offence somehow represents a break with civil behaviour. So, too, it conflicts with the idea that we'd better put up with the norms that we have: of those shared social understandings discussed in some existing works on the significance of manners, despite the fact that such shared understandings are frequently ones that reflect social inequality.[49]

---

[49] For instance, Calhoun, "The virtue of civility". Otherwise, Calhoun argues, deciding not to treat others civilly and so deciding for ourselves the bounds of civility, we impose our sense of our 'rightness' despite the fact we may be wrong and risk undermining the very system of civilities that protect the marginalised and oppressed from overt hatred. She suggests that those who are members of disadvantaged groups tend to receive less civil treatment than others, so there is reason to keep following the norms regardless, since giving them up would result in even less civility for such groups. Taking offence and negotiating these norms, I am suggesting, may not present that threat.

2.4. In defence of negotiating social norms

Some readers might think that the whole business of negotiating social norms is suspect, particularly if it is done though taking offence and especially when it is taken over contested norms. By contrast, I suspect that fewer are worried about those who tut at queue jumpers. For the rest of this chapter, then, I seek to take the teeth out of a set of permutations of this objection.

I begin with doubts over the role of social norms themselves. One might hold that imposing social norms on the way in which we relate to each other is itself oppressive or limits freedom. On such grounds, one would deny that taking offence is an appropriate strategy, given that any imposition of social norms is deemed inappropriate or morally indefensible. Here, John Stuart Mill's worries about the pernicious effects of social pressure would, no doubt, be cited.[50] Yet none of us exist within a social world that is free from social norms and their accompanying social pressures. A large number of norms already structure our social interactions. Take our knowledge of how close we ought to sit to each other, how much eye contact to make, or when it is the right time to shake hands. Think of how sensitive we are to minor transgressions of this sort of norm: the discomfort you would feel if I sat just that little bit too close or looked into your eyes a little too long. In short, then, taking offence to renegotiate social norms, or even inculcating a culture where more and more people take offence—were that an accurate description—would not be to impose norms on some previously norm-free canvas. Instead, it is a bid to change the details: to alter or replace particular social norms or their social meanings.

So, too, people taking offence does not make people unable to act as, or say what, they like. It merely means that our doing so has costs. Many of those costs, including being criticised or not being invited to events if you keep it up, are precisely what you would normally expect for doing those things that violate our norms of respect or of what is appropriate. Imagine if, without good reason, someone repeatedly got a little too close to others for comfort, ignored people when they tried to shake her hand, or referred to someone by a nickname that they found offensive. Where the behaviour is deemed beyond the pale rather than merely impolite or disrespectful, as may be the case

---

[50] Mill, *On Liberty*. For an analysis of Mill's notion of social pressure and which influences count, see Wilkinson, "Mill's *On Liberty*", pp. 220–223.

for some behaviours condemned in the so-called culture of taking offence, then the usual costs escalate.

One might respond that we ought never to police each other's behaviour in these ways and, instead, should let others behave however they like. However, social norms are what enable us to move around our social world, they let us predict how others will behave, know which side to queue on, how we might offend others or gain their trust, and a myriad of other clues about how to interact successfully. Further, social norms let us portray ourselves in a particular way: we know what signals certain behaviours send to others about the kind of person we are, or our values, for instance. Thus, it is hard to reject social norms altogether. At the least, doing so would require some new way to coordinate social relations so that we can understand how others are likely to behave and choose behaviours that convey what we intend.[51] Where we do not already know a person well, that need is still more pressing. One might make a still stronger claim, following Michael Hechter and Karl-Dieter Opp's view that "without norms, it is hard to imagine how interaction and exchange between strangers could take place at all".[52] Alternatively, Margaret Urban Walker observes that our social norms make us feel at home through the shared expectations that they generate: "Shared expectations are a roof over our heads and a floor beneath us; they provide reasonable assumptions about where we are safe and where we belong".[53] That is not to say that the precise shape of the norms of a society is always desirable, after all, the norms may be discriminatory. Rather, the claim is that some set of norms is necessary for a society to function.

Another objection to taking offence, or at least, to a society where more and more people grow prone to taking offence, is that it would increase the overall number of social norms in play, even if one thinks that taking offence over existing norms is acceptable. For example, one might think that the proposal that we stop performing microaggressions or instances of everyday sexism is a matter of imposing a whole new set of social norms limiting ever

[51] For example, see again Buss, "Appearing respectful" and Calhoun, "The virtue of civility", on how social norms enable us to express or communicate respect or disrespect.

[52] Hechter & Opp, Social Norms, p. xi; see also Sunstein's claim on social norms that "Social life is not feasible—not even imaginable—without them", in "Social norms and social roles", p. 917. As an illustration of the costs, Olberding examines the unpredictability that emerges where some find that norms don't apply to them straightforwardly by virtue of their group membership, "Subclinical bias".

[53] Walker, Moral Repair, p. 146. Resentment plays a central role in protecting these norms for Walker, and she includes in the appropriate scope of resentment violations of norms at which I argue that we should take offence. Chapter 4 returns to carve out a distinct place for offence, including where the act is small and where the person is not responsible.

more areas of behaviour. Yet this variant of the suspicion about social norms fails to take into account just how fine-grained and numerous are the social norms that already dictate our social interactions. Social norms already dictate details like precisely how close we sit; what topics we discuss in public, amongst family, or at dinner parties; how to blow our noses or wipe our mouths after eating.

An opponent may continue that, nonetheless, in such campaigns what is proposed is that there be yet more norms, or that these norms extend into new areas of life that were previously norm-free. However, that is to assume that the behaviour found objectionable is ungoverned by existing norms, or social practices. Often that is mistaken: at the least, what titles we use, what questions we ask, and the like are ordinarily norm governed. Consider dating, where there are clearly a set of existing social norms around how forceful a man should, or could, be when faced with a woman's lack of interest, as well as around how to appropriately communicate interest. Further, even were it the case that the overall number of social norms increased, that may not necessarily be for the worse. For a start, social norms are useful: through the shared language that norms provide we can achieve a great deal, in terms of quickly and easily getting across how we feel, what we believe and which groups we identify with, how we want to present ourselves, what we think of others, and so on, and all without having to know all the details about particular individuals and what they think. Social norms thus offer a useful and likely essential shortcut in our social interactions. As such, acting to reinforce norms that keep social cooperation going and to renegotiate those that pattern our social interactions in unjust ways, looks defensible and even desirable.

2.5. On negotiating through offence

In order to show that taking offence is unjustified or inappropriate, it seems that one would have to object to something particular about taking offence as a reaction, rather than dismissing norms in general. Perhaps, for example, taking offence is a particularly bad way to tackle social norms. However, it does not appear so, given the way in which taking offence intervenes in social norms. Taking offence targets the social norms that structure our relationships and imposes the normal costs of transgressing social norms, or of following social norms with particular social meanings. You have stepped

beyond the bounds of what is deemed appropriate behaviour. A legal intervention would seem both out of place and disproportionate. But it looks appropriate when others react by withdrawing, seeking to impose social costs
that indicate you violated the norms or followed an objectionable norm. On
the one hand, by not following shared norms you impose, or at least risk imposing, costs on others; for instance, the fraying of social norms, or a loss
of shared social meanings or of social ease. You fail to follow along with the
usual terms of interaction. That looks like it justifies imposing a social sanction, all else being equal. On the other hand, by contrast, in cases where we
lack shared social norms, say, when members of one group generally interpret some behaviour directed towards them as disrespectful where it is
widely regarded by others as acceptable, then some negotiation is required in
order to find a set of norms and practices that permits our social interactions
to be grounded on genuinely shared understandings. Taking offence can be
an appropriate part of that renegotiation.

Two lines of objections might arise, one from the costs of taking offence
and the other from the fact that offence is an emotion. On the first, one might
deny that offence is an appropriate or justified strategy because there is more
to the taking of offence than the bids to alter norms described above, such
that offence is more costly than I have made it appear. One might point to the
shaming of particular individuals or the attempts to impose all manner of
additional costs on those who offend, such as losing a job or having an article
retracted, that often draw popular attention. These costs go over and above
the usual reputation or relational effects of failing to follow social norms such
as refusing to shake a person's hand.[54]

However, these escalations in costs are not a central part of the kind of
taking offence that I am discussing, and certainly they are no necessary component. Very often, including in the social movements I discuss, our use of
offence in everyday relations is far smaller in scale than the cases that have
tended to draw media attention.[55] A great deal happens on campuses or
workplaces and takes the form of discussion, spreading information and the
like, rather than online targeting of particular individuals. Further, recall

---

[54] For examples, see Ronson, *So You've Been Publicly Shamed*; for a list of various criteria by
which to limit public shaming, see Billingham and Parr, "Enforcing social norms". I return to public
shaming at greater length in Chapter 6.

[55] Some evidence is provided by a study of more than a hundred people's reactions to offensive
content on Facebook: "Where they did respond to things they took exception to they generally did
so non-aggressively by ensuring through various methods that they no longer had access to such
posts"—a form of withdrawal; see Tagg et al., *Taking Offence on Social Media*, p. 8.

that this book's defence is restricted to those who are defending their own standing and that of their group. Many egregious cases of public shaming go beyond that to include taking up the causes of others. Indeed, this might be one reason why the shaming can end up appearing egregious, in so far as one takes moral grandstanding or desiring to virtue signal to be a serious threat.[56]

There are also internal reasons drawn from the purpose of the practice of taking offence itself to limit how extensive such costs become.[57] If the point is to reshape social norms and social meanings, then the goal is to reconfigure the way in which people relate to each other and not that we cease to relate at all: that we use different words, make different assumptions in our interactions, and so on. However, imposing too high a cost might instead lead to the suspension of relations by creating conditions where it is no longer possible for people to engage: perhaps, on the one side, because the costs are so severe that one is resentful and, on the other, because the person who takes offence ends up entirely alienated from the person who offends.

What, the opponent might continue, if a social norm is best challenged or a new norm best proposed by having individual scapegoats and so casting some out for their transgressions, even at the cost of an ongoing relationship? After all, the goal is to reconfigure relations amongst groups as a whole, rather than those amongst each and every particular individual. Still there is reason not to embrace that strategy or, at least, to be cautious. Return to the idea that what is happening is a reshaping of the social meanings of certain acts. If one makes transgressing the new or altered social norm too costly, one might aggravate a danger already facing attempts to make such changes; namely, that there is an available social meaning to not following such norms, of being the apparently courageous rebel or 'straight talker'. The costlier that transgressing becomes, and especially, the more apparently disproportionately costly, the more likely we are, I suspect, to see others as courageous for going against the norms. It is not very courageous to risk a raised eyebrow. In contrast, to some, risking an internet flaming looks brave.[58]

---

[56] See Tosi & Warmke, "Moral grandstanding".

[57] I will not yet commit to a view on what counts as disproportionate costs for an individual. Doing so would require assessing the ways in which the behaviour committed contributes to injustice, along with what difference it makes that one benefits from injustice as a member of some privileged group. For instance, I suspect that we may be liable to bear costs that seem excessive if one looks only at the particular action committed, but well within the bounds of what costs we should bear to correct the wider injustice. I return to the issue of costs in Chapter 6.

[58] It will be an empirical matter, and likely a context sensitive one, as to whether scapegoating is the most effective strategy, given both this alternative meaning and a worry about the backlash where norm enforcement appears excessive. The odds, I suspect, are not likely to be in favour of scapegoating. With thanks to Jennifer Page for pressing me on this point.

There is a different form that an objection from costs might take, starting instead from those costs experienced by the offended party. If I withdraw in reaction to some offensive act that you commit, then I too suffer the social costs accompanying the diminution of our relationship: withdrawal seems a two-way street. So, too, to take offence may be emotionally taxing or demanding and it can be risky for the offended party: others might reject one's offence or the offending party might escalate their behaviour in response to the accusation, perhaps growing angry. These costs may make it less likely that people would take offence.

One could observe in response that to take offence is not always particularly costly: to raise an eyebrow or not laugh at a joke is not emotionally taxing and, often, will not be socially risky. Yet, at this point, a 'goldilocks' problem arises for my defence of the social role of taking offence. In cases where offence poses little cost on the offended party, it may also not look especially effective: such minor forms of offence taking may do little to encourage others to comply with norms that have been transgressed against, or to push the renegotiation of social norms. Thus, an opponent may ask whether a social defence of offence is restricted only to cases where the balance of costs happens to be just right: low enough that someone would likely take offence, yet high enough that the offending party would change their ways. How common, one might wonder, is such an asymmetry of costs?[59]

There are good reasons to discount this balancing worry. One ought not to underestimate the effect of small and comparatively costless acts expressing offence: to realise that one has mis-stepped and offended another can be socially costly and can encourage us to reform our behaviour, even where the act by which that is conveyed is subtle. As a result, the costs of performing an act do not straightforwardly map onto the costs it imposes on another.

The goldilocks problem also overlooks the asymmetry in positions of the two parties—the potentially offended and the offender—before offence is taken. If another person affronts you, then you face a threat to your social standing in this interaction. The offending party, on the other hand, as yet faces no challenge or threat to their standing—until the offended party takes offence. When another takes offence, that suggests that the offending party commits some social misstep or acts inappropriately, which is itself a threat to the offending party's standing: hence why sometimes people are offended

---

[59] With thanks to Chris Mills for pressing this point. Another line of response is to observe that often we do engage in costly signalling behaviours, as when we blame others: see Shoemaker & Vargas, "Moral torch fishing".

when others take offence at what they do. Further, this asymmetry mitigates the idea that the offended party might not be moved to act unless the cost of their doing so is very low: the person who is affronted already faces a threat to which they have reason to respond, such as through taking offence. Failing to reject an affront itself can be costly in terms of one's standing and in terms of its emotional toll. Finally, the problem as formulated above treats an interaction between two parties in isolation. That will often be misleading. Withdrawal may be a two-way street between the offended and offending parties, but we should not overlook the fact that, sometimes, taking offence can be an act that draws one closer to one's group, even as it pushes the offending party out. It is an affirmation of the norms that one's group follows.

The second line of objection turns to what offence is: one might see it as a 'mere' emotional reaction, and not a calculated attempt to change the norms of a society.[60] In particular, when an individual takes offence, they do not aim at norm change but, rather, simply react to an affront. To reply, sometimes, in a sense, that reaction is all that occurs. For instance, offence can be taken at some idiosyncratic affront, say, being teased as the 'baby' of the family. The offended party may have no particular thoughts about social norms, nor their general treatment. Yet even in such cases, still, what renders the tease comprehensible is a background of social norms; in this case, regarding what is infantilising. Even without the offended party directly considering the background context of social norms, to take offence still reveals which norms are in play and to which norms the offended party herself is committed. So, too, in many other cases—likely the majority—our offence is taken at affronts that strike us in familiar ways: offended by a degrading joke, a microaggression, or similar, people know the background context of their experience, and their reaction is informed by that context.

Perhaps this reply fails to fully address the root of the objection; namely, the thought that an *emotion* ought not to be taken to play such a role within our social relations. One might propose that, instead, we should simply present others with reasons to change their behaviour, replacing any emotional reaction. But reason and emotion are not mutually exclusive strategies and nor are emotions 'mere feelings': some emotions communicate to others information about our values and commitments.[61] In particular, as earlier

---

[60] With thanks to Richard Child for this objection.
[61] For one critical discussion of the distinction between reason and emotion, see Fricker, "Reason and emotion".

discussed, emotions are commonly regarded as playing a significant role in sustaining social norms. Further, offering others explicit reasons can be a blunt and socially awkward approach. Much of our social negotiation occurs not through the explicit offering of reasons but, rather, rests on far subtler forms of negotiation. The analyses of offence and face offered by sociologists and sociolinguists demonstrate this, often examining cases where one individual seeks to subtly convey to the other that they have mis-stepped, perhaps though a joke, a pause, or an indirect story.[62]

The juxtaposition of having an emotion and calculated intervention also fails to hold up to scrutiny. Depicting our emotions and their expression as always without purpose and control is inaccurate. Consider a footballer who expresses great distress at missing an easy goal intending to make his team's fans less enraged. Often, we moderate our emotional reactions or their expression, sometimes in order to produce desired effects in others: say, refraining from yelling or crying, or purposefully expressing contentment. In addition, we might be able to become more or less inclined towards certain reactions. In this case, it seems that we can shape our orientation towards our standing. That calculation would be a step back from the one-off expression, in seeking to become the kind of person who notices affronts to a certain degree and informing oneself as to what counts as an affront. Still, it would shape the emotions that we tend to experience. The next chapter defends the cultivation of a pattern of attention where people do notice a subset of affronts to social standing.

I might now face an objection from the opposite direction. Am I proposing that we use offence strategically, such that we take offence to get what we want? It might be doubted that this is consistent with taking it to be justified to pay attention to one's standing. Perhaps I muddy the waters by making it a strategic move to take offence. Or it could be objected that inauthentic offence, where I take offence in order to achieve some calculated goal, would fail. The person we took such offence at might see through us, or they might seek to frustrate our calculated goal by deliberately not responding to our taking offence, repeatedly ignoring it.[63] However, my claims about our being able to shape our taking offence happens upstream of a particular instance where I react. Namely, I shape how I come to orientate myself towards

[62] On the last, see Michael Haugh's case of Sally and her tale to Peter of the ex-boyfriend, "Impoliteness and taking offence", pp. 40–41; Haugh also gives case of using sarcasm, p. 40; see also the discussion of online offence taking in Tagg et al., *Taking Offence on Social Media*.
[63] Thanks to Andrew William on this point.

my standing, and then in how I manifest my reaction. While we may have reasons to shape an inclination to take offence given its social role, as I continue to argue in the following chapters, that is not to claim that the attitude in a single instance is driven directly by those reasons. Further, while it is true that inauthentic emotions can be hard to pull off, it does not follow that we should never fake taking offence: doing so might sometimes be the best thing to do all things considered, as with any emotion. For instance, I might fake feeling pride in an important achievement that I don't particularly value, since my friend has attained the same and I know that her ability to take pride in this thing that matters to her will be undermined by my failing to do so.

Taking offence is thus a tool that can be used in our social relations to reinforce social norms or to renegotiate them, especially where these norms shape or constitute our social standing, by setting out what counts as respectful treatment and what counts as others acknowledging that standing. However, that does not tell us if and when we should use this tool, nor the limits on so using it. The defence of taking offence is far from complete. In particular, one might ask how can we tell when someone is justifiably or reasonably contesting a norm from when they are not? Indeed, one might even insist that this last is really the central, defining question of any treatment of taking offence, rather than the nature of taking offence itself. So, too, one might ask, *who* can demand changes to norms—what about odd individuals who, say, want to be greeted with six kisses rather than the usual (around here) one?[64] Chapter 4 addresses these questions. Finally, not enough has been said about the weightiness or normative significance of social norms around appropriate behaviour, nor of the demands for change to such norms. That absence is especially pressing when assessing the reasonableness, let alone the proportionality, of the costs imposed by taking offence. It is to these questions that I now turn, with an account of the social construction of our standing in society.

[64] With thanks to Peter Schaber for this example.

3

Do sweat the small stuff

On the nature and significance of social standing

Is it defensible to pay attention to one's social standing—particularly, atten-tion of the kind and degree that would incline one to take offence? To take offence and, certainly, to be inclined to take offence, reflects a particular pattern of attention or orientation towards your social standing.[1] You take your standing to be significant enough both to keep track of within social interactions in a way that means you notice affronts, and to react to such affronts by taking offence. Otherwise, that others act, say, in rude or incon-siderate ways, make dismissive remarks and derogatory jokes, or subtly put you down, might simply pass without note. But does social standing have the kind of significance that could justify taking offence when others ignore, attack, or diminish one's social standing? Could it even be that we ought to cultivate our attention in such a way that we are inclined to take offence?

Many would be sceptical, despite the last chapter's defence of offence as a means by which to negotiate social norms and practices. A popular view of taking offence casts it as a result of oversensitivity or even narcissism: take the coining of the term 'generation snowflake' to describe those purportedly in-volved in the so-called 'culture of taking offence'.[2] Some might instead favour disregarding the great majority of affronts offered to our social standing.[3] In this chapter, then, I defend both the significance of social standing and the desirability of taking offence at certain affronts to it against a background of

---

[1] For other discussions of orientation and attention, see, for instance, Lillehammer, "Who is my neighbour?" which analyses indifference in terms of the orientation towards an object it reveals; or for a depiction of modesty in terms of how we direct our attention towards our good qualities, see Bommarito, "Modesty as a virtue of attention".

[2] See, on 'cultures of victimhood', Campbell and Manning, "Microaggression and moral cultures"; "The new millennial 'morality'"; for further critiques of offence see Lukianoff and Haidt, *The Coddling of the American Mind*; or Fox, "Generation snowflake". Martha Nussbaum describes being angry at affronts as revealing a 'hypersensitivity born of morbid narcissism', in *Anger and Forgiveness*. Another source would be the sceptical responses to microaggressions in particular, see, for instance, Haidt, "The unwisest idea on campus".

[3] Perhaps even endorsing a Stoic ideal such as that defended by Nussbaum, *Anger and Forgiveness*.

On Taking Offence. Emily McTernan, Oxford University Press. © Oxford University Press 2023.
DOI: 10.1093/oso/9780197613092.003.0004

social inequality. To do so, I also tackle a persistent challenge to relational or social egalitarians: namely, that they tell us too little about what it is to live as social equals, especially when it comes to relations among citizens rather than relations between state and citizen.[4]

3.1. Between excess and deficiency

Clearly, we can pay too much attention to our social standing, getting it wrong in either the amount of standing that we claim relative to others or the degree of attention that we pay to our standing—or both.[5] For those who get the amount wrong take, for example, a sexist husband who gets offended when his wife makes some small joke about him in public because he holds that wives ought to be deferential to husbands. Or imagine a professor who deems himself due constant acts of deference from more junior academics and students in order to acknowledge what he takes to be his own greatly superior standing, say, their making fawning comments about his brilliance or demonstrating detailed knowledge of even his unpublished works. Consider, too, a minor celebrity who becomes offended when others don't recognise her or fail to ask for photos. While these last examples are light-hearted, below I examine how claiming greater than equal standing can produce stark injustices.

To illustrate getting the degree of attention wrong, take people who regard the actions of others that have nothing to do with them to be all about them and their standing. Martha Nussbaum, for instance, offers Seneca's case of being offended because he thinks some remark is about his own age, when his interlocutor may mean nothing of the kind.[6] Even if we think people shouldn't offer a certain type of affronts such as ageist comments, someone might become oversensitised to the possibility of such affronts, to the point of seeing them even where none are offered. Another variant of this complaint arises in the criticism of 'generation snowflake', where some hold that

---

[4] Jonathan Wolff labels this vagueness an 'abiding problem', "Social equality and social inequality", pp. 213–5. See also Fourie, "What is social equality?" p. 109; Schuppert, "Non-domination, non-alienation and social equality", p. 444. Similarly, Fabian Schuppert comments that there has been a focus on vertical (state-citizen) relations rather than horizontal (citizen-citizen) relations, "On the range of egalitarian justice". For an interesting account of why relational egalitarianism appears vague in this respect yet why that doesn't matter, given the emphasis is instead on diagnostic precision, see Axelsen and Bidadanure, "Unequally egalitarian?"

[5] The notions of excess and deficiency introduce a virtue framing, to which Chapter 6 returns.

[6] Nussbaum, *Anger and Forgiveness*, pp. 137–8.

it is a product of mere oversensitivity in that people are attuned to the sorts of slights that they ought to instead simply overlook; not because they are mistaken about their standing but simply because we ought to rise above such small infringements upon it.[7]

What might be more controversial is the thought that we can pay *too little* attention to our social standing or, at least, that the right attention to our standing is anything like the degree required to notice non-egregious affronts. Following Martha Nussbaum's adapted Stoicism, one might think that it is better to pay minimal attention to social standing, barring violations that are severely harmful such as sexual assault or harassment.[8] On her view, we ought not to care whether others do or do not offer us tokens of respect and consideration, hence disregarding insults, acts of impoliteness, putdowns, or slights. Such aspects of what she terms our 'relative social status' ought not be given undue weight in the way that taking offence would seem to do.[9] How admirable, one might think, to rise above such petty concern for social standing. So, too, rising above these affronts might make our lives go better, given the myriad opportunities to feel slighted in our daily lives, say, where fellow commuters shove past us to grab seats; colleagues talk over us in meetings; or family members make dismissive remarks about our life choices.[10] Society might also benefit if we paid less attention to our social standing, ignoring or even ceasing to notice ordinary rudeness, slights, or lack of consideration. Caring about such slights, you might think, could only increase a society's degree of conflict and unpleasantness.[11]

If disregarding one's social standing was a result of getting it wrong about the amount of social standing one is due, say, thinking oneself inferior or worthless, that might be undesirable. Yet our ideal might instead simply be directing her attention away from her standing in comparison to others; in parallel to Nicolas Bommarito's depiction of the modest person as directing her attention away from her good qualities.[12] Alternatively, perhaps she

---

[7] E.g., Fox "Generation snowflake".

[8] Her list: "improper termination of employment, negligent medical treatment, harassment on the job, theft, sexual assault, even homicide", Nussbaum, *Anger and Forgiveness*, p. 139.

[9] Ibid.

[10] For this observation see also Nussbaum, drawing on Seneca declares, "Detachment is urgently needed if life is to go well", *Anger and Forgiveness*, at. p. 140. See, too, Simpson, "Regulating offense, nurturing offense", for a claim that once we so cultivate our attention, then we won't be able to stop seeing the slights.

[11] See the various panics about generation snowflake, e.g., Lukianoff and Haidt, *The Coddling of the American Mind*; Fox, "Generation snowflake".

[12] Bommarito, "Modesty as a virtue of attention".

simply does not regard the way in which others respond to her perception of her standing as significant; rather, she is confident enough in her standing that affronts from others cannot shake it.

Indeed, it is not only Stoics who might resist attending to social standing. On the face of it, a concern for one's social standing appears to lead to an unattractive attention to details such as how long another shakes your hand for, say, or who buys the first round of drinks, or what title is used, along with other minutiae of our social interactions. Further, within ethics, defences of social standing's significance are rare. Macalester Bell comments that "judging by how little is written on the topic, it seems that most contemporary ethicists think that status, esteem, and deference are of little moral importance".[13] One might even be tempted towards a clear separation between that which is a matter for ethics and that which is *merely* socially fitting or appropriate. The realm of the socially fitting, one might think, is only about what we are used to, with little or no moral weight to any transgressions against the normal order and little significance to its overall arrangement. As such, attending to any transgressions, or to how the social order is arranged as a whole, would be a mistake.

Against this deflationary view, I defend relative social standing as an appropriate object of concern and the character of those who take it to be such. Directing our attention away from our social standing or taking affronts to be insignificant or irrelevant to our social standing would be a mistake given, first, the way in which our social standing is up for negotiation and, second, the importance of affronts, and of resisting these, in constructing our social standing.[14] In particular, I defend a concern for one's standing as a *social equal*: to claim standing as a social equal is what it is to get the amount of standing one is due, correct.

As to what is the right degree of attention, our social standing, equal or otherwise, is made out of the cluster of social norms and social practices that

---

[13] Bell, *Hard Feelings*, p. 99. Of course, Bell's own work is an exception, e.g., "A woman's scorn", *Hard Feelings*. Further exceptions include Buss, "Appearing respectful"; Calhoun, "The virtue of civility"; Olberding, *The Wrong of Rudeness*; along with a set of political philosophers discussed shortly.

[14] But the concern that I defend is not one that motivates anger, ordinarily understood, nor even Nussbaum's anger that takes a 'road of status', seeking down-ranking of the other as payback, in her *Anger and Forgiveness*. The person who takes offence is not seeking to 'down-rank' the other, nor seeking payback, but rather resisting the lowering of her own standing through withdrawal and estrangement. I stick with the psychological characterisation of anger as leading to engaging with the other, in a way that offence does not: see Chapter 1. Hence, it is only Nussbaum's case against a concern for relative social standing that is of interest here. In Chapter 6, I consider how offence imposes costs, but these are not down-rankings.

shape and structure our relations as we navigate our social interactions. As suggested in the last chapter, and defended in §3.2, this endows ordinary everyday behaviours like shaking hands, making eye contact, or using titles with significance: underlying norms and practices endow these behaviours with social meanings, and these behaviours both partly constitute and sustain such norms and practices. As such, we are neither being oversensitive nor narcissistic when attending to our standing and the behaviours of others that largely constitute our standing. To attend to our social standing to the correct degree is to attend to such details of ordinary interactions.

3.2. Social standing as an equal, part I: Why the 'small stuff' matters

The significance of our social standing emerges out of what it is like, in practice, to live a life with standing as a social equal—or not. Over this section and the next, then, I depict six features of a life with standing as a social equal, compared to a life that is marred by pervasive hierarchies in social standing: receiving and offering similar tokens of respect; freedom from unwarranted intrusions; a sense of belonging; having status as a knower; unobstructed access to socially valued contributions and attributes; and having the power to set the terms of one's interactions. I draw on political philosophy and feminist philosophy since, unlike in ethics, there relations of status and deference have been a core concern. However, I extend the discussion beyond political philosophers' usual focus on tokens of respect and epistemic injustice.[15]

Some notes on the description to follow. First, offence is not appropriate for all the injustices depicted below but only some; for others, anger at grave injustice might be more appropriate.[16] Second, I describe only the social aspect of the ideal of social equality: of how we ought to treat and regard one another in our social interactions. Clearly, there are significant and essential

---

[15] Notably, by relational egalitarians, see for instance, Anderson, "What is the point of equality"; Miller "Equality and justice"; Wolff, "Fairness, respect, and the egalitarian ethos", along with republicans addressing deference and domination, e.g., Pettit, *Republicanism*. See also the literature on epistemic injustice, e.g., Fricker, *Epistemic Injustice*; Dotson, "Tracking epistemic violence"; Bailey, "On anger, silence, and epistemic injustice".

[16] For arguments in defence of anger at injustice, see for instance Lorde, "The uses of anger"; Spelman, "Anger and insubordination"; Frye, *The Politics of Reality*. Of particular relevance here is the defence of anger as a response to epistemic injustice offered in Bailey, "On anger, silence, and epistemic injustice". For a dissenting view, see Pettigrove, "Meekness and 'moral' anger".

political, legal, and economic aspects to possessing social equality, such as all having the vote or being treated as an equal before the law. Further, these others are intertwined with the social aspects. However, I examine the distinctively social dimension insofar as it can be pulled it apart from these others: that irreducibly social aspect, in that it can (and often does) persist despite formal equality before the law, and even legal and institutional attempts to bring about more substantive forms of equality. Third, some liberal egalitarians might be uncomfortable with the thought that a state ought to do anything about some of the hierarchies or acts that I am about to sketch. But the thought here is precisely that many of these social dynamics lie outside state control and that we, by doing things like committing microaggressions or taking offence, are the ones who variously sustain, negotiate, or shift such hierarchies.[17]

I begin with handshakes, perhaps the most popular example for those political philosophers who defend ideals of social equality, along with other gestures commonly understood to express respect or deference like eye contact, the use of titles, or bowing. Often, these gestures are central to characterisations of living as a social equal: we are told that a society of equals would mean that everyone shook hands or used the same title, say of 'Mr', not 'Lord'.[18] Sometimes we are also offered a set of behaviours that characterise relations between social unequals: those flattering, fawning, obsequious, or excessively deferential on the one side, and degrading, dismissive, condescending, or humiliating on the other.[19] Such characterisations are widely regarded as offering an inadequate or at least incomplete account of what it is to live together as social equals even once one adds an accompanying depiction of what relations to avoid; namely, oppression, domination, and unjust status hierarchies.[20] Yet they do capture the first significant dimension of our

[17] See, for example, Anderson's arguments against "any single official standard of worth" from a liberal egalitarian perspective, "Expanding the egalitarian toolbox", p. 145. Then again, Anderson suggests in the same piece that upwards directed contempt would be a way to affect hierarchies.

[18] See for instance Miller, "Equality and justice", p. 232; Fourie, "What is social equality?" pp. 107–8, 112; or in the introduction to a recent collection on social equality, Fourie et al., "The nature and distinctiveness of social equality", pp. 2–3. On meeting other's eyes, see also Phillip Pettit's comment on domination, "The powerless are not going to be able to look the powerful in the eye", *Republicanism*, p. 60.

[19] For similar lists see Runciman, "'Social' equality"; Anderson, "Expanding the egalitarian toolbox", especially on hierarchies of esteem, at p. 144–5 and of command, including "groveling and self-abasement", at p. 146; on "forelock tugging" and condescension, Miller, "Equality and justice", p. 225.

[20] See footnote 4.

social standing: the kind and extent of **behaviours communicating respect and consideration** which one receives, and that one is expected to provide.

To have standing as a social equal is to anticipate and receive tokens of respect and consideration from others, such as handshakes, and to offer others similar tokens, rather than ones unequal in kind or amount. By contrast, in a society with unequal social standing we would expect to see excessive deference, along with condescension, flattery, snobbery, and so on such that the tokens of respect and consideration given to one group would be greater than those offered to others whether in degree, kind, or both. Further, members of such a society would widely regard the uneven pattern as expected and fitting, so being inclined to penalise members of the group with lesser standing when they fail to offer the deference deemed to be due to members of the group with higher standing. In short, they'd take these to be norms in their society: expected patterns of attitudes and behaviour that people are often motivated to enforce.

One might doubt that we ought to attend much to such tokens, at least before we find extremes of overt disrespect, or cases where certain groups have to engage in demeaning or degrading behaviours. Admittedly, the individual tokens of behaviour by themselves and devoid of context would lack significance. There is often no one single specification of which behaviours would manifest equality of standing. Shaking hands may be a way to signal respect to a stranger given the norms in play within a particular society, whilst being a strange way to, say, welcome your lover home. Nor are handshakes an essential expression of respect, abiding across all forms of social organisation. Rather, which features of our social interactions matter for social standing depends on the particular social norms and practices in play in a society, or subgroup within a society, in certain interactions, where these norms and practices come with particular social meanings, to be read as instances of respect or disrespect, consideration or its absence.[21]

Such variability does not detract from the significance of these tokens of respect. As Sarah Buss and Cheshire Calhoun argue, and as discussed in the last chapter, social norms around polite or appropriate behaviour like shaking hands and making eye contact are what provide a 'shared language' by which we can convey our respect.[22] We can't, as Buss observes, wander around stating 'I respect you, I respect you', but our social norms

---

[21] In pithier form, from sociolinguistics: "There is, in other words, no linguistic behaviour that is inherently polite or impolite"; Locher and Watts, "Relational work and impoliteness", p. 78.

[22] Buss, "Appearing respectful"; Calhoun, "The virtue of civility".

let us express such sentiments by, instead, shaking hands or phrasing our questions politely.[23] Further, having our everyday interactions characterised by tokens of equal respect looks desirable. When you have social standing as an equal with others and do receive such tokens, then your life within society is characterised by a certain ease, with attentiveness to your interests and to what would be received as respectful behaviour. In addition, your sense of self-respect, insofar as that rests on others treating and regarding you with respect, may be shored up by others making such gestures. These gestures demonstrate to their recipient that they are subjects of such regard; by contrast, to be the object of other's disregard and disrespect may be corrosive of one's sense of self-worth.

At the very least, the importance of tokens of respect and consideration is clear where these are *unevenly* distributed, even in the absence of extremes. Norms about what is polite, appropriate, or respectful behaviour not only offer us ways to show others respect—or disrespect—but also let us express differing degrees of respect or communicate messages of lesser regard. Take Calhoun's example of 'ladies first' norms, where the token of consideration comes with the social meaning or message that women are lesser than men, needing greater protection or special treatment.[24] Or, as Marilyn Frye depicts following one such norm of holding doors open for women:

the message is that women are incapable. The detachment of the acts from the concrete realities what women need and do not need is a vehicle for the message that women's actual interests and needs are unimportant or irrelevant.[25]

As another example, Adam Cureton observes that those with disabilities can experience acts of apparent consideration that express a pitying attitude, so diminishing their social status.[26] These norms pattern our social relations in ways that realise social hierarchies. Further, they are constant reminders that some have greater standing than others, in ways that might act to subtly undermine a person's own conception of what she is owed or of what she is capable.

[23] Buss, "Appearing respectful", p. 802.
[24] Calhoun, "The virtue of civility", pp. 262–3.
[25] Frye, *The Politics of Reality*, pp. 5–6.
[26] Cureton, "Offensive beneficence", pp. 85–6.

One may think that we could nonetheless do without such tokens altogether, even if we shouldn't accept unequal distribution of such tokens, hence seeking to eliminate and not reform the practices by which we offer others tokens of respect. Handshakes could then be a distraction for those desiring to characterise a life living as social equals, despite their prevalence within depictions of social standing. Still, I think, there does seem to be something more attractive in a society where we do offer affirmations of our respect of, and consideration towards, others.[27] That society is one where the value of social equality is expressed and reinforced through daily interactions.

The next two dimensions of social standing concern one's 'place' in a society. The second dimension is that you are **free from unwarranted intrusions**: you are given space.[28] Cureton argues that restraint, in staying out of others' way and their affairs, forms a core part of our common sense understanding of respect; one found, he observes, in common expressions such as 'mind your own business' as well as in those norms of politeness that protect our privacy.[29] By contrast, those who are members of groups with unequal social standing, especially those subjected to overlapping forms of disadvantage, may face a constant string of intrusive microaggressions along with other unwarranted intrusions.[30] To illustrate, women face intrusive interruptions more often than men; women in same-sex relationships are asked inappropriate or intrusive questions about their relationships, such as 'Who's the man in the relationship?' or 'Can I watch?'; and white people touch black people's hair or ask to do so.[31] As another example, Cureton describes how acts of (apparent) consideration, say opening the door for someone with disabilities, can be disrespectful intrusions given that they involve the assumption that such assistance is desired.[32] Some of the norms challenged by

[27] See on this point, Olberding, *The Wrong of Rudeness*.

[28] Note the term 'unwarranted': not all intrusions are unwarranted—consider the close friend asking a personal question of a kind that it is inappropriate for a stranger to ask.

[29] Cureton, "The limiting role of respect", esp. pp. 365–7.

[30] Some, but not all, microaggressions take the form of unwarranted intrusions, and some unwarranted intrusions are neither apparently innocuous nor unintentional, as many definitions of microaggressions, though not all, require. See McTernan, "Microaggressions, equality, and social practices" for a discussion.

[31] Lindsay Pérez Huber and Daniel Solorzano argue that "racial microaggressions are a form of systemic, everyday racism used to keep those at the racial margins in their place"; "Racial microaggressions", p. 302. For these examples: on the first, see the following meta-analysis, which distinguished amongst kinds of interruptions, highlighting intrusive (and so dominating) ones as more common from men, especially in natural (rather than laboratory) settings: Anderson and Leaper, "Meta-analyses of gender effects". On the second, see research on microaggressions targeting the LBGT+ community, e.g., Nadal et al., "Sexual orientation microaggressions".

[32] Cureton, "The limiting role of respect", p. 394. See also, for a full account of what he terms 'offensive beneficence' and the ways in which it can be disrespectful, Cureton, "Offensive beneficence".

the 'Me Too' movement started by Tarana Burke also fall into the category of addressing unwarranted intrusion, especially where this movement has extended to, for instance, workplace sexual harassment or dating norms, say, asking an employee out on a date or overly 'friendly' touching.

Some also face overt and violent forms of unwarranted intrusions owing to their lack of perceived standing or the understandings of their social role or position. For instance, take cases where white people call the police on black people for no good reason, where that imposes a significant risk of police violence, given the institutional racism of the police.[33] As another example, consider the physical and sexual violence sex workers face: in studies across a range of countries the murder rate of female sex workers is reported to be between twelve and sixty times higher than that of the general population.[34]

The third dimension is feeling that **you feel that you belong**, are welcome, or are seen and valued across a wide range of social spaces. That would range from being regarded as a plausible candidate for jobs, insofar as your qualifications and experience are fitting for that job, or for friendship, in so far as your personality and interests align with the other. By contrast, some might be shunned altogether merely because of their group membership; find themselves excluded from relations or opportunities; face 'othering' forms of microaggressions; and/or be regarded with disgust or distain.[35] Experiencing unwarranted intrusions too can give one the sense of not being welcome, but that is not the only way in which this feeling can be induced. Conversely, feeling unwelcome is only one of the costs of experiencing an unwarranted intrusion; for instance, such intrusions might lead to a loss of a feeling of safety, the risk or infliction of harm, or a violation of privacy.

With these second and third dimensions of social standing, there are clear injustices, like having the police called on you for no good reason and so being exposed to police brutality; not being hired for a job due to prejudice; or experiencing violence. These patterns of inclusion, at least where they affect who holds which jobs or social positions, are commonly found objectionable by egalitarians.[36] However, less starkly unjust acts also have significance,

[33] For one discussion of disproportionate police violence against black men, and the impact on citizens' reliance on calling the police in black communities, see Desmond et al., "Police violence". For a collection of data on police killings, see https://mappingpoliceviolence.org.

[34] For a critical discussion on these studies and a consideration of murder rates in the United Kingdom, see Cunningham et al., "Sex work and occupational homicide".

[35] For a description of microaggressions as 'othering,' see Nordmarken, "Microaggressions", at p. 129.

[36] Often this is captured with an appeal to substantive equality of opportunity. Perhaps oddly, violence tends to receive less attention. For one exception, see Young, *Justice and the Politics of Difference*.

especially where they are cumulative. Having enough social standing enables you to move around a social world with less interference from others. You get to, say, walk down the street safely and without harassment, go to a bar and sit alone without comment, not think twice about what seat to take on a train, don't have to dodge out of other's way every time, and do not have to carefully choose what you wear, or how you speak, to head off possible blame, to avoid being targeted, or to otherwise appease others.

In contexts of relational inequality, some groups are especially liable to un-warranted intrusions and/or exclusion.[37] Even if some members of the group escape these experiences, that liability shapes their relations to others and what it feels like to be a member of a society. Take the woman who walks home at night with keys between her fist just in case, the same-sex couple who never hold hands in public, or the black man who never wears a hoodie. Even where these precautions might not have been needed, such that nothing would have happened to that particular individual had they not acted in these ways, they still shape how they experience their social world and their place within it. One could see intrusive and excluding acts as again about respect for others: it is dis-respectful to inflict an unwarranted intrusion on another and exclusions often express disrespect. However, there is more to the injustice than the disrespect that such acts convey: intrusions and exclusions shape the kinds of lives we can lead, the kinds of goods we can attain, what opportunities are open to us. In short, then, they can contribute to the oppression of a group.

A fourth dimension of social standing, and one that is the subject of a large literature, concerns our **status as knowers**. When you have standing as a so-cial equal, your views and testimony are given due or appropriate considera-tion by others. Here, appropriate consideration does not mean equal: to defer to the climate change expert on a technical detail about climate change would be, for instance, to grant the appropriate consideration to her opinion. By contrast, those lacking equal social standing may face epistemic injustices. Miranda Fricker, for instance, describes having one's testimony discounted on the basis of one's group membership, or lacking the terms even to describe one's experiences.[38] Kristie Dotson describes 'testimonial smothering' where the speaker, realising the audience won't take up their testimony as a result of pernicious ignorance, changes what they say.[39] Conversely, a social group

[37] See footnotes 31–4 for a small sample of the relevant evidence; see too surveys of experiences of microaggressions, such as 'the microaggressions project' discussed in Chapter 2.

[38] Fricker, *Epistemic Injustice*.

[39] Dotson, "Tracking epistemic violence".

with privileged social standing may receive or assume greater epistemic standing.[40]

The significance of these sorts of injustices is indisputable. For instance, Fricker considers the case of Carmita Wood, who suffered aggressive sexual harassment from her boss before the term was coined and yet received no unemployment benefit on quitting her job given the lack of reasons that she could offer (other than 'personal') for leaving her job, in the absence of that concept.[41] The harms involved are various, from lacking epistemic resources to be able to make sense of one's experiences, to being systematically disbelieved in ways that hamper one's access to legal justice.[42] But these epistemic injustices are not only a manifestation of unequal social standing, rather they also constitute a dimension of what it is like to have unequal standing: to be dismissed and discounted; to be frustrated in one's abilities to make one's situation known to or understood by others; to be silenced.[43]

Those are subjected to systematic marginalisation and disadvantage may also face dynamics of discounting and obscuring with respect to their **socially valued contributions or attributes**: access to such sources of social value forms a fifth dimension of social standing. So, as Iris Marion Young describes, one often finds professions that have been associated with the marginalised, oppressed, or disadvantaged group discounted in terms of their social value (nursery workers, teachers, nurses), where professions associated with the dominant group may have their value overinflated. That is often reflected through the respective economic rewards of these professions but also through the ways in which a society tends to frame the importance of the work done and the status of those who carry it out. Or, in cases of cultural imperialism, the culture of the dominant group is taken as the (valued) normal, while others are devalued or treated as 'other'.[44]

These, too, affect social standing, in the sense that our 'face', or that image of ourselves that we seek to present to others in particular contexts, draws on those attributes and traits that are socially valued. In socially unequal societies, members of different groups have unequal access to approved

[40] Fricker, *Epistemic Injustice*, on the privileged man being given greater than average epistemic standing. See also Solnit, on mansplaining, 2014. José Medina analyses the 'active ignorance' of privileged groups in his, *The Epistemology of Resistance*, ch.1.

[41] Fricker, *Epistemic Injustice*, pp. 149–52.

[42] Fricker, *Epistemic Injustice*.

[43] For a compelling account of the wrongs of being silenced see Dotson, "Tracking epistemic violence".

[44] Young, *Justice and the Politics of Difference*.

social traits and attributes, and those towards the bottom of social hierarchies find that the approval these traits and attributes tend to bring with them is diminished or attenuated by their group membership. As a result, those at the top of social hierarchies have more ways to construct a self-image that is imbued with 'approved social attributes', to borrow Erving Goffman's terms.[45] Those at the bottom find themselves with fewer possibilities, and may find their presentation of certain self-images more likely to be contested or rejected: a dynamic one also sees in some forms of epistemic injustices, where some marginalised groups find their claims to epistemic authority constantly undermined by their audiences.

Again, here, I have drawn on the concept of 'face' from sociology and sociolinguistics that was introduced in Chapter 1.[46] This understanding of standing contrasts with political philosophers' far thinner notion of 'equal respect' for others. Such equal respect is, perhaps, due others by virtue of their citizenship or personhood or some associated capability, such as the ability to form and revise a conception of the good. But, with that conception comes no sense of valuing of the other for what they are like and what they do. Our sense of our standing in society is thicker than a notion like 'equal respect' looks like it is able to capture.

3.3. Social standing as an equal, part II: The power to set the terms

On the account thus far, social standing is largely constructed through the social norms and practices that structure our interactions with each other and the social meanings of these, say that a bow would be an act of deference or that this way of interrupting is an assertion of dominance within a conversation. That is to say that we are located in hierarchies of social standing by the various ways in which people in fact respond to us (the patterns of behaviour resulting from social norms and social practices) along with what behaviours we take to be expected of us and of others (the social norms) and the social meaning of these norms and interactions. To care about social standing, then, is to take as significant the everyday interactions that

---

[45] Goffman, *Interactional Ritual*, p. 5.
[46] Face is defined as "an image of self delineated in terms of approved social attributes"; Goffman, *Interaction Ritual*, p. 5. See also Qi, "Face", on the relation between a person's construction of their self-image and how others receive it.

shape such standing. From these patterns of intrusion, exclusion, disrespect, and lack of epistemic standing or uneven valuing of other attributes arise injustices of the kind that centrally concern relational egalitarians, like oppression, violence, and domination.

As suggested in Chapter 1, it would be a mistake, if one made by some political philosophers, to regard social standing as a fixed amount, akin to, say, one's income, and something that we should think about allocating or distributing through state intervention.[47] The account of social standing above as constructed out of the details of social interactions of a kind that the state could (and should) play limited roles in distributing—at least beyond the acts of violence and overt discrimination—already disrupts such a conception. But that pattern isn't the whole picture: our social standing is also about what we can *do* within that pattern and our varying capacity to negotiate our standing.[48] Those with high social standing have power over others to set the terms of their social interactions, without thereby being at risk of significant social costs or retaliation when exercising that power. By contrast, those who have low social standing have diminished power to set the terms of their social interactions, and risk greater social costs when attempting to do so.[49]

To illustrate this sixth and last dimension of social standing, consider a professor who turns to a student and says "call me Bob, not Professor Smith". The professor has the power to set the terms of their discussion, here, as informal. By contrast, the student lacks the equivalent power to set the terms of their discussion as similarly informal.[50] That isn't to say that they can't call their professor 'Bob' unprompted. But that option isn't open to the student in the same sense as it is for the professor: when the professor does it, there are no risks of social penalty, and there is little the student can do to resist this move without being made to appear ungracious or unduly formal. By contrast, when the student does it, the professor has the socially supported option of taking offence or correcting the student. Indeed, the professor can

[47] Usually implicitly, as in the general discussion of equal respect, sometimes explicitly, for a paradigm case, see Lippert-Rassmussen, *Relational Egalitarianism*.

[48] This section is simply one illustration of Young's important observation of the weaknesses of the distributive paradigm, especially where it reaches beyond material goods, in her, *Justice and the Politics of Difference*.

[49] Here I draw on the distinction between power over and power to, for one discussion see Pansardi, "Power to and power over".

[50] Another example of the same phenomenon might be the use of formal as compared to informal terms of address in France, of 'tu' or 'vous', where the higher rank person can choose which to use. With thanks for Jennifer Page for suggesting this case.

set the terms of interactions of whole groups of people (all the students in his classroom), simply through a statement. Of course, a student might try for the same—'I'll call him "Bob" then everyone else will'—but his bid is easily frustrated and comes with risks of social penalties, such as the professor embarrassing him or others refusing to engage with the bid to change the terms of interaction.

For another illustration of how such power is exercised, Miriam Locher asks, "Isn't all impoliteness a form of power?" and Jonathan Culpeper examines how those of us with higher social standing in some contexts get to be impolite without risking much objection. So too, we can limit the ability of others to respond to us impolitely in return, given the retaliation we might then inflict.[51] This should look familiar as a feature of our social interactions; for instance, consider the unwarranted intrusions like invasive questions just sketched: the rudeness goes one way, the powerful can ask these, where the less powerful cannot. The senses of 'can' and 'cannot' here, are not, of course, physical or logical impossibility. Rather this is a matter of how social organisation enables, or disables, certain kinds of interventions in our interactions. For some, in some settings, to challenge the way in which they are treated can be costly: whether to reputation, in terms of the risk of escalation of the impolite behaviour, or even physical harm.

For one last illustration, Amy Olberding relates the experience of bias and microinequities to manners. For her, 'mannerly micropractices' such as listening to others, introducing them to new people or shaking hands, are expressions of social cooperation.[52] Where these are absent, or frustrated— say, when another fails to shake our hand or to listen—that is a failure to so cooperate. If that happens repeatedly, for instance, as a result of widespread bias, that entails a loss of a power over our actions: as she describes the experience where others fail to give your acts uptake through listening, say, or shaking a hand when offered, "uncertainty of response transforms doing into attempting . . . I speak not to participate, but to attempt to do so."[53] Another dimension of this social cooperation is how we usually collaborate in others' presentations of their selves. But again, Olberding observes, some groups find that their presentations of particular aspects of themselves, as befits a context, is resisted, or aspects of their selves that they seek not to make salient

---

[51] See Culpeper, "Reflections on impoliteness", where Locher's remark appears.
[52] Olberding, "Subclinical bias", p. 289. Her paper examines the situation of women in philosophy.
[53] Ibid., p. 292.

in this context, are attended to: as in her case of the pregnant woman running a conference who finds the fact of her pregnancy constantly referenced.[54]

In a society where all have equal social standing, then, we'd have roughly equal amounts of the power to negotiate our social standing. Equal here does not mean the same: a person having the ability to say "please take your shoes off in my house" need not violate relations of equality. Consistent with social equality, within narrow contexts or in special cases, some may have power over others to set the terms of the interaction, where there is good reason for so doing. But over the set of social interactions that we engage in, there must be no systematic favouring of one group over the other. Further, in no context would someone have unjustified or wide-ranging control, and nor would we find members of certain groups subjected to violence or severe social costs such as reputational damage for making claims to standing or attempting to negotiate terms with others. An inability to negotiate in the setting of terms without undue costs to one's standing or risk of harm is one way in which social inequality is made manifest. It is also something that makes one's social world feel more hostile and less one's own.

To draw the account of social standing together, I present two levels of salient norms and practices in constructing our social standing. The first level, sketched in §3.2., produces a clustering of relevant behaviours: the norms about what behaviours express respect or what counts as an act of deference or as an intrusive question, or whose testimony is believed to be reliable. Then there is a second level outlined in this section: those norms, practices, and social roles that enable—or restrict—our capacity to shape interactions as we desire, to set terms, where that term setting can include determining what kinds of first level norms are in play (such as formal or informal ones).

Having lower social standing can be expressed by doing badly in one or in many of these dimensions. Take being a middle-manager as compared to a low-ranking employee in a capitalist firm within a society with a poor social security net, and little funding for employees to take companies to court for wrongful dismissal. The relation between manager and underling could be characterised by the manager inflicting unwarranted intrusions of various kinds, or an anticipation of unequal tokens of respect and consideration, with the underling engaging in flattering behaviour, say, or the boss displaying condescending behaviour. However, it would be unlikely that dynamics of exclusion play a significant role in this relation as the case is

[54] Ibid., pp. 295–6.

described. Or consider how in some societies certain women might receive tokens of respect and consideration, especially where they have otherwise privileged identities (white, straight, able-bodied, say) and perhaps even, outside of those spaces that are still dominated by men, experience little exclusion. Yet nonetheless such women may lack equal epistemic standing and be subjected to unwarranted intrusions including violence and the threat of violence.[55]

On this account, there is space for non–group related hierarchies in social standing within particular settings. Consider an academic who is constantly mocked after falling over during his job interview, whose daily life in his department is characterised by lack of respect, open mockery, and no one taking his views particularly seriously since he appears a ridiculous figure. That academic lacks social standing but not by virtue of any group membership. Or consider the family member who is the target of every joke at family gatherings but not for any reason that touches on her social identity. Yet such examples can be tricky to construct. Often, although not always, we end up dragging in some dimension of disadvantage to make the case realistic or implicitly draw on a background social inequality. Indeed, the case of the academic may rest on underlying ableist norms.

Non–group related, or idiosyncratic, hierarchies differ from group-based ones. Often that difference is one of degree, with systematic group-based hierarchies being characterised by more severe intrusions, exclusion, epistemic dismissal and so forth, as well as of spread across a life, with systematic social inequality less constrained to particular contexts than the idiosyncratic forms. To illustrate, the academic of the tale above eventually changed universities, and finds himself well-regarded by his new colleagues; such moves often do little to assist the person facing group-based discrimination. Further, systematic social hierarchies often encompass a greater set of the dimensions of standing. In particular, lacking power to set the terms of one's social interactions, and especially finding that others have power over one when negotiating these terms, looks to be primarily a feature of systematic cases. Last, in idiosyncratic cases, unlike systemic cases, disrespect lacks a connection to, and grounding in, other kinds of inequalities, such as persistent economic inequality or political inequality.

With this account of social standing in view, it ought to be clearer the sense in which I draw on a notion of 'face' to understand the idea of social standing,

---

[55] For an analysis of misogyny, see Manne, *Down Girl*.

in contrast to those political philosophers who have thought of it in terms of some static amount or quantity.[56] Our standing is constructed out of, and negotiated through, particular interactions. But that ought to give those of us who care about social equality reasons for some limited and cautious optimism. As Locher and Watts describe this sort of social power:

> it is not a static concept, but is constantly renegotiated and exercised in social practice. All interlocutors enter social practice with an understanding of a differential distribution of social status amongst the co-participants, but the actual exercise of power is something that we can only witness in the interaction itself.[57]

We can resist the 'line' the other assumes, and in so doing, resist the way in which our social standing plays out within a particular interaction.[58]

3.4. Defending the significance of affronts

Social standing is significant and the person who pays attention to her standing is not mistaken about its importance. Further, to pay attention to one's social standing entails attending to the details of one's social interactions: it is out of such details that our standing is constructed. Nonetheless, one could still doubt that we should pay the kind of attention that leads to offence at others ignoring, mistaking, or attacking our standing on particular occasions. Why, one might ask, would any one affront matter? Further, when and why is *offence* in particular the right response to certain details of standing? Over the rest of this chapter and the next, I outline when taking offence at affronts is a morally justified way to stand up for one's standing; namely, where one's standing as a social equal is transgressed against, but that affront does not in or by itself cause severe harm to one's welfare or well-being.

I begin with what makes affronts significant, since when we take offence, we respond to an affront. Given the arguments above, our social standing is made up out of the pattern of social interactions and what 'moves' are open to us within that pattern: of how others treat us and reveal the way in which

---

[56] Goffman, *Interaction Ritual*, then, rather than Lippert-Ramussen, e.g., *Relational Egalitarianism*.
[57] Locher and Watts, "Relational work and impoliteness", p. 81.
[58] As Erving Goffman describes the image we project or assume through a particular interaction, *Interaction Ritual*.

they regard us and which interventions against the pattern of behaviours are permitted or penalised. In the absence of such interactions we would have no social standing.[59] Hence, affronts are significant insofar as they contribute to that broader pattern. All the same, one might object that the contribution of any one affront is too small to be worth considering, let alone be worth reacting to; even if a heap of sand is made up of grains of sand, still no one grain of sand forms a substantial part of the heap. Still less important, this opponent might continue, are small or minor seeming affronts. Even if one admits that individual acts are significant to our standing where they are egregious—say using a sexist or racist slur or deliberate attempts to marginalise another—a sceptic might insist that affronts cannot be significant when they are as small seeming as failing to use the right title to address someone, explaining things to them that they already know, or asking some intrusive question.[60]

However, that mistakes the possible role of individual affronts in our social relations, however small they may be. An affront can reinforce one's unequal standing: again, the pattern of such affronts partly constitutes unequal standing. But an affront may also introduce unequal social standing into a context where it had not previously been salient. Consider cases where someone puts another 'in their place' in some new setting through drawing attention to some characteristic that might not previously have been as noticeable, but that connects to a broader social inequality. The noting of one's 'token' status or being 'othered' is a common experience for members of underrepresented groups.[61]

Small-scale affronts may even be particularly well-suited to playing such patterning roles: they are less risky for the individuals who perform them than larger-scale acts. This feature is often noted in the case of microaggressions: being small-scale, they are often hard to pin down, and

[59] While other forms of inequality—political, legal, economic—often underpin and reinforce social inequality, our interactions are where such inequalities are converted into social inequalities, say where people are condescending or dismissive of those with lower incomes.

[60] I draw here from debates over microinequities, e.g., Brennan, "The moral status of microinequities", and microaggressions and cumulative harm, e.g., Friedlaender, "On microaggressions", Fatima, "On the edge of knowing". These debates also tackle how small scale or incremental acts relate to larger scale harms. A similar discussion of how small-scale acts can contribute to injustice to that which appears below also appears in McTernan, "Microaggressions, equality, and social practices", but focused on microaggressions.

[61] For instance, microaggressions are sometimes described as performing this role of 'othering': see Nordmarken, "Microaggressions", p. 129. A similar mechanism can operate in the absence of group-based hierarchies, too; for instance, sometimes our indiscretions of a kind apt to lower our standing follow us into new settings (say, a new group of friends) when stories of these are told again.

are hard to draw attention to without appearing to overreact.[62] So, too, psychologists sometimes claim that microaggressions may be every day or common partly as a result of being hard to resist and fairly costless to commit.[63] Another example would be making offensive jokes as Chapter 5 examines: for jokes too, one faces the problem of being seen as over-reacting if one resists the affront. Such every day patterning is important in constructing social hierarchies, in contributing to the way that social hierarchies can intrude across a life, becoming a background feature of interactions.[64] Finally, a multitude of subtle gradations in standing are most aptly conveyed by small-scale acts, and not those larger in scale. Social inequality comes in forms other than degradation and violence. Sometimes, for instance, the relevant range for a particular subgroup might be, in general, facing condescension and being belittled.

As a consequence of the significance of affronts, however, sometimes we find moments where, by resisting an affront, we can claim equal social standing or, at least, more equal standing in some particular setting or type of interaction. Our social standing can be up for negotiation in particular social interactions. Consider correcting students who fail to use one's title 'professor' at the start of term or conveying to a colleague that a certain sort of comment about one's personal life is off-limits. Alternatively, take Michael Haugh's example of a woman, Sally, who subtly conveys that she takes offence at a new partner's snobbish correction of her, through telling a tale of an ex-partner's similar shortcoming.[65] Social standing, then, is a thing to which we can lay claim, although that is by no means to say that our social standing is whatever we say it is. For our social standing to change, our bids or negotiations must have uptake from others. Sociologists and sociolinguists at times appear to take our social standing as constantly in flux and up for negotiation in each and every interaction or, at least, that is what they emphasise in their accounts. But while our standing is up for negotiation, that negotiation

[62] For one analysis, see Fatima, "On the edge of knowing", on the resulting bind on people's response to microaggressions, and even doubt of over what has really happened. On micro-inequities being innocuous and so their invisibility, see too Brennan, "The moral status of micro-inequities".

[63] E.g., Sue et al. describe the 'invisible' nature of these acts as "preventing perpetrators from realizing and confronting" them and their effects, "Racial microaggressions in everyday life", p. 272. Pierce argues that microaggressions being every day and subtle explains their power, "Stress analogs in racism and sexism".

[64] This argument also appears in McTernan, "Microaggressions, equality, and social practices".

[65] Haugh, "Impoliteness and taking offence", pp. 40–1. In general, the linguistic studies of social interactions are full of careful ways in which people express offence, attempts to save 'face' or avoid the appearance of offering affronts to others—a helpful corrective perhaps to the kinds of public shamings emphasised in popular discussion on offence.

is severely constrained by our standing, in what moves we can make, and which moves would have uptake from others. In light of the discussion of our varying capacities to set the terms of our interactions, some will be far better placed to negotiate than others and some bids are more likely to be accepted than others. Sometimes, a claim for greater standing can even be treated as ludicrous or absurd.

Some will also face greater costs in negotiating than others: having lower social standing often renders bids for standing riskier. Sometimes, the likely costs will be to someone's social reputation or perception, and to the possibility of having uptake for one's contestations of other's behaviour: take the characterisation of 'humourless feminists' or the trope of the 'angry black woman'.[66] At other times, the risk is of escalation to stronger attacks on one's social standing, sometimes even to violence. Consider the experience of women who find street harassment escalates where they resist the act: the man yelling from his car might start with 'give us a kiss' but escalate to serious insults and threats if the woman doesn't perform the acceptable responses (say, acting flattered or claiming to have a boyfriend). Alternatively, take the recent case of the couple subjected to a homophobic attack on a London bus: a group of male teenagers first demanded to see the two women kiss and, when they refused, the teenagers threw coins, before the situation escalated into a violent attack.[67]

But, sometimes, others are willing to inflict these costs partly as a result of feeling threatened, and so precisely because social standing is up for negotiation. It is possible to resist attributions of lowered standing, and by doing so, in a hierarchical society, one threatens to bring down the other party's inflated standing—inflated by contrast to one's own. That also makes sense of the strength of the reactions we often see against what look like comparatively minor requests for modifications of social norms, such as a change in the terms used to address someone. Out of the pattern of interaction comes our social standing and so, within particular contexts an individual might make a difference. Take the lecturer who insists students use her title 'Professor' rather than calling her 'Miss', making use of professional power to correct an unequal attribution of standing based on gender. However, I suspect that where individuals succeed in this contestation, especially where it is not by virtue of a privileged aspect of identity, that act will often be part of

---

[66] For a discussion of the former, see for instance Bergmann, "How many feminists"; for the latter, Jones and Norwood, "Aggressive encounters and white fragility".

[67] BBC News, "London Bus Attack".

a wider contestation of such norms: here, could consider the spread of information about which sorts of everyday degradations, putdowns or attacks are deemed unacceptable; or campaigns to use gender neutral terms like 'actor', not actress'. Against that background, bids for standing are more likely to be read as instances where a behaviour is found offensive, rather than a particular individual being taken to be 'oversensitive'.

3.5. Resisting by taking offence

Thus far I have defended social standing as significant and, as a consequence, the significance of particular affronts to it. One way in which we can respond against an attribution of less standing than we deem ourselves due is to take offence. The next question is why and when we should take offence in particular in the ongoing process of negotiating our social standing, now that we have reason pay the kind of attention to our social standing that may well produce offence. What makes *this* negative emotion justified?

In the last chapter, I outlined how taking offence can be a way to stand up for one's standing. Namely, the withdrawal that often results from offence conveys that one cannot commit this sort of affront yet have social relations continue unhindered. Sometimes taking offence can thus act to reinforce compliance with an existing social norm or extend to which groups or contexts an existing norm applies. That can help maintain socially beneficial social norms: say, norms to show respect and consideration to all or to treat each other as epistemic authorities where appropriate.[68] In this role, the defence of offence extends beyond those who, by virtue of their group membership, frequently experience affronts to their standing of social equals, since it shores up such shared norms. Alternatively, taking offence might act to alter a social norm or replace it with another. By taking offence, we can sometimes influence the social meanings of an act: turning it from what we do around here to something that is regarded as conveying a particular (and controversial) message, especially where offence taking becomes widespread through a social group.

---

[68] In defence of these beneficial roles of politeness and civility norms see Buss, "Appearing respectful"; Calhoun, "The virtue of civility". Olberding, in *The Wrong of Rudeness,* characterises their arguments as 'do no harm' arguments for politeness norms, and herself offers a positive defence.

In light of this chapter's argument, resisting affronts in this way can be morally justified not only because social standing is a thing to which we can (collectively) lay claim and taking offence is a way in which we can make such claims,
but also because social standing pervasively shapes our lives in important ways.
As such, to be inclined to be offended by an affront to one's standing *as a social
equal* manifests the right kind of pattern of attention; it shows we are attending
to the sort of thing that we ought to care about.[69] In so doing, we would not be
claiming more standing than we are due, nor paying excessive attention, given
the importance of such standing for how our lives go. The case for thinking offence morally appropriate, then, extends beyond its social role in negotiating
norms and practices.

In some cases, the defence to be made of taking offence is stronger than its
being one appropriate way to negotiate social relations and manifesting a fitting
concern for one's social standing: namely, in those cases where offence is taken by
those who already face pervasive social inequality and at affronts that target the
dimension of their identity or position by virtue of which they experience that
inequality—and still more so where these affronts are familiar ones. Members
of marginalised and oppressed groups tend to face affronts to social standing
that look quantitatively and qualitatively different. Members of such groups
are more frequently subjected to affronts to their social standing as equals; as
one illustration, consider the surveys of the microaggressions that members
such groups confront in their daily lives and the earlier arguments over how
these pattern social relations in unjust ways.[70] In addition, threats to standing
are more likely to get uptake from others where they chime with existing social
inequalities: to be accepted by an audience as 'merited', say, or to be ones that the
target cannot show that they reject, without suffering consequences. Further,
these affronts contribute to the background pattern of social inequality, perhaps
especially where they are familiar. A novel discriminatory remark, say, may not
have the same impact as a common, widely shared one that ties into more familiar tropes and stereotypes about that group.

Hence, those who already face social inequality in taking offence at
affronts can act to resist an act that, however incrementally, contributes to
a pattern of injustice. That makes offence ripe for a feminist defence akin to

---

[69] See, on patterns of attention, Bonmarito, "Modesty as a virtue of attention".
[70] See "The microaggressions project" discussed earlier; but also, Sue et al., "Racial
microaggressions"; Nadal et al., "Sexual orientation microaggressions".

those offered for anger, bitterness, and contempt.[71] Sometimes our emotions serve as a way to resist or protest injustice or inequality. In this case, where members of one group are commonly attributed less social standing than members of another, taking offence is a way to resist that patterning. For instance, the woman offended at a sexist joke rejects the ordinary patterning of relations within a patriarchy, wherein women have less social standing than men and, as Merrie Bergmann observes, where women are the traditional objects of humour within our culture.[72] To take the joke as offensive, not humorous, resists: even without others knowing that she is offended, or without her influencing the future behaviour of others a woman who takes offence at a sexist joke rightly attributes to herself more standing than others attribute to her. That act, then, is one of direct insubordination against a social hierarchy, of a kind that might help preserve her sense of standing.[73]

The next chapter continues this justification of taking offence under conditions of social inequality, carving out space for offence as a distinctive way to resist injustice, in contrast to anger, and considering what we should do where certain groups are likely to find their offence gets little uptake.

---

[71] For a taxonomy of these arguments, see Macalester Bell's depiction of feminist defences of negative emotions, "A woman's scorn". As examples, see Frye, *The Politics of Reality*; Lorde, "The uses of anger"; Bell, *Hard Feelings*; Spelman, "Anger and insubordination", amongst many others.

[72] Bergmann, "How many feminists".

[73] Serving the role of 'emotional insubordination' that Bell outlines as part of the feminist defence of emotions, "A woman's scorn". She points to Spelman's "Anger and insubordination". As Chapter 4 examines, offence is a particularly direct act of insubordination.

4

The limits of justified offence

On anger, intent, and uptake

On the account offered thus far, taking offence can be fitting and morally appropriate only if the affront in question targets 'you and yours', it pertains to your standing as a social equal; and the offending party bears a relation to you sufficient for you to be estranged from them. Then, to take offence can be to stand up for your standing and, further, it reflects a justified attention to one's standing. Against background of social inequality, taking offence can be a way of resisting an act that contributes incrementally to injustice. This chapter turns from the general case for taking offence, to the details of particular interactions. I ask, when exactly is it justified to take offence? What if the offending party didn't intend the affront, others disagree over whether an act is offensive, or one's offence will be misinterpreted? I will assess a series of potential limits on the justifiability of taking offence drawn from the way in which offence plays out in our interactions; later, in Chapter 6, I consider the limits on the costs that offence should impose.

On the one hand, given the previous chapter's arguments, offence may appear to be a response that is simply too small in scale for those cases where an affront contributes to, or stems from, unjust social hierarchies.[1] Anger, after all, is the emotion that is more commonly associated with reacting to injustice. The first task of this chapter is thus to carve out a distinct space for offence and not only anger as a morally appropriate response to affronts to equal social standing.

On the other hand, it is far more common to regard taking offence as an *over*reaction than an underreaction. Taking offence is sometimes regarded as a manifestation of some oversensitivity to being affronted, or even taken to

---

[1] A stronger variant of this objection would be to claim that it is offensive even to suggest that those who resist everyday sexisms or microaggressions might be taking offence. The re-characterisation of what offence is, in Chapters 1 and 2, should undercut that objection: to take offence resists an affront to one's social standing.

On Taking Offence. Emily McTernan, Oxford University Press. © Oxford University Press 2023.
DOI: 10.1093/oso/9780197613092.003.0005

be the product of seeing affronts where there are none to be found.[2] While the previous chapter defended the general significance of one's social standing, still, the justifiability of taking offence at any particular affront can be challenged. Indeed, the popular criticisms of offence-taking often focus on details of individual cases; of interest here are the subset where the offending party defends themselves on the grounds that they didn't mean the act as it has been interpreted, or where it is held that it is unreasonable to interpret the act in the manner that provokes offence. The second task of this chapter, then, is to examine whether (and how) facts about the offending party's intent, or about how an affront is generally understood, influence the justifiability of taking offence.

Third, resistance from others when one takes offence raises another kind of possible limit on justified offence: this time on pragmatic rather than moral grounds, concerning whether offence can be justified all things considered. When reacting to another taking offence, sometimes people mischaracterise what has gone on, say, as a matter of mere emotional upset. At other times, the person who offends may be spurred into being yet more offensive. When offence faces such resistance and, more so, failures of recognition, one might doubt that taking offence could still count as one way to stand up for one's standing. Worse, it seems likely that the less powerful or marginalised are most likely to face resistance and these failures of recognition. Drawing on Marilyn Frye's work on anger in the face of failures of uptake, I defend a persisting role for taking offence in the face of such reactions.[3]

4.1. Anger, offence, and the act

I begin with the thought that offence is simply not enough of a reaction. Since a pattern of social interactions can produce and constitute an unjust social hierarchy, to react to acts such as microaggressions or unwarranted intrusions is to react to injustice. Offence may seem to be an emotion more appropriate for social missteps than injustices. At the least, when offence is taken at unjust acts, one might think that it reveals a failure to fully realise

---

[2] See the articles damning 'generation snowflake' and accusing those in the apparent 'culture of taking offence' of being oversensitive, e.g., Campbell & Manning, "The new millennial 'morality'"; Lukianoff & Haidt, *The Coddling of the American Mind*; Fox, *I Find That Offensive!*

[3] Frye, *The Politics of Reality*.

and reflect the significance of what has occurred. This thought motivates this chapter's first candidate limit on justified offence:

The no injustice limit: Offence should not be taken in response to injustice, nor at acts that contribute to injustice.

However, to reject offence in contexts of injustice is to give too little weight to the socially constituted injustices that emerge out of the ordering of everyday interactions, examined in the last chapter: a subset of what appear 'social missteps' in part constitute unequal social standing. It also gives too little weight to offence's role in negotiating the social norms and practices that shape our everyday interactions, defended in Chapter 2. To withdraw from another person and, especially, to convey to others that one is withdrawing, can be a highly effective way to clarify and negotiate the terms of our social relations. At the least, it is to resist an attribution of less than equal standing.

Anger has tended to be the focus of those addressing emotional reactions to injustice.[4] So, one might still regard anger as the better or more appropriate reaction to affronts to standing as a social equal, as compared to offence, where such affronts are made against those who experience oppression and domination. Indeed, Alison Bailey defends a 'resistant knowing anger' as an appropriate response to epistemic injustices, and Mark Tschaepe, drawing on Audre Lorde's work on anger, proposes anger as one tool with which to tackle microaggressions.[5] Offence, one might think, is instead more appropriate when taken at acts like others snubbing us or failing to shake hands.

Offence is not alone in also being taken in less morally or politically significant contexts, however: sometimes people get angry when others step on their foot or their computer freezes. Below, I will defend offence as a particularly apt way to respond to a subset of the affronts to equal standing which contribute to injustice: those affronts that are rendered significant by unjust broader contexts. Without that context, the act would have a differing meaning or communicate a different message: one which either did not threaten social standing or that did so to a far lesser degree, akin, say, to being merely rude to someone. For this subset of affronts, the core of my defence is

---

[4] E.g., Bailey, "On anger, silence, and epistemic injustice"; Frye, *The Politics of Reality*; Lorde, "The uses of anger".

[5] Bailey, "On anger, silence, and epistemic injustice". On anger and microaggressions, see Tschaepe, "Addressing microaggressions and epistemic injustice". Responding with a tactical case against anger as responding to microaggressions, see Rini, "How to take offense".

that taking offence offers us a way both to directly defend our social standing and to respond to the particular act's threat to that standing. Thus, offence merits a place as one of the emotions appropriately involved in responding to injustice.

To clarify this line of argument, first, I do not thereby claim that anger is inappropriate in these cases. My argument is not that there is no place for anger over acts like microaggressions but, rather, that there is also a place for offence: anger or offence could be morally justified, and people might experience one, both, or neither. Second, affronts lacking a relevant connection to patterns of unjust social inequality, say where we find an individual affront to another as an individual would still be conceptually appropriate instances at which to take offence. However, taking offence at these individual affronts would be less likely to be morally justified, except indirectly, as a means by which to support the wider system of social norms, as Chapter 6 discusses. Such offence-taking might be better regarded as socially, rather than morally, valuable.

To illustrate the kind of significance of the unjust broader context that I have in mind, take standard rape jokes. These are a subject of interest within the literature on morality and humour, which address whether an immoral joke can be funny or whether the person who finds it funny is open to moral criticism. To give one example, Noel Carroll considers the joke that 'rape is an assault with a friendly weapon'; as another, take T-Shirts with the slogan, 'Stop rape, say yes', written on them.[6] Merrie Bergmann argues that jokes like these rely on an audience sharing sexist background assumptions and may also exacerbate these beliefs.[7] To make sense of these jokes, and for the jokes to succeed, depends upon an undercurrent of sexist beliefs, say, that women do not always mean 'no' when they say 'no'; along with the background of gender-based violence. Without that background context, rape jokes would simply introduce an unpleasantly violent topic into conversation in a way that people would find startling, rather than amusing. Further, many of these jokes depend on taking rape to be not that serious in order for the way in which they trivialise or normalise rape to amuse. As evidence, consider the lack of equivalent jokes about physical assaults: there are no T-Shirts with

[6] Carroll, "Humour".
[7] Bergmann argues sexist beliefs must be held to understand such jokes (perceive the incongruity) or they add to the 'fun effects' of the incongruity in her "How many feminists", p. 70.

'stop physical assaults, say yes' written on them. If there were, they wouldn't be found funny.[8]

Another illustration is Derald Wing Sue's experience of being asked along with an African American colleague to move from the front to the back of the plane to rebalance the aircraft after three white men sat down at the front. Without the particular details of the history of racial injustice in the United States, especially the Jim Crow segregation laws, one might still find this an affront and even, given underlying racial injustice in society, a racist one: why do *they* have to move? However, given that historical context, there is a deeper social meaning to the act, worsening the severity of the affront.[9]

So, with these illustrations in view, offence is appropriate where acts present a threat or attack to one's standing as a social equal. By themselves, and without the context of pervasive social injustice, the acts described above might not do that, or may not even make sense, as in the case of the rape joke. The context of injustice makes the act into one that attacks standing; especially, one that presents a serious threat to standing or one that attacks one's standing as a social equal. In the case of microaggression on the aeroplane, consider, by contrast, the lack of affront if it were necessary for someone to move and a white person was selected at random. These acts may also contribute to harm for the person experiencing them, especially cumulatively. The psychologist Chester Pierce initially coined the term 'microaggression' in order to describe the harm done to his African American patients in facing a barrage of small, every day "putdowns and degradations".[10] The sexist rape joke might intrusively capture the attention of a rape survivor, as well as demonstrating to her that others fail to regard the harm that she suffered as serious. But the harm done tends to emerge from the pattern of acts experienced, say, the repeated microaggressions or the frequency of dismissals of rape's seriousness, while the individual act is itself a threat to one's standing, given the background context.[11]

---

[8] Carroll might disagree, since he argues that one could laugh at rape jokes in the absence of sexist commitments, say, by finding the wording witty, see "Humour". Yet on perhaps the most popular theory of humour, the incongruity theory, to find something humorous is to find it a benign transgression. At the least, then, finding a rape joke humorous manifests a lack of commitment to regarding rape as a serious harm. Chapter 5 returns to humour.

[9] Sue, "Racial microaggressions", p. 295. Sue depicts his experience as one of feeling "resentment, irritation, and anger", reflecting his "everyday racial experiences", at p. 275.

[10] See for instance Pierce, "Stress analogs of racism and sexism".

[11] Threats to standing do not always harm: they may not succeed in lowering one's standing and even where they do, that may not always be harmful.

As to why not take anger to be the sole morally justified or appropriate response to acts that constitute injustices or that contribute to patterns of injustice, the simplest response is to observe that our emotional lives are not so simple, nor so one-dimensional. Often, we feel a range of emotions when confronted by injustice: say, anger but also grief or despair. Sometimes, one might be both angry and offended. To give a fuller response, however, there are also good reasons to see offence as particularly apt when it comes to the relevant set of acts.

First, this is a book concerned with the details of our social interactions that may add up or combine into injustice. It might be that a single nongrievous but unwarranted intrusion would not amount to an injustice by itself, and yet when most members of a group continually experience such events that creates restrictions and limitations that contribute to the group's oppression. However, that does not suffice to turn each and every unwarranted intrusion into a significant injustice: the injustice stems from the cumulative effect. No one act produces the injustice; as another illustration, no one inappropriate remark makes a hostile environment. But some defences of anger focus on the starker wrongdoing, of evil or single grave injustices.[12] There is room left, then, for offence at the inappropriate remark or the non-grievous intrusion. By comparison, acts like violent intrusions of bodily integrity may instead provoke anger: taking offence may sometimes be crowded out as a reaction, since severe physical harm displaces one's attention from the threat to one's standing.

Second, and relatedly, the justified anger taken at the kinds of acts I discuss—such as microaggressions, exclusion, and other everyday experiences for members of marginalised or discriminated against groups—often targets the pattern, not the one-off act. To illustrate, Saba Fatima advises us to "think big" when it comes to microaggressions: to consider not only intentions but also the structures of racism, sexism, and other forms of pervasive injustice.[13] Christina Friedlaender describes how a microaggression can be a "tipping point" such that the person responds with anger where they react to the *cumulative* harm of the many microaggressions that they experience.[14] The anger is at what such acts reveal and the broader structures that these acts support.

---

[12] Consider, for instance, the appropriate attitudes defence of anger at evil, and the focus on the case of slavery in Bell, "Anger, virtue, and oppression".

[13] Fatima, "On the edge of knowing", p. 154.

[14] Friedlaender, "On microaggressions", pp. 15–16.

Offence, by contrast, *is* taken at the particular act. Therein lies a reason to think taking offence both appropriate and distinct from anger in these everyday but patterned acts: offence is a way to respond to this one act, offering a direct challenge to it. Further, anger demands of or from the other recompense, or the rectification of harm, or payback.[15] Yet often the one affront is not by itself what harms the individual and, sometimes, the central injustice is not whatever harm might be attached directly to a (non-egregious) affront. Offence, on the other hand, aims at resisting a particular act: failing to accept the offered slight to standing and pushing back against the attribution of lesser standing. In addition, as Chapter 2 detailed, offence is an emotion well suited to negotiating our norms around social standing. By contrast, anger threatens to cause far more of a rupture in relations; albeit one that admits of repair through acts of atonement.[16]

The third and last reason in favour of offence, and not only or always anger, is that anger pushes us towards engagement. Yet it is a common thought that we should not require of those already burdened that they do more work, as being angry, explaining that anger, and ensuring its uptake by others, requires. Offence, by contrast, communicates through its estrangement and withdrawal. As a result, offence looks less demanding of a person's time and attention than anger: to remove oneself from the situation or raise an eyebrow, say, looks neither onerous, nor calls for continued attention to the offending party. Indeed, where we are significantly offended, we often remove ourselves from the costs of engaging further with that person even in future. Thus, taking offence can be justified as a response to affronts to our standing as social equals, even for acts that contribute to injustice—although it is not the only appropriate response. The first proposed limit fails. There is, however, another limit on when offence is appropriate as a response to injustice, arising simply from the fact that offence is an emotion taken at affronts to social standing. For those injustices whose central or main wrong is unrelated to one's standing as a social equal then, to take only offence would be to fail to perceive or judge the situation at hand clearly or in its entirety.

---

[15] See the discussion in Chapter 1 on accounts of anger in moral psychology.

[16] Sometimes offence too demands an apology or atonement, but not always. At times, to apologise for one's offensive remark can be undesirable or even worsen the affront, even when sincere: take cases where the last thing that the offended party wants is yet more attention being drawn to her, or to the aspect of her identity that lowers standing in this particular kind of context, against a background social hierarchy. A misplaced or slightly misworded apology may increase offence.

4.2. Contesting offence

The rest of this chapter, and the next, addresses the more familiar thought that, rather than offence being too weak a reaction, it is too much of one, and so the various ways in which those who are offended find that others reject or resist their offence. I begin with three cases.

(I) FUTURISTIC STAFF

"Three haircuts, facial piercings, neon manga tattoos . . . I don't know if it's a boy or a girl but I want to have sex with it." A comedian made this joke about staff in a London restaurant and it was found offensive by a member of his audience, who assumed that the joke concerned a person who was transgender and referred to that person as 'it'—a clearly degrading way to reference someone. The comedian did not intend that implication; instead, he saw the joke as being about how futuristic and alien the staff appeared. In response to having caused offence, the comic removed the joke from his set.[17]

(II) THE 'FACT'

Richard Dawkins, an outspoken atheist, posted on Twitter: "All the world's Muslims have fewer Nobel Prizes than Trinity College, Cambridge. They did great things in the Middle Ages, though." That caused widespread offence. But Dawkins tweeted, "You can attack someone for his opinion. But for simply stating an intriguing fact?"[18]

(III) DELIBERATE SLUR

Suppose that person A uses a slur when talking to another, person B. A is not a member of the marginalised group to which the slur refers but B is.

---

[17] Stuart Goldsmith, personal communication, 2019, September 27. The joke might also have been taken to be offensive on the grounds that it objectifies someone in their place of work.

[18] Richard Dawkins, "All the world's". Reported in Miekle, "Richard Dawkins criticised".

A knows that this word is considered a slur. A's use of the slur causes offence, but A doesn't care.

In each case, some at whom the affront was aimed take offence, or it is likely that they would do so. Further, their equal social standing is affronted: something is said that draws on negative group-based stereotypes or prejudices, and it conveys a derogatory message. Hence, these acts meet the criteria for when offence is justified laid out thus far: there must be an affront to equal social standing; it must be an affront to 'you or yours'; and the offended party has to bear some connection or relation to the offending party such that they could be estranged. So, too, in all cases, the groups subjected to the affront are ones that commonly face similar affronts.

However, other than in DELIBERATE SLUR, it could be thought that features of the situation ought to mitigate or undermine the offence taken. Indeed, when we are accused of causing offence, we very often deny that the other ought to be offended, offering two types of reasons.[19] One type concern the person who offends, including claims that the offending party didn't mean the act or utterance φ in the way that the offended parties have taken φ; or that they did not know that φ would be found offensive by others.[20] Take FUTURISTIC STAFF, where the comic intended to joke about the alien nature of the staff, but unintentionally invoked a degradation targeting people who are transgender. Such features are sometimes offered as excuses by, or for, the offending party, but they are also presented as criticisms of those who take offence. Sometimes, a lack of intent or ignorance is taken to suggest that others ought not take as much, or even any, offence.

The second type of reason concern the act at which offence is taken, especially, disputing whether it is offensive. Sometimes, people object that nobody could 'reasonably' take φ to be offensive, or that doing so would manifest a mistaken oversensitivity. Take cases where people say that what they have said is 'simply' or 'merely' a fact and so ought not offend, as in THE 'FACT'.[21] Sometimes, this second type of reason draws on the first; for instance, insisting that the offended party knows the act 'wasn't meant like that'

---

[19] An exemplar of each of these is humour, the subject of the next chapter; for instance, that a person being humorous makes what they say a less apt target of offence than if they had 'meant' it; or that a joke, since it is a joke, is not offensive.

[20] Fatima examines the denial of intention in the case of microaggressions, such as "I don't think he meant it like that" or the offering of benign possibilities, "On the edge of knowing", p. 153.

[21] In this case, the claim may be disingenuous: a past pattern of behaviour may suggest that the aim was to provoke. With thanks to Stephen John for drawing my attention this phenomenon.

and taking it that how the act was intended ought to determine its meaning. The literature on microaggressions provides a rich set of examples. For instance, returning to Sue's example of being asked with an African American colleague to move to the back to rebalance the plane, the flight attendant took her intention to trump Sue's interpretation. As Sue describes, he said:

> 'Did you know that you asked two passengers of color to step to the rear of the "bus"?' The flight attendant replies, 'Well, I have never been accused of that! How dare you? I don't see color! I only asked you to move to balance the plane. Anyway, I was only trying to give you more space and greater privacy.'[22]

Such reactions are often efforts to block another's offence from seeming justified: to undermine the reasonableness of resisting the offered affront.

Below, I address whether either feature can render taking offence unjustified or, at least, less justified. My focus still remains on those who take offence, rather than those who cause it. The issue at hand is the justification for taking offence under these conditions—and not how factors such as a lack of intent or disagreement over what is offensive might alter our moral assessment of the offending party.

4.3. "But I didn't mean it": On intention and blame

Let's begin with the claim that what the offending party intended to communicate should influence whether their act is found offensive. One might even hold that the offender's intended meaning cancels out an audience's competing interpretation as, for instance, in FUTURISTIC STAFF, where the comedian intended to joke about how alien and futuristic the staff appeared, rather than anything directly regarding gender identity. Or one might opt for a more restricted claim that the intended meaning makes some difference, such that the comedian in FUTURISTIC STAFF ought to elicit less offence than person A in DELIBERATE SLUR. Take THE 'FACT', too, which had the clear aim of provoking a reaction: its author may seem not only to intend to present a fact, but for the audience to draw negative conclusions about the religion targeted. As the second potential limit on when offence is justified, one might endorse the following:

---

[22] "Racial microaggressions", p. 275.

The good faith limit: If an agent A did not intend to affront B's standing as a social equal, then B's taking offence is unjustified or, at least, less justified than it would be had A intended the affront.

This limit would account for that common response on the part of the offending party: 'but I didn't mean it like that!'. But it also mistakes the significance of the offending party's intention: in order to determine whether it is apt to take offence at some act or utterance, φ, the relevant question is not what does an agent intend by φ, nor what does it mean but, rather, is φ an affront to someone's equal standing? What justifies taking offence is that it resists a threat to standing, so what counts is whether the act *is* or functions as an affront to standing. A speaker's (or actor's) intention alone does not answer that question, rather, whether something functions as an affront to standing depends primarily on the social understandings of that kind of act or utterance within a particular context.

Expressive acts are not alone in being ways that standing can be shaped without any particular agent's so intending: consider how implicit bias leads people to rate the CVs with men's names over those with women's names, and those with names deemed likely to belong to white people over those deemed likely to belong to black people.[23] As further illustration that the social function of our acts need not be tied to our intentions, take social norms. Norm following can be done without people really thinking about it: say, out of unthinking habit, I join a queue, or I leave an empty seat between myself and another passenger on the train when sitting down, without forming any particular intention to do so. Yet by following these norms, I act to reinforce them, even without thinking about it. I contribute to the pattern of behaviour that underpins our expectations that people will continue to act like this. For certain norms, this unthinking compliance contributes to the unequal patterning of social relations.

One might hold that whether someone intended to cause offence would make *some* consistent difference, say, worsening an affront. At the least, oughtn't FUTURISTIC STAFF elicit less offence than DELIBERATE SLUR? Admittedly, knowing that a person intended to offend can sometimes make some affront more offensive. Suppose, to illustrate, that Amy thinks that

---

[23] On the women/men case see Steinpreis et al., "The impact of gender"; see also the survey of research in Jost et al. "The existence of implicit bias"; on stereotypical 'white' and 'black' names, see, again, Jost et al., "The existence of implicit bias", esp. p. 49. These and many other examples of implicit bias are discussed in Saul, "Ranking exercises".

Bertie simply slips up in assuming her to be heterosexual. Then it turns out that he did know Amy was bisexual but opted to slight her because he thinks that bisexuality isn't a 'proper' sexuality. Finding that out, Amy may then take more offence; indeed, she may even take offence where she did not before. It is revealed that Bertie intended to insult her, in addition to his failing to recognise her for who she is. So, too, in THE 'FACT' the context shapes the offence taken, in that the offended audience suspects that they know what discriminatory attitudes the author intended to invoke. Hence, while lack of intent does not appear to reliably block an act from functioning as an affront or threat to standing, intent may still increase the degree of affront that an act presents. Direct insults can be more offensive than accidental missteps.

Work on politeness and face provides a possible explanation. Usually, we collaborate in other's construction of their 'face', or the way in which they wish to present themselves in a setting.[24] Deliberately affronting another's sense of their standing breaks with this collaboration. As a result, intent may worsen the affront by increasing the degree of disregard for another's standing that it is perceived to express. But, still, intent does not always worsen the offensiveness of an act. Indeed, sometimes, performing an affront unintentionally can sometimes be more offensive, being a greater affront to one's standing as an equal. For instance, it might communicate that you did not even bother to find out that the act would be offensive, such is your lack of respect or consideration for another. Perhaps the comedian in FUTURISTIC STAFF could be accused of such disrespect in failing to find out about the common kinds of degradations that those who are trans experience. The ignorance of privileged groups is not always innocent.[25] As another example, sometimes the carelessness of forgetting to abide by some commonly observed norm, and one that is easily followed, reveals just how little regard one has for another. A person's intent by itself, then, neither settles the degree of offensiveness of their act, nor the justifiability of their taking offence.

The better way to capture the difference between a person who offends deliberately, and one who does not, likely lies beyond the bounds of this book: it might change our assessment of the offending party's blameworthiness. In DELIBERATE SLUR and THE 'FACT', the offending party deliberately sets out to offer affronts to standing, while in FUTURISTIC STAFF, the offending party does not. That may affect whether we blame the offending party or, better, for

---

[24] See Olberding, "Subclinical bias", on the importance of this collaboration.
[25] See Charles Mills on the culpability of white ignorance, e.g., "White ignorance".

what we blame them: culpable ignorance in the FUTURISTIC STAFF case but, in the other two, their ill-will and deliberate action.

It could be thought that we find here an alternative limit on when offence is justified, and not just a feature that alters the moral assessment of an offender, namely,

> No offence without blame: For taking offence to be justified, the offending party must be morally responsible for causing offence such that she is, in principle, open to blame for it.[26]

This limit could include as justified cases of offence-taking both those where the agent deliberately offends and those where the agent offends through their culpable ignorance or negligence. The latter, too, are failures to collaborate in another's construction of their 'face' and so insults, even if the content of the affront is not intended. By contrast, taking offence would be unjustified where the other party is not open to blame for their act. Precisely which cases fall under that description would depend on one's broader account of moral responsibility. To illustrate, it might include cases where the agent could not have been expected to do otherwise, or where the act cannot be attributed to the agent in the right way.

The blame restriction on justified offence does have some apparent pull. After all, when people offend, sometimes they defend themselves by appeal to factors salient for whether they are to blame or reasons that at least may diminish the degree of negative appraisal that they face; for instance, saying 'I didn't mean it', or 'I wasn't thinking'. Further, on some theories of blame, to take offence may appear to be one way to blame someone.[27] To illustrate, on T. M. Scanlon's theory of blame as relationship modification, the person blamed has done something reflecting "attitudes towards others that impairs the relations that others can have with him or her" and the blamer modifies her relations accordingly.[28] Taking offence could be a relationship modification of the right sort since, on his view, blaming may or may not

---

[26] This connection is not without precedent: Feinberg, *Offense to others*, after all, connects offence and resentment, and resentment is one of blame's paradigmatic reactive attitudes, see Strawson, *Freedom and Resentment*. With thanks to Manuel Vargas for prompting me to consider the relation between blame and offence.

[27] If not all, especially those that regard blame as a distinctive emotional response centred on resentment and anger, as some seem to have interpreted; Strawson, *Freedom and Resentment*. But offence may be a reactive attitude in Strawson's sense.

[28] Scanlon, *Moral Dimensions*, p. 128. However, against this view, defending a reactive attitudes account without relationship impairment, see Wolf, "Blame, Italian style".

involve feeling the standard reactive attitudes: for instance, one might simply fail to offer the friendly greeting that one usually would. Another example is Angela Smith's protest theory of blame, on which one modifies the relation to the other as a way of "*protesting* (i.e. registering and challenging) the moral claim implicit in her conduct, where such protest implicitly seeks some kind of moral acknowledgement on the part of the blameworthy agent and/or on the part of others in the moral community".[29] Taking offence, could be one way to so protest. Indeed, amongst her examples of blame, Smith offers cutting off contact with an unreliable friend and 'dispassionately "unfriending"' someone on Facebook, both of which look like manifestations of offence.[30] Finally, Shoemaker and Vargas offer a signalling theory of blame, where what unifies blame is its function as a costly way 'to signal the blamer's commitment to a set of norms.'[31] Offence, too, can signal one's commitment to—although sometimes one's rejection of—a set of norms.

Yet there is some distance between the practices of taking offence and blaming. First, one can take offence at another's acts without blaming them, and even where they aren't blameworthy. Take the very young child who parrots the offensive—say, racist, sexist, or ableist—views of her parents. One may be offended, but without blaming the child. As another example, take the Microsoft chatbot Tay which, after interacting with other users on Twitter, produced a series of racist tweets. One might be offended, yet the chatbot is not to blame.[32] Or take any case of innocently caused affronts, lacking even culpable ignorance on the part of the offender; say, someone who is unaware of the local norms, and reasonably so, and whose behaviour was intended to be polite but is read as offensive.[33]

Despite the lack of blame, these acts may offend; nonetheless they may constitute affronts to one's standing, since another's blameworthiness is not required for their acts to threaten our sense of social standing or how we wish to present ourselves in some setting. Of course, in many cases like these, there will be someone to blame for these affronts: the designers of the chatbot, say,

---

[29] Smith, "Moral blame and moral protest", p. 43.

[30] Smith, "Moral blame and moral protest", on Facebook, p. 32.

[31] Shoemaker & Vargas, "Moral torch fishing", p. 1.

[32] Whether one is offended by these tweets depends on if one regards a chatbot, or perhaps its programmers, as participating in social interactions, so taking offence makes sense as it would not for a natural phenomenon.

[33] In order to be innocent, that ignorance can't reflect or reinforce underlying social hierarchies of race, class, gender, disability and so forth. Often, one ought to have known and done better, see Mills, "White ignorance".

or the parents of the child. But the point is that offence tracks the act, rather than who is to blame for it.

Second, there is reason to think that being offended at someone may not suffice, by itself, to blame them, for those who regard blame as having a distinctively moral dimension: as addressing moral norms or moral wrongdoing, or as making some moral claim on others. Offence is usually taken at violations of social, not moral, norms. Despite the interplay between manners and injustice, often we take offence simply at rudeness with little wider significance. Indeed, offence is not always an appropriate reaction to violations of moral norms if these violations do not concern one's presentation of self. At the least, then, other reactive attitudes like resentment look more widely appropriate than offence within our blaming practices.[34] So, too, often what is sought in taking offence is not a moral acknowledgement, as Smith suggests blaming demands, but a change in our social interactions. What is primarily at stake is not one's moral status, but one's social status: consider that when I offend, I may primarily feel embarrassment, not guilt. Thus, I suggest that offence is better viewed either as a "blame-like interpersonal practice" to borrow Shoemaker and Vargas' phrase, or as a potential part of a blaming practice, but perhaps one that is, by itself, insufficient.[35] Reactions of offence may still form a part of blaming: I might, for instance, be both offended and resentful. But the gap between blame and offence is wide enough to undermine the notion that for offence to be justified, the offending party must be to blame for their offensive act.

4.4. "But *that*'s not offensive": Disagreement and the offensive

To ask what is offensive, is to ask what constitutes an affront to one's social standing. For offence to be justified, an affront must also be to one's standing as a social equal. However, whether particular acts count as affronts to equal standing is up for debate: sometimes, some take offence and others deny that they should. A recent illustration would be the dispute over whether widely inaccurate or inept renderings of national recipes, from undercooked sushi rice to poor imitations of Banh Mi, are offensive, perhaps in constituting acts

---

[34] Perhaps always appropriate, but see Scanlon, *Moral Dimensions*.
[35] Shoemaker & Vargas, "Moral torch fishing", p. 18. They admit that this signalling function appears in other practices too.

of disrespect or disregard for the group in question.[36] Such disagreement might motivate the following limit on justified offence:

> *The correctness requirement*: For taking offence to be justified, you must be right that the act at which you take offence is an affront to your standing as a social equal.

Surely, one might think, offence could only be justified if there is such a thing as being right that one's standing as a social equal has been affronted. Hence, we need some account of when it is right to find something to be such an affront. This proposal might also capture the thought that offence's justifiability is under threat in cases where there is widespread disagreement over whether some act is offensive.[37] If many others disagree with your taking my act to be offensive, surely that gives you a reason to reconsider whether you are right to take it to be an affront to equal standing. Previously, I argued that what counts is the social meaning of an act, not the offending party's interpretation, and the same might look like it holds for the offended party too. If most deny that some act, φ, is offensive how then could one be justified in taking offence at φ? To do so would seem out of keeping with the act's broader social meaning.

I will defend an alternative account of what makes an act offensive. Rather than relying on popular opinion, I propose that we look to a group's shared understandings of what counts as an affront to equal standing towards members of that group; for instance, regarding what manifests a lack of respect or constitutes an unwarranted intrusion. More precisely, an act, φ, is offensive to members of a group in a way that can justify their taking offence, under the other relevant conditions, only if: (i) members of that group tend to take φ to be an affront to their standing as social equals and (ii) their doing so is neither unreasonably demanding, nor requires that the other party degrade or demean themselves in a way that would be incompatible with the other party conceiving of themselves as social equals too.

In order to motivate this account, I begin with the other options. To start, the answer as to what is correctly read as offensive cannot be simply that the

---

[36] To illustrate, see the Oberlin College case reported in Staufenberg, "US university accused".

[37] As opposed to the justification of taking offence, all things considered, which I address in §4.5, where there is widespread disagreement there is, of course, likely to be more push back and resistance.

offended individual decides for herself.[38] One can be mistaken in taking offence; for instance, mishearing an innocent word as a slur. One can also mistake which affronts are appropriate candidates at which to take offence. Take someone with highly idiosyncratic ideas about what counts as respectful, who prefers a form of greeting that nobody else could reasonably be expected to know about; or someone who has an inflated view of the kind of deference to which she is entitled.

Nor is the right answer that there is an objective fact of the matter to uncover about whether some act is, or is not, offensive, in being an affront to one's standing as a social equal. Often, there is no one answer as to whether some act is respectful, or even demeaning or degrading, that abides across different societies or even across different kind of relationships and kinds of interaction. Expressions of consideration and respect, for instance, depend on underlying social meanings to turn an act into something that conveys that particular message; and while a handshake may often convey such respect it won't always, as say when one is greeting a former lover. So, too, one and the same act, even within the same society or kinds of relationship could convey a different message depending on who performs it. Consider, to illustrate, the difference between a Jewish joke as told by a person who is Jewish, where it is inoffensive and as told by an anti-Semite, where it becomes offensive.[39] Thus, any answer to what counts as offensive must make room for social understandings about what a type of act conveys in a particular setting. That would be as objective a standard as one could reach.

One might wonder whether there are at least a handful of universally disrespectful acts; perhaps including nonconsensually spitting in someone's face. Some acts might seem fundamentally at odds with human dignity. But, at best, these are few and far between and I suspect that most candidates (say, calling people animal names) are culturally specific. Much the same is true of many, although perhaps not all, acts of intrusion and exclusion.

Simply to appeal to social understandings still does not settle the issue, however; often, the social meaning of particular acts is contested. Take whether holding a door open for someone counts as a gesture of respect. Marilyn Frye depicts this act as one that reflects women's inequality: we give women gestures of consideration that reveal we think them weak and which

---

[38] Although for a nuanced defence of a version of such a position, emphasising the individual's opinion when determining if an act counts as a microaggression, see Rini, *The Ethics of Microaggression.*

[39] For one discussion of in-group vs. out-group jokes, see Anderson, "Racist humor".

fail to track what they need.[40] So, too, Adam Cureton observes that holding a door open for someone with a disability might be found disrespectful, in its assumption that such assistance is required.[41] But many think that to hold a door open is simply to be polite. Thus, the question arises of how one could determine 'the' social meaning of any act.

A majoritarian approach may be tempting at this point, on which whether an act is offensive depends upon if a 'reasonable person' or 'most of us' would understand some act as an affront. Yet the majority's understanding is likely to be shaped by the norms of the dominant group: it is a common critique of the idea of a 'reasonable person' that it amounts to the dominant and privileged perspective of a society.[42] That dominant group may not regard as affronts what members of marginalised groups commonly experience as such. Further, the dominant group may be liable to characterise some acts as affronts to *equal* standing, what are instead acts not in keeping with their anticipation of being treated as having higher than average standing. A recent example could be the offence that some white people took at journalist Jon Snow's remark that he'd never seen so many white people, when reporting on a rally in favour of 'Brexit'. Offence is taken here at a (reported) fact. What appears to lie behind the offence is a conception of being white as 'standard' or 'normal': the kind of feature we don't point out within racist societies—despite such observations being common practice for members of other racial groups.[43]

The above suggests that a group's social position is relevant for settling whether 'the' message conveyed by an act is one of equal or unequal standing, in that one ought to privilege the social understandings of disadvantaged groups in the relevant respect. One could here draw on standpoint theory and its arguments that marginalised groups, given their social position, have knowledge and epistemic authority that those with privileged social positions lack.[44] Belonging to a marginalised group can mean that one see facets of

---

[40] Frye, *The Politics of Reality*.

[41] Cureton, "The limiting role of respect", p. 394.

[42] To illustrate, one area that this worry arises is in cases of sexual harassment, where there is a dispute over whether it is a 'reasonable man' standard to be applied, or a 'reasonable woman standard' to determine the offensiveness of conduct. For one discussion see Adler & Peirce, "The legal, ethical, and social implications". For a critique of 'reasonableness' in defences of provocation and self-defence, see Lee, *Murder and the Reasonable Man*.

[43] 'Brexit' was the term given to the UK's exit from the European Union. Adding to the offence may have been also the implicit message that people in favour of Brexit were racist. See BBC, "Jon Snow".

[44] On standpoint theory see, for instance, Jaggar, "Feminist politics and epistemology"; Collins, "Learning from the outsider within".

social experience that others miss, including some of the complex ways in which unequal social standing gets constructed and enacted through particular interactions. That is echoed in the work of Derald Wing Sue, who depicts disputes over microaggressions in terms of two different perspectives, one that denies and one that recognises the experience of microaggressions, just as, he suggests, the tale of a lion hunt gets told from the point of view of the hunter and not the lion.[45]

Even without making a full epistemological commitment to standpoint theory there are reasons to attend to the understandings of a socially disadvantaged group, rather than the perspective of the dominant group in the relevant respect, in order to determine which affronts offend against equal standing. First, we have additional reason to attend to the claims of groups that have been historically and are currently disadvantaged or oppressed. These groups are less likely to have been the ones who set the terms of what is generally counted as polite, respectful, intrusive and the like, given their members have tended to lack power and standing. So, too, one can reasonably expect current norms around standing to systematically mark members of such groups out as having lesser standing. Hence, where members of such groups propose new norms, or differing interpretations of acts as compared to the common view, we have good reason to give such claims extra weight as compared to those of the dominant group. Such claims look more likely to be revisions in the right direction: towards a more socially equal society.

Second, as the last chapter argued, one dimension of social standing is having the power to set or negotiate the terms of social interactions. What equal standing demands in this dimension is, roughly, that we follow another's preferences about how to interact with them, unless we have good reason not to; for instance, refraining from asking questions they find inappropriate. Amongst the good reasons not to abide by the relevant norm would be that what the other demands of us is unduly burdensome, demeaning, or degrading. However, what is not required is that some abandon their power to negotiate the terms of an interaction and opt instead for the dominant or most widely shared understanding of what would count as respectful, non-intrusive, and as inclusive when it comes to how they are treated. One way to motivate this last point, in addition to the last chapter's arguments, is to consider how ordinary is such a demand. We are used to abiding by norms in our social interactions and used to changing these where other groups have

---

[45] Sue, "Microaggressions and 'evidence'".

differing understandings of these norms or their social meanings. Why not here too? Take the way that we might greet others: I might kiss a French colleague on the cheek, hug a young American colleague, or shake hands with an older British colleague. I use the form of a person's name that they'd prefer, be it a nickname, first name, or surname. The goal is to treat others in line with what they take to be a respectful, fitting greeting.[46]

Clearly, unlike the greetings cases, affronts to equal standing are often harmful. Affronts are often not only manifestations of a marginalised or oppressed group's inability to set the terms; for instance, some affronts can be a denial of the other's very identity. The task here, however, is determining what is offensive, rather than articulating the full harms done by others treating one as lacking equal standing. Still, one part of that harm is the manifestation of one's lack of power by contrast to the other's power to fail to track one's interests and to do so without penalty; to ask rude and intrusive questions; to override one's preferences and sense of one's own identity.

The account I offer then of how to determine what an act conveys is a predominantly group-affected one. What we should follow are a group's own shared understandings of what counts as, say, an intrusive or disrespectful question; or which terms are inappropriate to use. It may be that individuals can also make claims to particular idiosyncratic treatment. However, they can only do so where it is reasonable to require that others find out about their particularities; for instance, we might abide by a colleague's niche preferences around politeness norms, say, addressing each other using titles and surnames. It would be inapt, however, for this colleague to take offence when another academic, unfamiliar with their personal preferences, adopted the wider academic group norm of addressing them by their first name. Individual claims to special treatment of this kind thus threaten be epistemically burdensome in finding out about these preferences, or can be unreasonable, or may reach beyond the demands of social equality in requiring more of others than one does in turn for them—say, in requiring others find out about one's long list of idiosyncratic preferences where most make few such demands. These features tell against individual, idiosyncratic demands being consistent with relations of social equality. There are resulting limits, then, to how many others we are expected to track individual preferences for, perhaps restricted to those with whom we are in close or repeated contact.

---

[46] There is a quirk in these cases that it is not entirely clear which greeting one should use in these cross-cultural cases: the other person ought, too, to defer to your preferences.

A question arises as to how the group-affected account can deal with the fact of disagreement within and between groups. Given such disagreement, one might think that a group-affected account gives no clear answer as to whether one is correct to take offence. So, different groups might conflict over what is respectful behaviour, including cases where each group has historically been oppressed and each is disadvantaged by the social norms currently in play. Sometimes, this conflict will be surmountable. The solution will often be to abide by the norms of the group with which one engages, with the parallel practice of different norms, as we do where we swop between different forms of respectful greeting for those of different nationalities.

Other times, however, the groups' respective understandings of an act may directly conflict. Take the offence of an ultra-religious person at having to sit next to a woman on an aeroplane, whose demands that the woman move, in turn, offend the woman. Here, the same considerations of what is burdensome or consistent with another regarding themselves as an equal are relevant as for idiosyncratic, individual demands. While there is variation in the social meanings of acts, the variation may not be endless. If a gesture is in nearly all contexts and by near all groups in a society seen as incompatible with social equality—and segregation is likely a good contender for that— then all else being equal the group demanding it is unlikely to be making a reasonable request where that request impacts on those outside the group.[47]

Some disagreements between groups may be both insurmountable and be ones where such constraints won't provide good enough guidance. Perhaps more troublingly still, groups can also sometimes be internally divided over the correct interpretation of a particular act. Take the collective of French women who defended men's seduction against the expansion of a movement against sexual harassment and abuse in the French version of the 'MeToo' movement, '#BalanceTonPorc'. This is a dispute over which norms around compliments and flirting are acceptable, with the collective objecting to men being targeted for acts like touching a knee or attempting a kiss.[48] The question arises of what we should do in such cases. What are the norms that one ought to adopt if some women accept a 'freedom to pester' as the collective

---

[47] There are obvious exceptions, as when protection and promotion of a vulnerable group's interests requires separation, as for domestic violence shelters.

[48] For a letter by the group, see Collective, "Nous défendons une liberté". In rough translation, against some men being targeted: "when they were only wrong to have touched a knee, attempted to steal a kiss, talking about 'intimate' things at a professional dinner or having sent messages with a sexual connotation to a woman whose attraction was not reciprocal".

puts it, while others do not? How could we adjudicate, as we must in deciding how to interact and whether to, say, 'pester'?

I suggest that both of the above kinds of group disagreement are simply part of the negotiation that needs to take place over which norms will be adopted, as the old norms are contested. Exchanges of offence, counter offence, and protest to others taking offence, are part of this process as some adopt new norms while others stick to the old. One might ask, still, who is taking *justified* offence in these instances of disagreement, especially of the kind found amongst French feminists? Surely, one might think, only one party can be right to get offended, and only one is right about what equal social standing demands: the freedom to pester, or the freedom from pestering. Once again, however, there is no one right answer as to what 'the' socially equal treatment would be. Rather, it can be that both sides in a dispute take justified offence: offence justified, in that each group or subgroup perceives an affront to their standing as social equals and neither makes a claim to greater than equal standing, nor imposes an unreasonably burdensome or otherwise objectionable requirement on others. In this case of the French feminists, each side perceives an affront to standing as social equals and neither is self-evidently mistaken, even if one finds one set of norms far more attractive than the other. On each side, the case for offence can be connected to underlying sexist norms. On the one side, the 'pestering' behaviour is taken to convey a message that women are sexual objects, not equals. On the other side, banning or policing the 'pestering' of women is taken to convey a message that women are fragile and in need of protection.

To take offence and to be justified in taking that offence thus does not require that one has the single, correct answer as to what could be proper or respectful treatment. Often, there is no one correct answer to be found. But, then, to hold that taking offence is justified only in the absence of disagreement would be mistaken: it would fail to accommodate the dynamic nature of offence as an intervention into one's social standing. Against a background of disagreement, what justifies taking offence is not that one is correct, but that there are social norms salient to one's standing as a social equal to be negotiated or reinforced. To engage in renegotiating social norms through taking offence does not require that all already agree with the norms that one proposes, not even within one's own group. Indeed, if all already agreed and abided by the norm, no such negotiation through offence would be required.

4.5. When offence lacks uptake

Taking offence can be risky. Sometimes when we do so, it backfires: we face social sanctions that could include being called 'humourless'; being excluded from future social invites in case we 'drag the mood down'; or facing increased attacks on our standing, or even one's person.[49] Occasionally, our offence may not even be understood as offence. Instead, taking offence gets misunderstood, by being conflated with being upset, anxious, or oversensitive, rather than being regarded as a claim to standing by resisting an affront.[50] One might think that we fail to resist a threat to our social standing when others either fail to see, or do not accept, our offence at some act that we deem an affront. Hence, where offence fails to get seen or accepted as offence by those at whom it is taken, that might threaten to undermine the justification for taking it. To state the limits in a strong form:

> *The acceptance requirement:* Taking offence is justified, all thing considered, only where one's being offended will be, or is likely to, be accepted by others rather than provoking a backlash.
>
> *The uptake requirement:* Taking offence is justified, all things considered, only where one's taking offence will be, or is likely to be, understood by others as offence, rather than being mistaken for some other emotional state.

Imposing the acceptance requirement would result in an apparently counterintuitive conclusion that it is more likely that we should take offence at those who mean well but accidentally offend, as in FUTURISTIC STAFF, than at those who are purposefully offensive, as in DELIBERATE SLUR or THE 'FACT'. When offence is taken at the former, the offending party is more likely to recognise that another is offended and more likely to change their behaviour accordingly; indeed, the comedian in question apologised and removed the joke from future iterations of the show. By contrast for the latter, where someone desires to cause offence, to take offence may only spur them on. Take the type of comedian who, having caused offence, makes it the defining feature of their work to continue to do so.

---

[49] See, for instance, on the trope of the humourless feminist, Bergmann, "How many feminists", p. 65, pp. 75–76.

[50] These are different to the social costs of rejected anger, except an overlapping idea that the person is 'hysterical' or irrational.

However, this conclusion might *not* be counterintuitive. One aim of this book has been to domesticate the emotion of taking offence by contrast to its current portrayal as part of an oppositional 'culture war' or as a novel on-line phenomenon. Much of our offence-taking is small-scale and addresses details of our social relations within ongoing relationships. Hence it is unsurprising that taking offence can be a more successful strategy where the person who causes offence is sympathetic, or closer to our line of thinking. Thus, the apparently well-intentioned person in FUTURISTIC STAFF is, after all, a particularly appropriate target of offence.

The acceptance condition as stated above ought to be rejected nonetheless: that an instance of offence is likely to get pushback does not undermine the justification for taking it. First, the defence of offence has been that it is a tactic for recognising and negotiating our social standing and some backlash does not undermine its capacity to play that role.[51] The justification of offence is not restricted to the impact on the offender. By taking offence at an individual one might shape the behaviour of others, even if not that particular individual: others might see a contestation of norms. Further, where there is a backlash we can learn something about which norms of a society, patterned in socially unequal ways, are particularly ripe for renegotiation. Others, by disputing the offence-taking, signal that there is something to resist: it is worth putting effort into pushing back. By contrast, sometimes where people make claims to standing, such claims are dismissed as absurd or humorous, rather than being attacked directly. A rejection, or even an escalation in offensive behaviour, demonstrates that the offending party (or others) take the resistance of the offended party to be a serious threat, in a way that their being amused does not. Second, even where backlash is widespread, as earlier discussed, simply to take offence, even if others resist one doing so, shores up one's sense of self-respect. It rejects, rather than internalises, another's characterisation of one as lesser, or their failing to collaborate in our self-image as we present and construe it.[52]

There remain a set of cases where justifying offence still looks difficult: namely, those where there are widespread failures of recognition. The uptake condition, then, may yet succeed, even if our taking offence need not

---

[51] Nonetheless, the costs that will be inflicted on the person who takes offence can make choosing not to do so, or at least not revealing that one does so, pragmatically wise. Chapter 6 addresses whether there can ever be a duty to take offence and the burdens on the offending party.

[52] Appeals to self-respect are a familiar feature of feminist defences of negative emotions, see Bell, "A woman's scorn".

be accepted by others. Yet in those cases where offence isn't read as offence—as opposed to cases where the offender directly disputes and so engages with the person who takes offence—we can draw on Frye's defence of the mapping role of anger. Frye argues that we learn something from when others do not receive or engage with our anger *as* anger, and from where they do. She provides the example of a woman angry at a car mechanic's needless car repair where the car mechanic fails to given the woman's anger 'uptake': rather than engage with her anger the car mechanic calls her a "crazy bitch", and so "changed the subject . . . to the matter of her character and sanity".[53] From the way in which women's anger fails to get uptake we learn something about their standing, especially, about within which domains women can claim respect. For instance, women can get uptake for their anger at, and on the behalf of, children, but not with regard to car repairs.[54]

In the case of offence, we also learn something about people's respective standing where this emotion fails to get uptake from others. In particular, where someone is read as taking offence then they are regarded as having the standing to negotiate over the rules of engagement for *that* type of interaction; for instance, over what counts as respectful treatment or as intrusive. That includes cases where one's taking offence is directly disputed, as where the offending party appeals to their good intention or ignorance. By contrast, where one's offence lacks uptake in general, one may lack the standing to negotiate. A group might find that certain interaction types or particular contexts are places where they lack such standing—although that can change. Perhaps, until recently, women and especially teenage girls lacked the standing to contest (what seem) minor flirtations, in that to do so would be regarded as absurd, a manifestation of one's being 'frigid', or a needless overreaction. Now, though, it looks like in the aftermath of the 'MeToo' movement, in some places they have gained the standing to be read as taking offence at, say, flirtatious remarks. To take offence, then, can still be a justified move, one important in the negotiation of standing.

A lack of uptake might have deeper consequences, as yet unaddressed. Sue Campbell argues that expressing our feelings and being understood by others can be essential in forming some emotions.[55] As a result, she argues

---

[53] Frye, *The Politics of Reality*, pp. 88–89.

[54] Lorde describes the reading of Black women's anger and the defensiveness it can prompt in white women in her, "The uses of anger". See also Bartky on the gender pattern of shame as a "corporeal disclosure of self in situation" in a patriarchal society, "The pedagogy of shame", p. 226.

[55] Campbell, "Being dismissed", e.g., her formulation on p. 55. Her focus is on the transformation of intended anger to bitterness where one is not listened to, esp. pp. 49–51.

that "many people's emotional lives are, in fact, dominated by a confusion that is an inevitable consequence of persistent lack of uptake."[56] What, then, if offence is widely mistaken, especially for a particular group that tends to be deemed merely hysterical, or oversensitive to hurt feelings? Is it possible, then, to take offence successfully, or without confusion? As support for the idea that offence is one emotion where some do indeed suffer the confusion that Campbell depicts, one could appeal to the widely discussed ambiguity of microaggressions. Those who experience microaggressions can find it hard to be sure of what they experience.[57] That ambiguity could be in part a result of the lack of collective uptake of offence experienced by those in marginalised social positions.

Offence, however, is often successfully conveyed. All the cases where some dispute that offence is appropriate are cases where taking offence gets some uptake, including cases where people insist that this sort of affront ought not be taken so seriously, or that in this case the affront was not meant 'like that' and so ought not be the target of offence. Often, these are precisely the sorts of responses levelled at those who object to microaggressions. In such responses, we find an engagement with the fact that someone takes offence, rather than a shifting of the subject to something else. I suspect, then, that we are not yet in a situation of sufficiently persistent failures of uptake to undermine offence-taking.

Instead, what we find is a series of popular books and articles that sometimes look like they could inculcate such a widespread mistake. In particular, those who seek to depict the apparent growth in people taking offence as a growth in 'victimhood' might promote such widespread misinterpretation. Rather than reading this emotion as we should and ordinarily do, when encountering, say, queue jumpers and unapologetic drink spillers—namely, as a matter of a reacting to a threat to our standing—we are encouraged to read it as revealing emotional vulnerability and hurt. This could render it less effective in the negotiation of social standing with others.[58]

That, however, is not yet a reason to cease to take offence but, rather, reason to resist the narrative whereby taking offence is dismissed as mere feeling, and an irrational one too; precisely the discounting of the role of emotions

---

[56] "Being dismissed", p. 55.
[57] For one discussion see Fatima, "On the edge of knowing".
[58] The range of failures of uptake for offence could be narrower than for anger. Anger is an indirect claim for standing, as someone who can hold the other to shared moral standards. By contrast, offence is a direct claim for standing, which might make it less vulnerable to misinterpretation.

in our social and political lives that much feminist work has criticised.[59] Further, now we capture one of the harms of these popular critiques of taking offence, in the way in which they mischaracterise offence. They threaten to undermine one route through which marginalised, oppressed, and historically disadvantaged groups could have their demands for recognition and respect acknowledged.[60]

There is one last challenge to address, if not to the justifiability of taking offence, then to the optimism about its potential effectiveness against a background of social inequality. This time, the issue is the unevenness in the uptake or reception of offence. Existing politeness and civility norms are often ways in which our everyday interactions are patterned in socially unequal ways. As a consequence, taking offence has been, and often is, used to reinforce the norms that underpin social hierarchies. So, too, in general, the offence of the powerful looks far more likely to be seen and to be taken seriously than that of those who lack power. Surely, one might think, we are more inclined to notice, and to care about, signals of offence from those who have higher social status, than those from people with lower social status. The 'currency' of offence looks like it will be unevenly distributed: the powerful will find these emotions more effective and impactful than will the less powerful.[61] That might mean that small-scale gestures like raised eyebrows would be an effective strategy only for the powerful: those to whose every gesture we would attend.

These remarks, however, don't render taking offence toothless for those with less social standing or power. The most powerful may get the *most* uptake, with more people sensitive even to their slightest raised eyebrow. Still, the signals of offence of the less powerful will nonetheless tend to be read as such, even when small in scale, and that suffices for offence to be used to renegotiate social norms. For a start, as observed above, those from marginalised or discriminated against groups often *do* get uptake (if a resisting kind). Consider the prevalence of contestations of claims to have experienced a microaggression in terms of whether it was right to take offence over that particular case. That is a reading of microaggressed party as offended, even if it is not an acceptance that they are right to have taken offence. It is also too

---

[59] For a history of feminist work on emotion see Fischer, "Feminist philosophy", and the many examples discussed over this chapter and the last.

[60] There is some parallel here to Campbell's argument that "bitterness, sentimentality, and emotionality disguise their own operation by suggesting that expressive failure lies with the individual" rather than being a collective failure, a result of other's failure of uptake, "Being dismissed", p. 55.

[61] With thanks to a referee for raising this issue.

simple a picture of society to think of social interactions as entirely determined by a single hierarchy. We are often in personal relations that crosscut
hierarchies (as partners, friends, colleagues). This rescues the possibility of
the less powerful deploying more subtle manifestations: a friend, colleague
or lover may be concerned by a raised eyebrow or small silence, even against
background hierarchies.

Lastly, as sociologists observe, our standing in an interaction is, within
constraints, co-constructed. The more powerful are far from impervious to
affronts: consider how often those occupying high social positions are offended. Nor are we immune to the feeling of having committed a social misstep, even when we are higher up in social hierarchies. We are all attuned to
how our self-presentation is received. As a result, even those who have more
standing are likely to be sensitive to subtle signs regarding how they come
across, including those that indicate that they have caused offence.

There is one last tricky case for the scope of justified offence: humour. That
will be the subject of the next chapter.

5

Only joking!

On the offensiveness of humour

Professor Tim Hunt, a Nobel prize winning biochemist, remarked during a speech at a conference:

> let me tell you my trouble with girls ... Three things happen when they are in the lab; you fall in love with them, they fall in love with you and when you criticise them, they cry.[1]

Hunt's words were reported on Twitter and caused widespread offence. As a result, he ended up resigning from an honorary position at a university.[2] Having initially published pieces critical of Hunt's remarks, *The Guardian*, a British left-wing newspaper, later published an article that offered as reason to exonerate Hunt that he was only joking, as evidenced by a recording of the proceedings wherein some people laughed.[3] The suggestion appears to be that the fact that Hunt was joking ought to have altered whether people take offence. What is puzzling is that it seemed obvious all along that Hunt was making a joke: the structure of his remarks, like his use of overstatement, reveal this.[4]

This case illustrates a general tension within our practices of taking offence. On the one hand, offence is frequently taken at jokes or other humorous remarks.[5] Take many of the cases of offence that receive popular attention, such Lindsay Stone who stuck up her middle finger and pretended

---

[1] As reported on Twitter by St Louis, "Nobel scientist Tim Hunt FRS @royalsociety says at Korean women lunch 'I'm a chauvinist and keep 'girls' single lab'", Twitter post, June 8, 2015, 8.37am, https://twitter.com/connie_stlouis/status/607813783075954688

[2] In cases like these it can be instructive to see what happens next. In this case, one woman who reported his comments has now had her job reduced, whereas Hunt's career shows little sign of damage, as reported in Fernandez "Female academic".

[3] McKie, "Tim Hunt".

[4] On linguistic analyses of jokes see this chapter, §5.2.

[5] I follow Noel Carroll in treating jokes as distinct from informal humour. On his view, jokes have a particular verbal structure, taking the form of a puzzle and a solution, "On Jokes", pp. 286–8.

On Taking Offence. Emily McTernan, Oxford University Press. © Oxford University Press 2023.
DOI: 10.1093/oso/9780197613092.003.0006

to yell next to a silence and respect sign in a Military Cemetery in the United States, or the frequent outrage over comedians who make offensive jokes.[6] Indeed, philosophers are far from adopting a uniformly positive view of humour. Some hold that humour essentially involves feeling superior to others or point to humour's deriding, mocking, and aggressive aspects.[7] On the other hand, the fact that someone was joking or being humorous is often appealed to in order both to defend the offending party and to criticise those who take offence. We ought not take offence, the thought goes, if someone was only joking. To take offence at a joke would treat as serious what was meant as nonserious, or reveals that one lacks a sense of humour.[8]

A similar tension over the precise relation between humour and offence also emerges in disputes over the right way to do comedy. Some comedians sign up to codes of conduct, promising not to tell rape jokes, homophobic jokes, racist jokes, or any other jokes that 'punch down' in targeting groups that already experience oppression or other forms of disadvantage; and so, not to tell many of the jokes that are commonly found offensive.[9] Others insist that it is in comedy's nature to be, potentially, offensive.[10] Still others dispute the fittingness of taking offence at jokes, arguing that doing so reveals a mistaken interpretation of what a joke is or does.[11]

This chapter's subject, then, is the nature of the relationship between humour and offence. In particular, the next time that you cause offence, would "but I was joking" be a good response to offer? When you offer that response, ought others cease to feel offended—or at least, feel less offended by your utterance? Conversely, is there something that explains why humour so often appears offensive? Much of this chapter consists of a search for reasons to

---

[6] For a discussion of the former see Ronson, *So You've Been Publicly Shamed?*; indeed, most of his cases are ones where offence is taken at jokes or humour. On the latter, comedians like Jimmy Carr and Ricky Gervais may spring to mind.

[7] Surveys of theories of humour commonly note the long suspicion over its role, from Plato onwards, e.g., Carroll, "Humour"; Olin, "Questions for a theory of humor", pp. 338–9; Morreall, "Philosophy of humor". This characterisation is at the heart of the superiority views of humour, e.g., Scruton, "Laughter".

[8] For one example consider the notion of the humourless feminist, as discussed, for instance, in Bergmann, "How many feminists", p. 65, pp. 75–76. For another, see Hannah Gadsby, *Nanette*, on the need to laugh to demonstrate that you do have a sense of humour when you are from a group commonly characterised as not having one.

[9] For one discussion, see Jeffries, "Is standup comedy doomed?"

[10] This brings to mind Gaut's depiction (but not endorsement) of the anti-moralist position on humour: "Sometimes it is the exquisite, carefully honed cruelty of a joke that makes it so irresistibly funny. Remove its cruelty, and its humor vanishes"; "Just joking", p. 52.

[11] For instance, Ricky Gervais remarked in a tweet: "Offence often occurs when people mistake the subject of a joke with the actual target. They're not always the same", Twitter post, March 30, 2017, 11.40am. https://twitter.com/rickygervais/status/847398023680245760.

think that the fact that a person is joking or being humorous ought to prevent or mitigate the offence that we would otherwise take, were an equivalent but serious utterance made.

Formulating these equivalent serious utterances looks tricky: one needs to be sure that the same content is conveyed and yet one argument of this chapter will be that jokes and humour might convey more than (seemingly) equivalent serious utterances, and can play more pernicious social functions. Nonetheless, some helpful examples can be found in studies into humour by social psychologists. As an illustrative pairing that was used in two studies, the non-serious utterance (joke) was:

> A man and a woman were stranded in an elevator and they knew they were gonna die. The woman turns to the man and says, "Make me feel like a woman before I die." So he takes off his clothes and says, "Fold them!"

The paired serious utterance was, "I just think that a woman's place is in the home and that it's a woman's role to do domestic duties, such as laundry, for her man".[12]

I first look for reasons to think that humour mitigates offence in accounts of humour but argue that on most views of what humour is we should be *more* offended by a humorous utterance than we would be by an equivalent, serious utterance. Second, I turn to the linguistics of jokes. While examining the language of jokes suggests that we ought not interpret jokes as we would interpret equivalent serious utterances, nonetheless, the way in which jokes function in conversation sometimes renders taking offence more, rather than less, apt than it would be for equivalent but serious equivalents. I conclude the chapter by addressing the flip side of this relation, of whether comedy is invariably offensive, or must risk being so, if it is to be funny.

Two clarifications before I begin. First, I address whether humour makes offence inapt, or lessens the degree of offence that would be appropriate, and not questions about the responsibility of the person who offends. As such, this chapter neither directly addresses questions of whether there can be good but immoral jokes, nor the moral appraisal of the person who tells the joke or the audience that laughs at it.[13] Second, while I focus on verbal jokes

---

[12] As reported in Ford & Ferguson, "Social consequences of disparagement humor", p. 81.

[13] There is a parallel here to whether art can be beautiful, but evil, as to whether a joke can be funny, but immoral, see Devereaux, "Beauty and evil"; Jacobsen, "In praise of immoral art". For such discussions see, for instance, Benatar, "Prejudice in jest"; de Sousa, *The Rationality of Emotion*; on

or humour, some of the following analysis would extend to other forms of humour, such as slapstick.

5.1. Theories of humour and the offensive

It might seem that it is something about the nature of *humour* that makes the fact that someone was only joking or is otherwise being humorous a good reason not to take offence. There are three main theories of humour: the superiority theory, the relief theory, and the incongruity theory.[14] Whilst these theories are treated as competitors, with the last the most popular, I incline towards pluralism: each theory best captures some type of humour, but no one theory captures all types of humour.[15] Regardless, on none would being humorous render a remark more innocuous. Indeed, on at least two out of three, humour may only worsen the offence.

First, on the superiority theory, humour is, as Roger Scruton puts it, an 'attentive demolition' of another.[16] When we laugh, that is an expression of our superiority over others or, sometimes, over our former selves.[17] Some humour fits this depiction, although it is hard to make this work for every instance: mockery looks like this, as does sarcasm, but often puns don't.[18] As a case where the theory does fit, take Kant's remarks, which Merrie Bergmann describes as a prime example of sexist humour:

> [a] woman who has a head full of Greek, like Mme. Dacier, or carriers on
> fundamental controversies about mechanics, like the Marquise de Chatelet,

whether we should attribute the attitudes of a joke to the person who utters it, say seeing as sexist, the person who makes a sexist joke, Johnson, "The 'only joking' defense"; Smuts, "The ethics of humor". I also don't address when a person who tells a racist joke, is a racist: for a discussion, see Anderson, "Racist humor". But these debates have indirect relevance in this chapter's discussions.

[14] For descriptions of the three, drawn on in what follows, see Carroll, "Humour"; Morreall, "Philosophy of humor"; Olin, "Questions for a theory of humor".

[15] Olin observes that all the theories are plagued by counter examples resulting from the diversity of humour, "Questions for a theory of humor".

[16] Scruton, "Laughter", p. 209.

[17] Morreall, "Philosophy of humour". This theory is traced back to Plato, with his suspicion about the malice in humour, as well as Aristotle and Hobbes: see for instance Carroll, "Humour", §1; Carroll, "On jokes".

[18] Carroll also notes puns as a counterexample to this view, in his "Humour", p. 346. But, then again, some of Freud's examples of puns do express superiority, *Jokes and Their Relation to the Unconscious*.

might as well even have a beard—for perhaps that would express more ob-viously the mien of profundity for which she strives.[19]

Where the theory fits, that an utterance is humorous clearly fails as a reason for others not to take offence: offence is taken at affronts to one's perceived social standing and, on this theory, humour essentially involves a claim to superiority. To claim that one was being humorous could only confirm that the other person should take offence; indeed, if it is a joke, an affront is being offered. To illustrate, mockery generally functions as a way to put someone down or to deflate their standing.[20] So, too, Noel Carroll characterises a 'nasty' strand of our humour, where we take aim at those who seem deficient or 'foolish', say where we are amused when people who fall over.[21]

Sometimes, humour may even make the offence greater than would be apt for some equivalent but serious utterance. Take sarcasm, which Drucker et al. depict as "an aggressive type of humour, whereby a speaker derides another individual, turning her or him into the victim of a humorous ut-terance", and that, as Scruton observes, "devalues and rejects in an unkind way".[22] Uttering, "So kind of you to join us", is sometimes a greater affront to someone's standing, than would be the serious and nonsarcastic utterance, "You are late". That is so not simply a result of the manner of the delivery but, rather, the way in which it makes use of the person who is targeted in order to amuse others. It is not only the content, then, that can make a humorous utterance offensive; sometimes an aspect of its deriding note stems from the intended humour.

The second theory is the relief theory of humour, on which humour acts as a release, freeing the energy that we'd otherwise use to inhibit ourselves or act seriously.[23] To offer a brief characterisation of a Freudian version, the emotions we repress most often are sexual desire and hostility. When we

---

[19] Kant, *Observations on the Feeling of the Beautiful and Sublime*, p. 78. As cited in Bergmann, "How many feminists", p. 64.

[20] A counterinstance, on the face of it, would be mockery amongst friends. Often, we are not of-fended when our friends mock us, perhaps because we don't interpret this as truly a claim of supe-riority. That might be because the mocking is usually reciprocal in friendship groups: groups where one person is always subjected to mockery, with little offered in return, have less benign dynamics. Another possible explanation is that amongst friends we tend to find teasing, rather than some more aggressive form of humour such as mockery proper. Distinguishing teasing and banter from aggres-sion see, for instance, Dynel et al., "No aggression, only teasing".

[21] Carroll, "Humour", p. 345.

[22] Drucker et al., "On sarcasm", at p. 551; Scruton, "Laughter", at p. 209.

[23] Carroll depicts this in terms of economies of energy, "On jokes"; as one of the main proponents, see Freud, *Jokes and Their Relation to the Unconscious*.

tell a joke, we let out the desire or hostility that, ordinarily, we repress—and so, what we enjoy in jokes indicates what is usually repressed in our serious talk.[24]

There might be something to this account: our jokes are indeed full of expressions of sexual desire and hostility.[25] Yet that does not suffice to make our humour more innocuous than our serious utterances. There is something troubling in the kind of hostility that jokes often reveal. It is frequently gendered for a start, as evidenced by the prevalence of the mother-in-law and wife jokes. Merrie Bergmann goes so far as to call women the "traditional objects of humor in our culture", and they may be one such.[26] But jokes also often target people on the basis of their perceived race or ethnicity, disability, gender identity, or sexuality, amongst other socially salient identities.[27] The idea that humorous utterances reveal repressed hostility, especially targeting nondominant groups, makes jokes look less innocuous, not more so.

One might respond that when someone makes a joke or finds some comment humorous, this reveals that ordinarily they do repress the feelings that the joke presents. Yet that does not alter the expression of those underlying feelings through a joke, nor the way in which that joke might degrade and put down the other. But, one might continue, suppose that a man tells a rape joke without realising the current of hostility that lurks beneath it. Perhaps he would have suppressed that hostility, had he realised what his joke reveals. Oughtn't we then be less offended than we would have been, had he directly conveyed such hostility? It seems not. Often, expressions of overt hostility are not cases where a reaction of offence seems apt; we seem more likely to feel anger, fear, or hostility in return or, perhaps, surprise. So, too, as the last chapter elaborated, offence does not track the offending party's intention; people are often offended at unintentional affronts, including minor rudeness or instances of everyday sexism.[28]

[24] But for a highly sceptical discussion of whether it is sensible to think about relief and release in such ways, see Carroll "Humour", pp. 352–3.

[25] Indeed, Olin observes that the relief theory gives us a "natural explanation" of the common themes of our humour, "Questions for a theory of humor", p. 341.

[26] Bergmann, "How many feminists", p. 63.

[27] Admittedly, and as I return to discuss, 'targeting' is too simple a way to depict how hostile content functions in jokes: for a discussion distinguishing 'racial jokes' from racist jokes and racially insensitive jokes, see Anderson, "Racist humor"; for a discussion of a variety of ways in which jokes can draw on sexist beliefs, see Bergmann, "How many feminists", pp. 70–74.

[28] If you think a joke is a sort of psychic release, and that repressed sexual desire and hostility is inevitable, then you might want to dissuade other's taking offence, lest the risk of causing offence leads people to find other, less optimal ways to release that tension. But that would be a good strategy only if jokes are benign: §5.3 will present some reasons for scepticism.

The last and most popular of the theories of humour is that of incongruity, on which humour lies in violated expectations. I adopt the benign violation version of this view from psychology.[29] On Caleb Warren and A. Peter McGraw's variant, humour results from three features: "(a) something must be appraised as a violation, (b) something must be appraised as benign, and (c) the appraisals must be simultaneously juxtaposed."[30] As to what counts as a violation, that might be a physical or other threat, such as an insult or the apparent physical attack of tickling. Alternatively, the violation might be breaking some social, cultural, or moral norm, such as when making a fart joke; or a linguistic rule, communication norm, or rule of logic, so capturing puns and absurd humour. By describing the situation as 'benign', they mean that it is regarded as safe, acceptable, normal, or 'everything seems okay'.[31]

On this theory, I take it that if someone takes offence at a humorous utterance then they don't find the violation benign: the second appraisal, (b), fails to occur.[32] The joke or humour fails for the offended audience. Hence, this theory has an advantage in that it explains why we often do find humour offensive where we don't find it amusing and where it violates social norms. Yet it offers no support to the claim that we ought not take offence at humour. People often find violations of social norms offensive: take the woman who sticks up her finger in a graveyard violating our norms of respect for the dead, or someone who farts at the table violating norms of politeness. That such violations are often found offensive makes sense in light of the arguments of Chapters 2 and 3: affronts to our social standing are often expressed through such norm violations. These social norms give us a shared language through

---

[29] The theory is originally attributed to Francis Hutcheson, see Carroll, "Humour". Morreall describes as the dominant theory in both philosophy and psychology, in "Philosophy of humor"; for its popularity amongst philosophers see also Carroll "Humour", p. 347. However, I suspect that the psychologist's account generalises more successfully across forms of humour than the philosophical variant which, given its focus on violations of patterns and expectations, tends to work best for traditionally formed stand-up jokes. Indeed, the psychologist's may generalise too successfully: Olin observes that this theory is likely to be too broad (where others look too narrow) and so is perhaps best understood as a necessary, not sufficient condition on humour, "Questions for a theory of humor", p. 343.

[30] Warren & McGraw, "Differentiating what is humorous", p. 410; adapted from Tom Veatch, "A theory of humor". See also McGraw & Warren, "Benign violations". While Warren & McGraw frame their theory as incorporating the other theories' insights, given the way they define humour it is best characterised as an incongruity theory, see "Differentiating what is humorous".

[31] Warren & McGraw, "Differentiating what is humorous", p. 411. The reasons to be found to meet this condition include lack of commitment to the norm or one's psychological distance from the violation, on distance for example see McGraw et al., "Too close for comfort".

[32] Bergman's account of sexist jokes has a similar caveat: that to find the incongruous funny, it "must not simultaneously be the cause of serious or painful concerns", "How many feminists", p. 69.

which to express our respect—or the lack thereof, as Cheshire Calhoun and Sarah Buss describe.[33]

Some also find jokes that make light of our *moral* standards offensive: take dead baby jokes that find humour from ways of interacting with dead babies ranging from shovels to blenders. Such offence-taking might, at first, appear to sit uneasily with the account of offence offered thus far, with its focus on social rather than moral norms. However, these jokes are transgressions against moral standards that do not involve actual violations—i.e., inflicting the harm, injury, or wrong in question—rather, they offer affronts to standing. They do so through manifesting a lack of consideration for those who might find the jokes hurtful, such as bereaved parents. More generally, such jokes also express a lack of concern for the kind of respectful treatment that we take it people are due in order to reflect human dignity; in the case of dead baby jokes, the respect that we take it dead human bodies are due. As such, these jokes can be found more broadly offensive.

The role of norms in our social relations also provides a reason why, indeed, violations of such norms may not be benign: an affront to one's social standing, that a background of norms lets us express, just is a threat to one's social standing. I side once again with the sociolinguists over a certain strand of political philosophers: our social standing is constructed up out of the details of our social interactions. There is nothing more to having social standing, in its distinctively social dimension—insofar as that can be disentangled from one's legal, political, or economic standing—than others tending to treat you as if you have that standing, you claiming that standing, having your claims respected, and so forth. Thus, humour, where it violates social norms that have to do with respect and standing, or that set of moral norms that have to do with our standing as persons, presents a potential threat to the standing of its target or subject. Of course, this is true only of some humour, not all: take jokes that violate norms of logic or absurdist humour.

In light of the above, one might ask why we ever find jokes with violations of such social norms amusing: aren't they always threatening? Here, there may be a helpful parallel to draw to the physical threat of tickling or pushing someone over. Who does it, with what assumed intention, and to what audience, makes a difference. Sometimes, threats are 'pretend', or we have reason not to take them as attacks on our standing, even indirectly. In-group jokes

[33] Buss, "Appearing respectful"; Calhoun, "The virtue of civility".

are a good example of the latter: if one makes a joke about one's own group it is more likely to be taken to be innocuous.[34]

Two objections might arise to this portrayal of offensiveness from within an incongruity theory. First, some may think that now the incongruity account itself faces a challenge from the fact that it looks possible to both find something humorous and yet be offended.[35] I here consider cases where one experiences both amusement and the emotion of offence, not merely someone thinking, "I ought to be offended by that", without taking offence in fact.[36] One possible example of genuinely feeling both could come from hearing the longstanding 'the Aristocrats' joke, where a talent agent asks a family, or the father of a family, about their act, what follows is a list of horrifying violations of taboos, and then comes the punchline, where the agent asks what the act is called and the answer is, 'the Aristocrats'.[37] Another example could be being amused by just how sexist or off-colour is some joke.

There may be ways to interpret these cases such that one does not experience both emotions, say, that the sexism is so ludicrous that the teller inadvertently sends up the very sexist notion that animates the joke, or Luvell Anderson's suggestion that we might be amused by the delivery of a joke and not its content, which could account for the Aristocrats case.[38] However, suppose that one did feel both emotions regarding the content, or at the joke itself. Then, one's experience fits poorly with the incongruity theory: I both experience the incongruity, and I don't—I see it as violation and benign, I see it as violation and not benign.

There are competing options here. One is holding that we can think, at the same time, that some joke is a benign violation and that is not, and hence have the conflicting emotions (or states) of amusement and offence. The one emotion, though, is likely to overcome or mitigate the other: if I am amused by a joke, I seem likely to become less offended by that joke. Further, the requisite perception here is hard to picture. The other option, that I prefer, is

---

[34] This will not be fool proof: suppose that someone who identifies as a lesbian wears the "Keep calm, watch lesbians" T-Shirt ironically—but in a setting where others may not realise that background context. For a discussion of in-group/out-group jokes, see Anderson, "Racist humor".

[35] Some may dispute that this is possible. Sometimes social psychologists on humour frame their discussions and experiments by assuming that there is a contrast between finding something amusing and finding it offensive. For instance, Dynel examines how teasing relies on knowing common ground, so the hearer finds humour, not offence, in "No aggression, only teasing".

[36] Note this is distinct from laughing: we can laugh for many different reasons including a desire to diffuse discomfort or make a situation seem okay.

[37] As repeatedly told in the movie, *The Aristocrats*. Thank you to the audience member in Durham who suggested this example.

[38] Anderson, "Racist humor", p. 505, responding to Bergmann, "How many feminists".

to simply to retreat to pluralism about humour. Insofar as we do have these experiences, what is going on is that we find humour in the release of tension, say, without taking the norm violation that the joke involves to be benign.

As the second objection to the portrayal of offensiveness on an incongruity theory, one might claim that the fact that the utterance was *intended* to be perceived as benign, makes it so. Successful humour—successful in being found funny—depends on others finding a violation benign, thus the person who offers the remarks must intend the violation to be benign, it seems, insofar as they intend to be amusing. However, that is too quick: the joker does not necessarily intend that the party who is offended finds the violation benign. Take sexist locker room humour that, once reported outside the locker room, offends, or take jokes that are intended to amuse one part of an audience at the expense of another. Further, even where the joker did intend the offended party to have found the violation benign, it is not necessarily up for the speaker to determine whether their utterances count as such; rather, as the last chapter argued and as §5.3 elaborates for humour in particular, that depends on how the utterance functions.

Hence, none of the three theories give us much to work with to defend the idea that because something is humorous, or intended to be, it is not the sort of thing at which we should take offence. On the superiority theory, and perhaps on the relief theory, that the utterance was humorous may only make things worse. Thus far, on the incongruity theory, we get an apparent explanation for what happens when we take offence: we do not experience the violation as benign. Yet that explanation is not one that means we ought not take offence, unless we can insist that the violation must be interpreted as benign. Chapter 3's arguments for the role of affronts in undermining social standing cast doubt on that, and the rest of this chapter further challenges humour's cast as benign. Ultimately, I will argue that on the incongruity theory too, that an offensive remark is humorous, or intended to be so, may worsen the affront.

5.2. Some linguistics of jokes

The nature of humour, then, cannot be the way to make sense of the thought, 'only joking!', where that is supposed to undermine or mitigate another's taking offence. Might something about the type of speech act would do the trick? Jokes look like a special sort of speech act. Usually, when we speak, we are serious. Sometimes we are not, and then our speech looks different: in general, we can tell when someone is joking.[39] Below, I examine whether what marks the one type of speech off from the other, or something about the nature of non-serious talk, would give us reason to think that jokes are inapt targets for offence.

Salvatore Attardo describes a distinctive feature of humour as being that it permits a kind of "decommitment" from, or retractability of, one's utterance: sometimes one can "discount one's remarks as having been uttered non-seriously".[40] As an example, Attardo offers Alf Walle's case of men attempting to pick up waitresses and doing so in a humorous way, in order to avoid embarrassment. Humour, then, can be used when attempting or trying out behaviour that would be socially risky, letting one have an 'out'.[41]

This might, at last, be a reason that accounts for the frequency of people's claims that they were only joking where others take offence. Sometimes such claims do make sense: they can be understood as efforts to retract the risky social move one has made. However, this does not make 'but I was joking' succeed as an all-purpose response to having caused offence. Rather, it could succeed, at best, only in those cases where the offence resulted from taking the remark to be serious—and where recharacterising the utterance as humorous would undermine that offence. Often, of course, 'but I was only joking', will not work in this way: the waitress being hit on may not find the suggestion that the man's suggestive remark was a joke much help in finding it less offensive. A retraction certainly won't work for cases where the audience already knew it was a joke, yet is offended.[42] As such, it will not in general let the professional comedian off the hook for their performances: we couldn't have taken their utterance to be serious. Nor would it let someone like Tim Hunt with his crying girls comment off the hook, given that his comments clearly had the structure of a joke. So, for instance, Hunt uses overstatement

---

[39] 'Dry' humour or wit is sometimes harder to catch.

[40] Attardo, "Humour in language", p. 9.

[41] Ibid., p. 9; from Walle, "Getting picked up".

[42] There are strategies of comedians that might permit an alternative form of decommitment, even where it is always apparent that they joked: consider ventriloquist dummies, where comedians often project a vile or offensive persona onto the dummy, or comedians who adopt personas for their acts. The claim seems to be that it is this character, and not I, who makes this joke. Would that succeed in making any offence taken, misplaced? It is an odd kind of distancing that occurs here: clearly, the comic is still the one making the joke. However, sometimes, the use of such devices could suffice to sufficiently change how a joke should be interpreted; for instance, where the persona is designed to send up those who have offensive beliefs.

in a way that is common to jokes, it was not the case that those who found him offensive thought that he really thought that *all* girls cry or fall in love.

Observing how jokes are constructed may lead to a potentially more convincing reason against taking offence at jokes. Certain features of our nonserious talk mark it out as distinct from our serious talk. In particular, jokes are widely held to be unusual in that they violate the Gricean rules of conversation.[43] Usually, our conversations are governed by the Principle of Cooperation: we will contribute what is required by the accepted purpose of the conversation. In particular, Grice claims that we follow maxims such that we do not say things that we think false or unjustified; we are as informative as is required and are relevant; and we aim for brevity and order, avoiding ambiguity. But jokes do not look like this. Often, when joking, we say things that are false or unjustified: take any kind of absurdist humour, the use of overstatement or exaggeration for comic effect, or the way in which stand ups tell stories that begin a true event but rapidly add details that make the story more amusing—but less truthful.[44] Often comedy trades off ambiguity; one classic example used to illustrate this by Morreall is Mae West's joke that "Marriage is a great institution—but I'm not ready for an institution."[45] So, too, he considers the use of comic rants where the humour lies in the extension of the joke well beyond what would be brief or to the point.[46]

Returning to our question of whether one ought to take offence at jokes, one might think that, as a result, interpreting any joke as offensive is to take it more seriously than it ought to be taken. It would be to interpret the person as really meaning the offensive content that the utterance invokes, when we ought to treat this speech differently. We ought not interpret the person as meaning what they say or, perhaps, we should not see the utterance as conveying the same information that a serious utterance would; say, for instance, that Hunt thinks that it is a bad idea to have women in one's science lab.

The above is partially correct, in that we ought not be too literal in interpreting jokes when deciding if they are offensive, but it is correct only in a limited sense. In particular, the various ways that not serious speech is marked apart from serious speech—such as overstatement, understatement,

---

[43] Grice, "Logic and conversation". For a discussion see Attardo, "Violations of conversational maxims and cooperation".

[44] In *Nanette*, Gadsby examines a flip case of this: where we don't add a detail (in her case, being beaten up) to in order make a story funny.

[45] Morreall, "Philosophy of humor", where this example is used to make the same point.

[46] Ibid.

absurdity and the like—ought to be accommodated when deciding if some utterance is offensive. So, what Tim Hunt says isn't offensive in its overstatement: his joke is not offensive because he thinks *all* girls cry or fall in love, and yet some do not. Rather, what is offensive is his invoking stereotypes, and expressing demeaning attitudes towards women. But from the fact that the usual rules of conversation do not apply, we shouldn't conclude that jokes cannot be taken seriously, in the sense that we do when we take offence.

It might be objected that one can invoke stereotypes or demeaning attitudes in order to make a joke, without thereby being committed to such beliefs and attitudes.[47] The fact that jokes do not abide by the usual conversational rules also troubles the thought that we ought to treat people as meaning, or as committed to, the underlying attitudes or beliefs when they joke, by contrast to if they offered the equivalent, serious utterance. Sometimes, these beliefs or attitudes are invoked in a spirit of playfulness; perhaps, one might continue, Tim Hunt doesn't really believe that women are more emotional or less able to work in labs. However, this is not a chapter about the correct moral judgement to make of the person who makes the joke, for which the person's commitments would be relevant. Rather, what matters is how the joke functions: in particular, whether it functions as a threat or affront to social standing, say, invoking stereotypes or a demeaning attitude. On a Gricean picture, one might think about humour as still somehow apart from our ordinary interactions: as a brief violation of the rules before ordinary conversation returns. But that view might lead us to underestimate how jokes shape our conversational context in ongoing ways, even where jokes appear 'playful'. Below, I examine how such shaping occurs, and hence why the suspension of the usual rules of conversation fails to give us reason to think jokes are inoffensive or, in other words, unthreatening to our social standing.

5.3. How offensive jokes function

Phillipe Schlenker suggests that when a slur is used without correction or dissent from others, then the background presuppositions of a conversation shift. A derogatory proposition, or set of these, are incorporated into the 'common ground' of the conversation; for instance, in the case of a racial

---

[47] It is a point of dispute over whether we need to hold attitudes, agree with them, or merely know about them, to find a joke funny. On this see Anderson, "Racist humor"; Bergmann, "How many feminists"; DeSousa, *The Rationality of Emotion*, ch. 11, on sharing sexist assumptions, pp. 290–292.

slur, that one race is superior to another.[48] While this is controversial as an account of the derogatoriness of slurs, one can take a looser interpretation of this idea of the common ground that our utterances might shape, in order to think through offensive jokes.[49]

So, when a joke is made, one thing that might happen is that it can shift or shape the background assumptions or common ground of our conversation.[50] That can increase the extent to which the joke affronts or threatens a person or group's social standing, and so the extent to which one may find it offensive, in my sense. Once the joke is made, we can come to think, or are further supported in our thinking, that this sort of thing is funny, and so—adopting the incongruity theory sketched before—that it constitutes a benign violation of the relevant norm; say, for a mother-in-law joke, an antisexist norm. The group who hear the joke and laugh have the common ground of their conversation grow to include that this sort of norm violation is acceptable, normal, or safe. This means that it is the sort of norm that we (the amused audience) have a certain distance from, and to which we are not that committed, given that these are reasons listed as features that determine what kinds of violations we will find benign.[51]

To illustrate, the benign violation theory is often used to explain the different patterns of humour amongst men and women such that men find jokes with sexist content more funny, and women find them less funny, accounted for by these two features of distance and lack of commitment. Perhaps unsurprisingly, women tend to be more committed to anti-sexist norms and less distant from the effects when such norms are transgressed against. Likewise, studies into rape jokes suggest that the men who laugh at these tend to find rape less serious as an offence, blame the victim for it more, and self-report higher proclivities towards it.[52] By introducing such jokes, one signals that around here the norms against discrimination about the wrongness of rape are not so strong or not ones to which 'we' are all that committed.

---

[48] Schlenker, "Expressive presuppositions", for a description of the process, see p. 242. Examining the idea of the common ground, see Stalnaker, "Common ground".

[49] On the controversy, see Richard, *When Truth Gives Out*, ch. 1. Anderson, in "Racist humor", has suggested that there might be connections between the work on slurs and offensive humour. In what follows, I explore one such connection.

[50] Bergmann offers a footnote suggesting a similar idea, that "laughing at sexist humor may suggest to others that it is acceptable to hold the beliefs that are presupposed by the humor" in her "How many feminists", at p. 79, in note 15.

[51] E.g., McGraw et al., "Too close for comfort".

[52] E.g., Viki et al., "The effects of sexist humor". In explaining these findings they suggest that "sexist jokes provide a situational norm which suggests that discriminating or even violent behavior towards women is acceptable", at p. 128.

It might be argued, once again, that merely drawing on sexist, racist, or otherwise offensive content in making some joke, or finding such jokes funny, does not mean that one *endorses* the underlying beliefs. Indeed, one issue with the original theory for expressives is that merely hearing some slur, and not correcting it or saying anything, does not necessarily mean that one signs up to the underlying derogation, nor that one incorporates it into the common ground of the conversation. However, in making or in laughing along with a joke that puts down some group of people, one *is* signalling agreement to thinking this sort of thing is acceptable, such that it isn't that important to be strongly committed to the relevant norms (say, to antisexist or antiracist norms). When you take it to be humorous—which you show through either by making the utterance with the intention of being funny or by reacting in ways deemed apt for humour—then you are finding the violation benign, and signalling to others that you do so too. Admittedly, sometimes people laugh at jokes they do not find funny. Laughter has other social functions. Nonetheless, by laughing, even without finding jokes funny, we still signal to others that we treat the utterance as a joke. Further, nor do we need to laugh, in order to signal that we treat a remark in question as a joke; for instance, at times, merely smiling at it might be sufficient, or simply not answering a humorous remark that has been framed as a question. With this function of our humour made visible, we can see why sometimes humour's role in our social interactions fails to be benign.[53]

Here, I do not claim that entering propositions into the common ground is the only thing that an offensive but humorous remark can do.[54] For instance, Merrie Bergmann argues that in the case of sexist humour: "Sexist beliefs are not just harmless props for jokes. Whenever somebody tells or laughs at a sexist joke it is an insult to those people who have been hurt and who will be hurt by sexist beliefs."[55] Indeed, sexist jokes are not alone in being insults if Bergmann's argument succeeds: mockery, too, often insults. Rather,

[53] At this point, an overlooked issue is worth remarking on: of what to think about jokes that 'punch up', like jokes targeting corrupt politicians or powerful figures. Much of the analysis would still hold: such jokes can offend, can still affront a person's standing. Of course, they wouldn't, insofar as they were truly 'punching up', threaten a person's standing as a social equal and so the dynamic of these jokes in social interactions is not objectionable in the way sketched above. Some might even be attracted to punching up jokes, as a way to bring down those with inflated standing. With thanks to Jennifer Page and Simon Kirchin for drawing my attention to this issue.

[54] A parallel again to slurs: Richard, *When Truth Gives Out*, argues that the use of a slur is often to attack someone and so a slur insults and denigrates, rather than entering propositions into the common grounds of our conversation, esp. pp. 21–22.

[55] Bergmann, "How many feminists", p. 79.

the thought here is that nonserious utterances sometimes do something that a serious utterance might not, with regards to what we hold in common. Namely, in finding a joke humorous, and in expressing that we do so, however subtly, we demonstrate we find the violation benign and that others do too. Merely not actively dissenting from an equivalent, serious, utterance with the same underlying propositions that the joke introduces, does not have the same effect.

Crucially, serious utterances do not always demand a response from us in the way that humour seems to: the person who tells a joke, anticipates acknowledgement of a particular kind and places an expectation on their conversational partner that they will respond in a certain way. Mere statements often do not do this, although certain serious utterances do, like questions. It will often come across as rude not to respond to a joke, in a way not always true of other kinds of utterance. As a result, in serious speech, someone venturing the view that, say, "women ought to do the laundry" does not necessarily shape the common ground, even if nothing is said to dispute that.[56] Jokes can thus be more problematic in that we are being asked to accept, say, the violation of an antisexist norm as no big deal, as acceptable. Where others find that funny, or even simply accept the utterance as a joke, they signal they find it so. This argument about social function may extend to informal humour too, but jokes are especially clear signals to others and ones that particularly demand a response from their audience.

5.4. The riskiness of humour

Claims along the line of "I was only joking" or "it was meant to be funny!" turn out to be little use when defending those who cause offence from those who take it. There appears to be no good general reason to refrain from taking offence merely given the fact that someone is joking. As a consequence, the fact that something along the lines of "just joking" is a popular defence to offer when our jokes offend may appear somewhat puzzling. Indeed, one might think that there must be something to this defence, given that we use it all the time, and so there must be something that this chapter has thus far failed to capture.[57]

---

[56] Such comments might, of course, have pernicious effects when made by powerful individuals or when widespread.

[57] With thanks to Simon Kirchin for pressing this objection.

I have offered two partial explanations, however. First, occasionally, saying you were only joking will let you off the hook in discounting one's remarks as nonserious, but only when the offence resulted from treating the remarks as serious. Second, given the suspension of the usual conversational rules, one shouldn't be too literal in interpreting a joke: Hunt ought not be taken to be offensive because he thinks that in fact *each and every* girl cries in laboratories or becomes embroiled in love affairs. That doesn't render his joke no affront to social standing, however: it remains an utterance at which it is appropriate to take offence.

We also ought not find it too surprising that claiming that one was only joking often fails to act as a successful defence of one's remarks. Usually, jokes are supposed to be read as such by their audience. To have to make explicit that you are joking reveals that you have failed to convey what you intended to in some social interaction: we only say 'only joking' when things go wrong. Consider a person who constantly finds himself having to explain that he was only joking to those with whom he interacts. Most likely, we'd think that he would do better to desist from his jokes. Our practices, then, are not so permissive to the bad, or misfiring joker as taking 'but I was only joking' to easily let one off the hook would suppose.

What, then, are the implications of this argument for offensive jokes and, especially, for the debate mentioned at the start amongst comedians over causing offence? It turns out that, just as some who oppose codes of conduct for comedians suppose, humour may indeed be especially likely to provoke offence. If one adopts the incongruity theory, then we have a clear account of why comedy often risks being offensive: it involves norm violations. Often, people experience the violation of social and moral norms as affronts. The relief theory too, once one sees that our repressed hostility often targets marginalised groups, also suggests that humour will be liable to offend. In the case of the superiority theory, humour is highly likely to offend, in so far as it is based on putting down others. Hence, the comedians who defend themselves on the grounds that comedy is invariably offensive or that engaging in it means risking causing offence are, to an extent, correct. Some forms of comedy look immune, in that few of us find the violations of norms involved in puns or absurdity offensive. But many forms of comedy are, indeed, risky.

It does not follow that people should therefore refrain from taking offence at risky jokes. Nor, however, does it follow that comedians and the rest of us ought never make jokes that could offend. Rather, offence is a natural consequence of getting that sort of risky humour wrong: offending others is precisely what we risk, when we make certain sorts of jokes or other humorous remarks. When others take offence, that reveals to us that we overstep the line between a benign violation and a nonbenign violation, and so affront others. Offence is a social mechanism by which others signal that we go too far, affronting their social standing, as they perceive it. That might be because we fail to see that our audience is committed to the norms that we violate, or our audience lacks the requisite psychological distance. Or it might be that the joker doesn't have the kind of standing from which to risk this sort of joke and be experienced as offering a benign violation.

Rather than desiring to reduce people's inclination to take offence at comedy, or finding their doing so objectionable, we should regard offence as one way to resist the way in which humour can introduce or reinforce social inequalities in our interactions, when it targets socially unequal groups. To take offence is to deny that some humorous remark or joke is benign: it is to dispute that 'we' around here agree with the humour's underlying derogatory propositions about a group, or it is to resist the discounting of the importance of the norms protecting the group's standing on which the humour may rely, and it signals that resistance to others. On this positive note on what offence can do, in the next chapter I turn from the possible limits on when offence-taking can be justified, to ask whether taking offence might be not only justified but required.

6

A corrective civic virtue

Weighing the costs and benefits of offence

The inclination to take offence is sometimes regarded as amongst the civic vices of our era: threatening free speech and open debate, undermining the education of the youth, and creating the wrong sort of future citizen.[1] Sometimes, it is also seen as a moral vice: Robin Barrow, for instance, describes taking offence as "one of the supreme self-serving acts".[2] Yet this book has defended taking offence as morally appropriate and socially useful, especially where it is used to resist an attribution of lowered standing by members of groups that frequently encounter threats to their social standing. This chapter addresses whether the defence of offence can be taken one step further, such that to take offence might sometimes be not only justifiable but morally required: must we take offence? Affronts, after all, can contribute to lesser social standing not only for oneself but also for others who share the relevant characteristics. On that basis, one might think that some have a duty to resist affronts to their standing as social equals, and to do so by taking offence.

A duty to feel an emotion on a particular occasion looks like it requires an improbable capacity to control our emotions at a moment's will, and hence is not something that I will defend.[3] Instead, however, we could seek to shape our emotions through cultivating the right dispositions: to be sensitive to the salient features of a situation; to perceive or judge such features correctly; and to react to some measured extent, through in a culturally understood set of behaviours.[4] As such, I take talk of a duty to take offence to be

---

[1] As some examples, see: Campbell & Manning *The Rise of Victimhood Culture*; Lukianoff & Haidt, *The Coddling of the American Mind;* Fox, "Generation snowflake".

[2] Barrow, "On the duty of not taking offence", p. 274.

[3] An unaddressed possibility is that we might have a duty to act as if we are offended, without being offended. Inauthentic emotion can be hard to pull off.

[4] For a description of strategies of emotional regulation to enable these changes, see Kristjánsson, "Can we teach justified anger", pp. 676–8, categorised into "situation selection and modification"; "attentional deployment" (e.g., distraction); "bootstrapping" (e.g., pretending to feel an emotion until we do); conative strategies (learning to feel differently); and cognitive strategies (changing the underlying beliefs of our emotions). For a defence of civic education to cultivate political anger in citizens,

On Taking Offence. Emily McTernan, Oxford University Press. © Oxford University Press 2023.
DOI: 10.1093/oso/9780197613092.003.0007

best interpreted as a duty to cultivate the disposition to take offence in this sense: to attend to how others treat you in social interactions; to regard such features of your social interactions to have significance where they are relevant to your standing as a social equal; and to react in a measured way when confronted with affronts to your equal social standing.[5] This invokes a virtue framing of whether one should take offence, common to discussions of other emotions like pride or anger: ought one be inclined to take offence, at the right things and to the right degree?[6]

In this chapter, I will defend an inclination to take offence as a civic virtue under conditions of pervasive social inequality, at least for those who are subjected to systematic injustice.[7] Where a society is disfigured by troubling hierarchies of social standing, an inclination to take offence, at the right things and to the right degree, would be desirable in order to secure the behaviours required both for a socially equal society and for one characterised by civility, that laws and institutions alone cannot achieve.[8] Making this case also requires tackling perhaps the most significant challenge to regarding offence as a virtue and, especially, a civic virtue: the costs that offence can impose on those who offend.

including through shaping expressions of anger, see White, "Making political anger possible". That emotions can be regulated can also be supported by appeal to the ways young children learn to regulate emotions, or the shaping implied by cultural variability in how emotions get expressed and when; for instance, take different cultural practices of grief.

[5] Here, I draw on Bonmarito, "Modesty as a virtue of attention" on virtues and patterns of attention, and Lillehammer, "Who is my neighbour?", on vice and one's orientation of concern. Hence, I emphasise the conative and cognitive strategies of the footnote above.

[6] For a small sample, Bell, "Anger, virtue, and oppression"; Cogley, "A study of virtuous and vicious anger; Bommarito, "Modesty as a virtue of attention"; Pettigrove, "Meekness and 'moral' anger". One might think that this makes my side of the case too easy to defend—surely most of us agree that *sometimes* being offended is apt, at the right things? But the range of 'right things' that I have and will defend include the very things that those opposed to or troubled by offence-taking most clearly reject: offence at seemingly small acts like microaggressions or other everyday forms of sexism, racism, homophobia, ableism and other forms of discrimination.

[7] I leave largely unaddressed whether offence could also be a moral virtue. Suppose one adopted Philippa Foot's emphasis on virtues as correctives to human weaknesses that make it hard for us to live or act well: see Foot, *Virtue and Vices*, ch. 1, where the historical roots of this idea are discussed. Then, one might defend offence as a corrective to our being tempted to seek increased social standing at others' expense. But arguing that would require, amongst other things, addressing how pride and offence relate and whether pride itself is a virtue.

[8] Here I remain neutral amongst the offered accounts of how one might cultivate such a civic virtue: virtue cultivation, norm cultivation, or situational manipulation. On norms, see McTernan, "How to make citizens behave"; McTernan, "Moral character"; on the opposing side in defence of virtue, see Callan, "Liberal virtues and civic education", Ben-Porath & Dishon, "Taken out of context"; for a discussion of the role of nudges here, see Niker, "Policy-led virtue cultivation". See, too, the debate within ethics about cultivating moral character, e.g., Doris, *Lack of Character*; Harman, "Moral philosophy meets social psychology"; on the opposing side, e.g., Athanassoulis, "A response to Harman"; Miller, "Social psychology and virtue ethics".

6.1. Offence as a civic virtue: Arguments from equality and civility

Amongst political philosophers it is common to hold that a state's institutions and laws alone cannot secure a fully functioning or flourishing state. For instance, if most citizens break a law, the state will find it too hard and too costly to effectively enforce that law. As a result, political philosophers tend to invoke either an ethos or, more usually, a set of civic virtues to be cultivated in citizens in order to secure the stable patterns of behaviour required to ensure, say, a well-functioning democracy, a liberal political culture, or merely a state's ability to function.[9] However, existing accounts of the civic virtues have typically focused on the virtues required for a *liberal* state to function or flourish, such as tolerance or open-mindedness; or those required for nearly any state's capacity to function, such as the disposition to be law-abiding or a willingness to pay taxes. What these accounts tend to neglect, then, are virtues that achieving *equality* would demand, beyond the willingness to pay tax, which would enable redistribution, or Rawls' suggestion of a general "sense of justice".[10]

Contemporary accounts of civic virtue are also often framed within a Rawlsian style of ideal theory: they examine what virtues would be needed to fill the gap between the behaviour needed for the state to function or flourish, and that which just institutions can secure, given general facts about human psychology and the possibilities of institutional arrangements.[11] As a result, these accounts largely fail to address what I will call the 'corrective civic virtues': the virtues that might be needed specifically to correct for the *existing* injustices within a state. Here, I echo Philippa Foot's phrase that, in general, virtues are correctives for human weaknesses.[12] The thought is that

[9] Kant's intelligent demons aside. See for example, Callan, *Creating Citizens*; Galston, *Liberal Purposes*; Rawls, *A Theory of Justice*; Rawls, "The idea of public reason revisited", p. 788; on the widespread return of virtue, Kymlicka & Norman, "Return of the citizen". An ethos is less usual, but possibly more empirically accurate, if interpreted as a cluster of social norms: see McTernan, "How to make citizens behave", McTernan, "Moral character". For an example of an ethos, see Cohen, *Rescuing Justice and Equality*.

[10] Callan, "Liberal virtues and civic education", first drew my attention to this fact. This oversight may reflect the largely distributive focus of contemporary egalitarianism, until recently. A notable exception being Cohen's egalitarian ethos, where all would be motivated to choose the most socially productive jobs, and pursue them, in order to benefit the least well off, without demanding unequalising incentives, *Rescuing Justice and Equality*.

[11] See Rawls, *A Theory of Justice*; "The idea of public reason revisited".

[12] Foot, *Virtue and Vices*. There will be some overlap of course: tolerance would play both a corrective role in a society marred by prejudice as well as appearing on the standard list of civic virtues. The difference is that tolerance will also be required in a society not characterised by injustice: in the case of taking offence, things are less clear.

so, too, we might require correctives for the social and political flaws and failings of our present society. If we start from where we are, against a background of unjust institutions and histories of systematic inequality, then the way we need citizens to behave and the attitudes that we require may go beyond that required from citizens living under just institutions.

Drawing together this book's arguments then, I propose that a disposition to take offence lies amongst these corrective civic virtues that are directed at inequality, in this case, a background of pervasive social inequality. Taking offence can help to secure equal relations amongst citizens of a kind and in ways that the laws and design of institutions alone could not. As Chapters 2 and 3 argued, our social standing is largely constituted through the pattern of social interactions we experience and the power we have to shape how we are treated and regarded, underpinned by social practices and social norms. These patterns and practices are often too fine-grained for laws to keep track of and, further, they are matters of our collective behaviour which are not easily handled through institutional arrangements. Laws cannot ensure the absence of the everyday slights and affronts that both characterise the everyday experience of members of marginalised and oppressed groups and, in part, constitute what it is to be a member of a marginalised or oppressed group in its social dimension. Offence can play an important role in renegotiating these norms and practices in a more equal direction, and in sustaining these more equal practices.[13] Further, the arguments of Chapter 2 give us reason to think that taking offence is an appropriate strategy by which to bring about those changes that we need and to sustain the better practices, once achieved. Chapter 3 further defended taking offence as reflecting a morally appropriate attitude, given the significance of social standing and the importance of details of social interactions in constituting our standing.

The conclusion that, as a result, the inclination to take offence would be a civic virtue could be resisted. It could be objected that taking offence is not *necessary* to correct for social inequality; rather, institutions might do the required work. Certainly, some of the larger scale harms of social inequality appear partially amenable to institutional solutions, including, for instance, introducing well enforced sexual harassment policies, antidiscrimination laws, or the improvement of implicit bias training for, say, educators and the police. Yet even if one is highly optimistic about the effectiveness of

---

[13] Or it can support bad norms—the defence of offence is of that which is taken to defend one's equal standing, and not that which claims greater than equal standing.

such institutional arrangements, some part of the behaviour that we need for a socially equal society—or even, a society free of the worst of pervasive social hierarchies—lies outside of the possible, or at least appropriate, reach of institutions. Take, to illustrate, the many affronts to standing as a social equal that people experience in informal social settings and in their intimate lives.

Could we be still more optimistic about institutions? Even if institutions cannot cover all the spheres of life where social inequalities emerge perhaps, nonetheless, living under just institutional arrangements would secure the right pattern of behaviour across our lives, such that people would not need to take offence. Joshua Cohen offers a parallel line of argument in the context of distributive justice. He argues that living under just institutions could cultivate egalitarian dispositions in citizens, such that they would choose to work to benefit the least well-off without demanding unequalising incentives.[14] In our case, one might hold that the knock-on effect of living with the right institutional solutions to social inequality would be that citizen's attitudes are shaped in more egalitarian directions. In particular, perhaps people would be less inclined to offer to others affronts to their standing, especially affronts based on their group .identity. What need, then, to take offence?

Against such optimism, improvements to institutions and laws are unlikely to eliminate prejudice and bias immediately, or even over the medium term. As a result, an interim corrective virtue may be required. Take the continued persistence of Irish jokes wherein the Irish are depicted as drunk or stupid, arguably long after the end of the widespread anti-Irish sentiment prevalent in the nineteenth century.[15] Another role for an interim corrective virtue would be to contribute to mustering the political pressure required to demand the reformation of institutions in a just direction. But also, living under just institutions might, rather than reducing an inclination to take offence, *increase* it: cultivating egalitarian dispositions, whether directly or indirectly, may inculcate that inclination to take offence. Being inclined to take offence at affronts to social standing as an equal reflects values that one would want citizens to internalise in a just society: in particular, a commitment to

---

[14] Cohen, "Taking people as they are?"

[15] There appears to be some residual prejudice, with the occasional instance such as the 2012 job ad specifying 'no Irish', as reported in Hickey, "Australian bricklayer employment ad". But it is not akin to the systematic prejudice once found, for instance after migrations to the United States and into England. For one discussion of the nineteenth century context, see Kenny, "Race, violence, and anti-Irish sentiment".

social equality. When citizens feel that their equal standing is affirmed and judge, correctly, that affronts to their standing as equals are a serious matter, then they look more, not less, likely to take offence if presented with such affronts.

This defence of offence as a corrective civic virtue grounded on the value of social equality may have limited scope. It looks most persuasive for societies characterised by severe and relatively intractable social inequalities, and when taken by members of marginalised or oppressed groups. The resulting proposal, then, could be of a civic virtue for members of such groups alone: restricted to those who experience affronts to their social standing as equals by virtue of their group membership, who find themselves facing unequal social hierarchies on the basis of race, class, gender, or sexuality, for instance, along with the intersections of these. It is members of such groups who, by protesting affronts, would nudge us towards adopting better social norms.

There might also be a weaker case to make for a general corrective civic virtue of offence on the grounds of equality, insofar as there is reason to find a general attentiveness to one's standing desirable. Whether it is so depends on one's view of human nature. Suppose that one thinks that people have a propensity to dominate others, or corresponding weaknesses towards flattening or fawning behaviours. Alternatively, one might hold that humans 'naturally' seek to produce social hierarchies, or to gain standing at other's expense.[16] If so, then even those who are not systematically marginalised or disadvantaged could have a civic duty to attend to their social standing in a way that would incline them towards taking offence. That attention would act as a check on the emergence of localised hierarchies or social inequalities produced by such human weaknesses, say, by encouraging resistance to an overbearing professor or boss, or a condescending midwife.

Claims about human nature, like the above, can be contentious. But in order to defend offence as a more general civic virtue, we could, instead, turn to the importance of a well-functioning civic society and so to the more familiar virtues of tolerance and civility. This returns once more to the defences of civility offered by Buss, Calhoun, and Olberding.[17] To function well, a

---

[16] See note 7 this chapter on the idea of virtue as a corrective for human nature, as in Foot, *Virtue and Vices*.

[17] Buss, "Appearing respectful"; Calhoun, "The virtue of civility"; Olberding, *The Wrong of Rudeness*.

society requires a set of norms and practices that structure social interactions and render our attitudes towards one another and the messages we convey through our acts, intelligible. One important subset of that communication concerns our respect and consideration for others. Without such norms we could not express our toleration and equal respect for others; at least, as Buss observes, short of inelegant and time-consuming direct declarations. Offence plays crucial roles in that system of norms around our social standing, enforcing and revising these norms. Hence, when being inclined to take offence shores up the norms that make our respect for, and tolerance of, one another expressible, it becomes a derivative or associated virtue of the virtue of tolerance or civility. Tolerance is commonly understood as a disposition to treat others in tolerant ways and to regard other's ways of life as permissible.[18] But to communicate these attitudes is important in order to sustain a system where all feel tolerated. For that, we require the relevant norms to be in play that let us express our tolerance. We may have duties as citizens to sustain these norms, such as through being inclined to take offence when others transgress against them.

Characterising offence as good for civility could strike some readers as counterintuitive. Pulling up others over regarding the minor details of their behaviour in social interactions, say, how they phrase questions or their eye contact, may appear to preclude the sort of forbearance that essentially characterises civility. Sometimes, too, the behaviours that we use to signal that we are withdrawing from the person who offends appear inconsistent with being civil. It isn't civil to refuse to appear where a person will be present in personal or professional life, if that is the way in which one conveys one's withdrawal. Indeed, it isn't civil even when all one does is turn away from someone, or pointedly fail to engage with the off-colour joke that they just told.[19] Alternatively, take the common response to the supposed 'culture of taking offence' where people claim they will now no longer engage in acts that they regarded as civil or polite—say, holding the door open for women or complimenting their appearance—out of fear of condemnation by those

[18] There is disagreement over how to characterise tolerance. Peter Jones argues that tolerance is needed where we object to another's way of life, rather than for those of which we approve, see his, "Toleration, recognition, and identity", p. 126. However, Galeotti offers a richer idea of what it is to tolerate another, as a matter of recognition—something which Jones observes seems to move beyond acceptance or regarding as permissible to positive appraisal: see Galeotti, *Toleration as Recognition*; Jones, "Toleration, recognition, and identity". For a historical perspective on ways to think about civility, and a defence of 'mere' civility, see Bejan, *Mere Civility*.

[19] This, however, may move to a different, less politically salient kind of civility: one needed for relations to be pleasant.

inclined to take offence. Surely, a critic may continue, increasing citizens' inclination to take offence could only lead to a reduction in civility, rather than being a way of shoring it up.

There could be a trade-off to make. Perhaps it is uncivil, in a sense, to take offence at microaggressions or inappropriate flirting, even though one ought to do so in pursuit of a more important political value; namely, equality. But, on the other hand, the thought that there is something uncivil about taking offence looks like may be confusing the civility that we need for a liberal, tolerant society that treats people well, with what would feel nice or easy in our relations with one another. It may well be uncomfortable for us when we offend others, but that doesn't necessarily threaten our treating one another with the kinds of respect or consideration needed for a tolerant society. Further, often, it is a mistake to regard demands for change regarding the details of how people treat and regard each other as in conflict with civility. Rather, taking offence can renegotiate the boundaries of what counts as civil. Taking offence is one of the ways in which we create and sustain a genuinely shared public culture of civility. To offer a microaggression is no act of civility, and nor is it civil make one's colleague uncomfortable through an unwanted sexual approach.

There are thus two grounds for taking offence to be a civic virtue: equality and civility. Neither establishes offence as essential for a functioning or flourishing society. There are other ways to revise norms and practices and to ensure that norms are followed; say, being indignant, angry, or simply offering reasons to others for why they should alter their behaviour. This book only defends offence as *amongst* the ways to negotiate our social standing. However, this limitation is far from being unique to taking offence: for other civic virtues, too, there are alternatives. To illustrate, citizens could be tolerant because they value tolerance, accept the importance of pluralism, and are disposed to act in tolerant ways. Alternatively, they could simply be entirely indifferent to others' beliefs and ways of lives. Which of these motivations is preferable depends on which attitudes and beliefs one desires to underpin the right kinds of behaviour: here, indifference, or a commitment to the freedom of others to choose a way of life. Likewise, it appears to me that both to care about one's standing as a social equal, and to be willing to participate in and support the system of social norms that enable a society to function and be marked by tolerance and consideration, have value. To be inclined to take offence at affronts to one's standing as a social equal would manifest these valuable commitments.

6.2. The costs of offence to the offending party

The depiction above of offence-taking as a civic virtue may strike those who object to a 'culture of taking offence' as overlooking the troubling costs of offence. Surely, one might think, nothing with such unfair and even nasty consequences for the offending party, and perhaps with broader negative effects for society, ought to be counted as virtuous behaviour or something that has overall social value—let alone something that one would want more of in a society.[20] This objection highlights something that appears to be unusual about the postulated civic virtue of apt offence-taking. The other civic virtues, such as being law-abiding or tolerant, are often about conforming your own behaviour to some desired norm(s), whereas to take offence is to seek to ensure that others conform their behaviour to such norms.[21] To become more tolerant or law abiding is clearly good for those around you: they will not experience so much prejudice from you, or they won't have to bear the associated costs of your breaking the law. By contrast, to become inclined to take offence at other's missteps appears to be costly to some of those around you, even if there are some broader social benefits. That could threaten the proposal of a civic virtue of offence-taking. Since arguments for civic virtue tend to be instrumental, to the effect that inculcating the virtue contributes to the functioning or flourishing of a society, the benefits of inculcating the (right) inclination to offence would need to outweigh these sorts of costs.

For some, it is simply the nature of the costs imposed that render an inclination to take offence not the sort of thing that one could have an obligation to cultivate—and perhaps might even make taking offence unjustified. Many of the behaviours that follow from taking offence appear to inflict shame or humiliation, especially in contexts where committing the affront in question is taken to reflect some belief, attitude, or tendency that is widely disapproved of or disdained.[22] Such behaviours might include 'calling out' an offensive act since that exposes people to censure, telling others about a person's offensive behaviour in order to inflict reputational damage on that person, or avoiding the person who offends. Further,

---

[20] See references in note 1, this chapter.

[21] The difference here shouldn't be overstated: on norms-based understanding, the civic 'virtues' are a collective achievement. By becoming law abiding I increase the chances that you are too, in that I contribute to this norm being in play and to others believing that the norm is generally followed.

[22] Taylor, *Pride, Shame, and Guilt*, defines shame as deviating from some norm and so diminishing one's "standing in the world".

inflicting shaming or humiliating punishments is often condemned, even when they are controlled through formal systems such as courts.[23] To impose shaming and humiliating costs without the protections of a court and its careful limits, as taking offence sometimes does, might seem still less justifiable.[24] Society does not flourish, one might think, if it is marred by shame and humiliation.

For others, the problem with offence's costs will not be their nature but, rather, the way in which these costs sometimes escalate.[25] To illustrate, Jon Ronson offers a series of stories of people whose offence-causing conduct 'goes viral' and results in their being publicly shamed: those who make one error and then find themselves subjected to widespread condemnation, lose their jobs, and suffer from long-term harm to their reputations. One is the case of Lindsey Stone, a woman who posed for a photo of herself swearing and pretending to yell next to a silence and respect sign in a US military cemetery, who suffered exactly these consequences.[26] Even where the actions of the offender constitute affronts to equal social standing, one might doubt that could justify such extensive consequences. Indeed, one might argue that merely the *risk* of consequences like public shaming and people losing their jobs renders taking offence hard to justify. Given the well-publicised cases where such escalation occurs, the imposition of significant harms appears a real possibility.[27] As such, to take offence appears morally risky.

Worse, for some people there appears to be very little possibility for public redemption after having caused offence. Worse still, which people fare worst in this sense may reflect background injustice. An instructive case is that of 'donglegate', which began as a standard story of social media shaming, with a man exposed to public scorn and losing his job as a result of making sexist jokes at a male-dominated technology conference, one of which concerned 'big dongles'. However, the woman who publicised the man's jokes on Twitter

[23] Arguments against such forms of social punishment include objecting to the "tyranny of the majority", Mill, *On Liberty*; Nussbaum's respect-based arguments against shaming or humiliating punishments in her *Hiding from Humanity*; and, recanting his previous support for shaming punishments, Kahan, "What's really wrong with shaming sanctions".

[24] Against this, some think that what is wrong with shaming punishments lies precisely in the relation 'between the state and the crowd' thereby created: see Whitman, "What is wrong with inflicting shame sanctions".

[25] The lack of proportionality in public shaming is the central concern of Billingham & Parr, "Enforcing social norms".

[26] Ronson, *So You've Been Publicly Shamed*.

[27] Again, as illustrated by Ronson's cases, ibid.

experienced not only public shaming but also lost her job after her company experienced online attacks. She also suffered from far worse public abuse, including threats of extreme violence.[28]

Still others would be most troubled by the broader social costs of the shaming and exposure of those who offend. This worry is sometimes framed as a threat to free speech: we would, or do, limit what we are willing to say or even what topics we discuss, for fear of causing offence and incurring its accompanying costs.[29] This adopts a particular, if plausible, interpretation of what free speech protects: one that extends beyond a right held against governments and their coercive interference with speech to include the ways that our fellow citizens might supress speech, especially collectively.[30] Where offence escalates into the kinds of excess depicted above, then such suppression of speech may be threatened.

To respond to this range of concerns about the nature, escalation and broader chilling effects of taking offence, I begin with a clarification of the costs in question. A running theme of this book has been that much of our offence taking is ordinary and every day; that it can be and often is contained to the small details of our interactions with another person, falling far short of the cases receiving the most popular attention where people are publicly shamed, endure lasting reputational damage, and lose their jobs. Taking offence is a part of the system of social norms that structures our everyday interactions, being a way to enforce norms around standing and what is appropriate or respectful treatment of others. That lack of escalation holds true even in many online contexts; for instance, a study into offence taking on Facebook found that a range of subtle interactions characterised taking offence and not instances of public shaming.[31] Thus, I could simply observe that the ordinary ways of displaying often mild or moderate offence—such as raising an eyebrow, not laughing, tutting, or some other small degree of withdrawal—escape the concerns raised above regarding the infliction of costs on offenders. Let us term these small, every day ways in which we resist

---

[28] As reported in Filipovic, "Sexism in the workplace". One might also think of the 'comebacks' staged by men whose wrongdoing was exposed through the 'MeToo' movement.

[29] For an instance of such a framing, see McWhorter, "Our oppressive moment", on the expansion of what is taken to be "beyond the limits of civilized discourse".

[30] E.g., Mill, On Liberty.

[31] See Tagg et al., Taking Offence on Social Media. As discussed earlier in the book, linguistic studies provide general support for this low-key description of what taking offence is like see, for instance, Haugh, "Impoliteness and taking offence".

other's dismissals, attacks and lack of recognition of our social standing, 'micro-defences'.[32] Certainly, such acts are insufficient to count as supressing free speech, even for those concerned about social pressure and Mill's tyranny of the majority.[33] If this is tyranny, it is an extremely weak kind. Nor do such costs appear strikingly disproportionate in the way that public shaming can, and nor would they suffice to claim that a society is marred by shame and humiliation.

These micro-defences, with their small associated costs, are the kinds of acts that this book primarily defends. After all, this is not a book about public shaming and nor should one conflate taking offence with acts of public shaming. Doing so would be akin to conflating individual anger with physical violence. While sometimes being offended may motivate people to contribute to acts of public shaming, much of our offence taking does not; just as often we are angry, yet do not engage in physical violence.[34] Thus, as some do for anger, one could simply say that the emotion is justified where expressed in certain ways, but not others.[35] Indeed, the conflation in the case of offence might be less plausible even than equating anger and physical violence: while the violent are nearly always angry, there is no particular reason to hold that those who engage in public shaming are nearly always—and maybe not even often—offended. Public shamers might, instead, be indignant, outraged, angry or frustrated; they might desire to demonstrate that their sympathies or moral convictions lie on the side of the shamer, not shamed; or they may simply be bored, or keen to keep those they admire or on whom they rely on side.

Appealing to the ordinary nature of offence alone might not suffice entirely to allay the above concerns about the costs of offence. First, even though there appears to be no necessary connection between taking offence and online or public shaming, sometimes what starts with offence does escalate to public shaming. Many of the cases that Ronson describes begin with someone being

---

[32] Samantha Brennan suggests the term 'micro-sanction' as a response to a micro-inequity, referring to a paper with Megan Winsby: see Brennan, "The moral status of micro-inequities". That would be a possible alternative label, but I think the acts in question here are better characterised as resistance than sanction.

[33] Likely Mill himself wouldn't count taking offence as coercive social pressure, given his comments on the permissibility of expressing distaste and feeling contempt in On Liberty. For a discussion of different interpretations of Mill's comments, see Wilkinson, "Mill's On Liberty and social pressure".

[34] For one discussion sceptical of the link between anger and violence, see Srinivasan, "The aptness of anger", esp. p. 139.

[35] Ibid., but see also Pettigrove's worry about the tendency to violence, "Meekness and 'moral' anger", p. 369.

offended but result in online shaming campaigns. Second, even in everyday cases of moderate offence, the consequences of causing offence can easily extend beyond others' eyebrow raising and tutting, to acts such as refusing invites to future events where the person will appear, inflicting reputational harm, or encouraging others to distance themselves from the offending party, amongst other larger-scale demonstrations of estrangement. What makes *these* costs of withdrawal acceptable, whether or not there is any general connection between offence and wider public shaming?

Answering, I begin with the threat of escalation to public shaming. Most worrying would be if there is, after all, some disposition to escalation residing in offence that renders public shaming likely or, at least, a significant enough risk to alter our calculation over whether offence-taking can be justified. To support that, one might appeal to Justin Tosi and Brandon Warmke on 'moral grandstanding', which occurs where a person makes a public expression because she "desires that others think of her as being morally respectable with regard to some matter of moral concern".[36] Offence, too, can be a way to signal our moral concern, or to demonstrate that we are on the 'right side'. Further, some of the dynamics that Tosi and Warmke depict as characteristic of grandstanding also appear when offence-taking escalates. In particular, we find 'piling on', where people repeat the judgement that something is offensive in order to join in; consider, to illustrate, the many cases where something offensive is reported on the social media platform Twitter, and then others agree with that reaction.[37] We also sometimes see 'ramping up', where people make increasingly strong claims about how offended they feel.[38]

However, even where it spreads, offence-taking generally differs from moral grandstanding and does so in significant ways. On my characterisation, offence is taken at affronts to one's own standing. As such, in paradigm cases, the primary drive of offence is not to demonstrate one's moral excellence or right thinking but, rather, to respond to a perceived slight or putdown to oneself. So, too, while one can be joining in with a group by taking offence, the dynamic in play is better characterised as people identifying with or expressing solidarity with their group, and hence seeing an affront to those like them to be an affront to them too, rather than the dynamic found in moral

---

[36] "Moral grandstanding", p. 200. Their reasons to find moral grandstanding objectionable do not straightforwardly translate to offence. They claim it undermines our moral discourse through promoting cynicism, outrage exhaustion, and failures to notice signals of injustice. One would have to make the parallel case for offence.

[37] "Moral grandstanding", pp. 203–208. For examples, see Ronson, *So You've Been Publicly Shamed*.

[38] "Moral grandstanding", section II.

grandstanding of appearing to others as if one possesses the right convictions. As a result, moral grandstanding is no inherent component of taking offence. In support, consider that it would often be a poor characterisation of a woman who takes offence at a sexist joke to think that she is centrally concerned with signalling her correct moral convictions. Indeed, in the contexts where she may be most likely to encounter such jokes—including, perhaps, male-dominated workplaces, locker rooms, sports venues, and mainstream comedy nights—what her taking offence will be taken to signal is not that she abides by the correct moral standards but, rather, that she fails to adopt the local norms: the social norms that we follow around here. Further, rather than approval, the woman is likely to experience social disapproval as a consequence of her taking offence.

The case for a distinction between moral grandstanding and taking offence is stronger still when one considers the many instances of offence taking that are unconnected to moral principles. After all, the woman responding to the sexist joke may be committed to the moral principle of equality. To illustrate, consider a professor who takes offence when a graduate student fails to show him the deference that he deems himself to be due. In taking such offence, the professor may offer no signal of moral respectability.

Some people might take offence in order to manifest publicly their moral sensibilities, of course, or might have mixed motivations, say, to defend their standing and to manifest their moral respectability. Suppose that a woman takes offence at a sexist joke but that joke was made at a meeting of a feminist campaigning group. If one objects to moral grandstanding in itself, and not only the escalations that it could provoke, then such mixed motivation cases will appear less morally desirable than a purer defence of one's own standing. But, still, given the ordinary nature of much of our offence taking, the idea that there is some slippery slope into excess ought to be resisted: nothing yet suggests that escalation is a likely risk. Given that the relation between moral grandstanding and taking offence is loose at best, it seems to be sufficient to answer the threat of escalation simply to say that acts of withdrawal beyond a certain extent are excessive, such that there is a line beyond which the justification of offence does not extend.[39] Clearly one can take excessive offence, or take offence and also be motivated to engage in public shaming, but these

---

[39] For one account of what factors might be considered in judging the proportionality of public shaming, some of which could have relevance for the limits on the degree of offence, see Billingham and Parr, "Enforcing social norms".

facts by themselves do not render taking a reasonable degree of offence un-justified: one fitting to the offensive act and social interaction in question.

To those concerned about silencing of our public debate and limits to free speech, it could seem that simply the *fear* of escalation, even if such escala-tion is no likely result of taking offence, makes taking offence a civic vice. But such a fear is too ill-grounded to count against cultivating an apt virtue of of-fence, especially when, instead, a state could educate citizens to be less fearful. Again, that fear underweights the ordinary side of offence which appears in all sorts of social interactions as we navigate our social worlds, from things our partners say to strangers who push in front of us. With that set of ordi-nary practices of taking offence in view, one can see how highly unlikely the escalation is; for instance, one might compare the sheer number of offen-sive remarks people make and the many instances where we take offence at others' acts, to the very small number of victims of public shaming. Indeed, cultivating the right inclination to take offence might even help mitigate the negative social consequences that could render it a civic vice. If one takes only an appropriate degree of offence, then objectionable public shaming ought not emerge, even were someone to—wrongly—regard offence as a sig-nificant motivator of publicly shaming another. Thus, cultivating the inclina-tion to take offence but only at the right things (at affronts to one's standing as a social equal) and to the correct degree (on which more below) remains desirable.

6.3. Justifying the costs of offence

The challenge of the apparent unfairness of the costs on the offending party, and the question of whether these costs can be properly justified, might per-sist however even for the small, everyday kinds of withdrawal that ordinarily characterise offence, whether micro-defences or moderate ones like leaving an event. Even without conflating offence with public shaming, the acts that follow from being offended often reveal to others that the offending party has transgressed against a norm and can involve a certain degree of exclusion, in that they express estrangement. That can be true even where the withdrawals are subtle, such as a raised eyebrow or not laughing at a joke, depending on the audience's sensitivity. As previously observed, this exposure might be found shaming or humiliating, depending on how the offending party relates to the underlying social norms and their meanings against which she transgresses;

for instance, seeing herself as falling short of her liberal commitments where she makes the wrong kind of joke, or finding herself identified with some group that she abhors. Is it a good thing for a society to encourage such exposure and its potential humiliations? One might object that the behaviour of those who take offence look like *punishment* and, worse, these punishments are carried out by the 'mob' rather than a carefully controlled legal system. If taking offence results in punishing another then an appeal to instrumental benefits alone may not suffice as a justification.[40]

Punishment is commonly regarded as the intentional infliction of hard treatment on a wrongdoer by an authority.[41] On a retributivist view, that is on the grounds that such treatment is deserved, or that the censure which the treatment communicates is deserved. For those of a less retributivist bent, punishment gets a different justification, for instance, as hard treatment for the sake of deterrence, or even to encourage reform.[42] However, many of the social consequences of causing offence would be poorly characterised as *hard* treatment, even if they are social sanctions: take not laughing at a joke, tutting, or raising an eyebrow, or even correcting someone. Further, offence itself does not involve a desire to inflict hard treatment on another, nor the view that such treatment is deserved: offence lacks a direct desire for 'payback' or for giving the other their due.[43] That is not to say that when we are offended, we cannot also feel an urge for payback or desire to impose costs to make things fair but, rather, that the latter is an additional sentiment: one found, for instance, where our offence begins to shade into anger. Emotions of estrangement or withdrawal such as offence are primarily about disengaging from the other. The urge for payback renders the other an object of increased concern and interest (if negative); the urge to withdraw, the opposite.[44] The

---

[40] Clearly, this requires that one adopt a thicker conception of punishment than one that simply equates it with any sanction, and a theory of punishment other than a simplistic consequentialist or deterrence view.

[41] This definition roughly follows Hart's classic definition of punishment, with hard treatment capturing the infliction of pain or unpleasant consequence, being intentional, targeting the offender, and imposed by an authority—although it (for obvious reasons) excludes the reference to the legal system. See Hart, "Prolegomenon to the principles of punishment".

[42] For one survey of views of punishment, and a defence of punishment as part of a communicative process of repentance and reform, see Duff, "Penal communications".

[43] To echo Nussbaum's characterisation of an aspect of anger in her *Anger and Forgiveness*. See Chapter 1 of this book for this argument. Offence may still be a form of censure, and one could ask if that is enough, in the absence of hard treatment or intention to payback, to still be a 'punishment'. I think if it is, it isn't the worrying full-blooded notion of punishment that motivated the objection to offence in the first place.

[44] Pervasive shunning of an individual might be a form of payback. But, again, it is worth noting that full withdrawal appears rare, even on social media: see the study of Facebook users from Tagg et al., *Taking Offence on Social Media*.

costs imposed by another's taking offence and expressing it are not akin, then, to punishment of a full-blooded retributivist sort, of the infliction of hard treatment with a desire for payback or the person getting what they deserve; presumably, for many it would be such a conception of punishment that would have motivated the concern that to take offence punishes.

Better, then, to think of taking offence as involving, in its resistance to an affront, a sanctioning of another. Some such sanctions are, I think, an inevitable result of living together. Our social interactions are, and must be, structured by social norms. For there to be social norms requires that people have expectations about how others will behave and that some are willing to enforce these social norms through imposing social sanctions on those who transgress. Insofar as we need social norms then, social sanctions will be part of our social lives.[45] Offence, and the norms that structure our relations equally (or unequally), are only a part of the broader set of norms that underpin our lives together.

Perhaps the question still persists of *how* (or why) the person who offends is liable to the social sanctions that the offending party may inflict, even if we can dismiss the idea that to take offence is to punish in a troubling, full-blooded sense. When we do not follow shared norms or when we follow norms that some others reject, why is it justifiable for another to alter their relationships towards us in order to encourage us act differently? Wouldn't inflicting costs to sustain a system of norms unjustly burden particular individuals? Even if the overall system of norms is valuable, one might ask why a particular individual ought to bear the costs to keep it going and whether, in imposing such costs, we treat offending individuals as mere means to an end.

One route to justification would be to argue that individuals are liable to the costs where they perform certain offensive acts: adopting, then, what Iris Marion Young terms the 'liability model' of responsibility.[46] Here is how that justification could go. If you affront someone's standing as a social equal, you harm them. While the idea that offensive acts harm might sound odd to those legal philosophers who sharply divide harm and offence, the offensive acts in question contribute to undermining a person's social standing as an equal. Such social inequality harms: the consequences of hierarchies in social standing include poorer health outcomes, unequal income and

---

[45] Sanctions, of course, can make things worse, in keeping bad norms going too.
[46] Young, *Responsibility for Justice*, ch. 4.

wealth, and a greater risk of violence and abuse.[47] So, too, evidence suggests that experiencing frequent affronts itself has harmful consequences; for instance, studies examine the relation between experiencing microaggressions and harms to mental and physical health.[48] Thus, by offering an affront to another's standing as a social equal the offending party can do harm. Hence, the social costs of offence that follow for the offending party could be justified consequences, in so far as they are proportionate to the harm done.

The problem is that the harm done by any single, one-off, affront is hard to quantify and, for the more subtle affronts, hard even to detect. For instance, work on microaggressions often observes that the harm done by small-scale 'putdowns and degradations' emerges from the repeated experience of similar instances, such that the harm is cumulative.[49] Further, we do not always intend to cause offence, or do not know that what we do will cause offence. On some accounts, that may undermine attributions of liability or blameworthiness, at least where the lack of knowledge is not itself something for which we are rightly held responsible.[50] As a result, depending on one's account of responsibility, it may appear unpalatable to hold that an individual who commits a one-off offensive act is liable to the larger scale retaliations that sometimes result where people take offence. Thus, while it may succeed for gross affronts to social standing, a liability model may struggle with offence taken at smaller affronts and those that are unintentional, especially where the harm of the affront stems from its connection to a broader social inequality.

The issues above are familiar in work on climate change, implicit bias, and microinequities, as well as microaggressions.[51] There, we find defences of

[47] As a small set of examples, on health, see for instance Marmot & Wilkinson, *Social Determinants of Health*; Pickett & Wilkinson, "Income inequality and health"; on the black/white wealth gap see Oliver & Shapiro, *Black Wealth, White Wealth*; for a discussion of studies on risk factors in intimate partner violence against women, including education levels and "ideologies of male dominance", see Jewkes, "Intimate partner violence".

[48] E.g., Nadal et al., "The impact of racial microaggressions on mental health".

[49] For philosophical discussions, see Fatima, "On the edge of knowing"; Friedlaeander, "On microaggressions"; McTernan, "Microaggressions, equality, and social practices"; Rini, *The Ethics of Microaggression*.

[50] Often, we ought to have known better, for one discussion of the culpability of white ignorance, see Mills, "White ignorance". See also Friedlaender for the same observation on blame and ignorance, in the context of microaggressions, and a more demanding distinction between "genuine ignorance" and "ought-to-have-known ignorance"; "On microaggressions", p. 11.

[51] See, for examples, on climate change, Cuomo, "Climate change, vulnerability, and responsibility", esp. pp. 700–703; on micro-inequities, Brennan, "The moral status of micro-inequities"; on microaggressions, Friedlaender, "On microaggressions"; on responsibility for implicit bias, Holroyd, "Responsibility for implicit bias".

the proportionality of responding to small harms that make up the greater harm. As one example, Christina Friedlaender draws a parallel to someone who steps on your foot, where one should have a proportionate reaction like feeling a small amount of anger at the carelessness. She then asks us to imagine a person who spends a whole day having her foot stepped on, resulting "in a constant state of pain". The question is what is the proportionate reaction for this repeated case: the same as the one-off foot stepping incident, or something greater? To Friedlaender, the constantly stepped upon person is justified in getting very angry at the particular individual who just happens to be the final straw after the day of being stepped on. The perspective of that last foot-stepper, thinking that the harm they have imposed is minor is, to her, wrong; the stepped upon person in her anger is correct, just as is the person who experiences microaggressions taking the harm done to be sufficient to feel anger.[52] To make this more palatable, Friedlaender proposes that happening to be the one who triggers the very angry reaction by offering the latest affront is merely a matter of bad moral luck.'[53]

Why, though, is the last footstepper or microaggressor liable to the reaction due to the cluster of cases simply because they committed the latest of such acts? Ordinarily, we are liable to some amount of defensive harm by virtue of being morally responsible for some unjustified threat. The correct specification of the harm done in this case appears to be a fractional contribution to the wider, significant harm. While that may be good reason to cease to so act, given that one contributes to a significant harm, the idea that one might be liable to larger scale retaliations that sometimes result where people take offence may yet remain unpalatable. However, again, often the reaction of offence is far from costly: a raised eyebrow, pointedly failing to laugh at a joke. These may be fitting ways to respond to the fractional contribution itself. As such, in its more small-scale manifestations, offence may have its costs justified under a liability model.

When it comes to justifying the costlier consequences of the withdrawal associated with offence or its signal that one has transgressed, Iris Marion Young's social connection model of responsibility offers a better route to take. On this model, one has a responsibility for the structural injustice to which one contributes, such that "one has an obligation to join with others who share that responsibility in order to transform the structural processes

---

[52] Friedlaender, "On microaggressions", pp. 15–16.
[53] Ibid.

to make their outcomes less unjust".[54] Rather than attempting to determine what (small) harm any particular affront inflicts on any particular individual, if adopting this approach one would instead consider how the affronts contribute, if often fractionally, to a broader system of injustice and not for just a single individual, but for a group.[55] Considering this broader context can justify the imposition of what would otherwise appear to be disproportionate costs. The last footstepper ought not be retaliated against as if they are responsible for the cumulative effect: they are not. But, by contrast, taking offence at acts like repeated microaggressions, and the resulting costs imposed—even where these are more significant than could count as proportional to the one-off act—can be justified by reference to the structural injustice, and without requiring an account of for what part or portion of the structural injustice an individual is at fault.

It is not only, then, the fact that agent A, who commits a microaggression against B, has harmed agent B individually and to some measurable degree which renders A liable to costs. By itself, this line of argument leaves the offended party open to the charge that so reacting will very often be disproportionate over the smaller scale details of our social interactions where the manifestation of their offence is anything other than subtle, or where it has a broader impact of exposing the offender to censure from others. Rather, agent A makes a small contribution to a larger injustice in affronting B. Further, that injustice is one that we have a duty to do something about, if we can. Insofar as taking offence, and so bearing the costs of the other taking offence at us, contributes towards reshaping the norms that promote such injustice, then agent A ought to bear the costs of B's taking offence. Further, A is no innocent bystander who can protest against being the one who bears the costs for the sake of a move towards justice: A does contribute, if in a diffuse and hard to measure way, to that background context of injustice through participating in the patterning of social relations that produces such injustice. A, then, is not being used as merely a means to an end.

This way of assessing the case of microaggressions may blend something of the 'backwards' looking liability model into Young's 'forwards' looking social connection approach. When someone takes offence, then they resist the way another treats them: something that might seem more familiar to a

[54] Young, *Responsibility for Justice*, p. 96.
[55] See, for instance, Fatima, "On the edge of knowing".

liability or blame approach to responsibility.[56] But that very resistance may contribute to transforming the structure: those underlying norms that shape our social interactions, often in ways that create or sustain social inequalities.

One might object that a social connection model still doesn't justify taking offence where doing so would impose heavier costs than ordinary, everyday kinds of withdrawal and the feeling of having mis-stepped—and so, nothing beyond the kinds of costs that a liability model could justify. There are ways other than taking offence to resist acts like A's that contribute to unequal social relations, and so to contribute to transforming the structure. For example, B might flag the offensive behaviour without directly targeting A, say, by later posting on social media that the act happened to them and that this sort of thing happens all the time, without naming A. One might think this would contribute to correcting an injustice through educating people about what counts as an affront, but without being as costly to agent A. Further, one could hold that costs are justified only where they are necessary to achieve some end: we should not impose costs on others where we need not do so.[57] Hence, one might doubt that we should express our offence at A: doing so would be costly to A, and we need not impose such costs.

To respond, there are limits to the extent of the costs that I defend: once again, my defence of offence is not one of public shaming, but of how offence is used to negotiate ordinary social relations. In addition, there is good reason to take offence directly, targeting the offender, rather than only deploying indirect strategies. Indirect, later reporting may fail to achieve the same end as the direct response of taking offence: namely, of targeting the local norms in play in some setting. For a start, those who read our indirect reports are a different audience. Insofar as we accept the thesis that social media is a place of polarisation, where people interact only with those who have similar views to them, they may even be the *wrong* audience: those already inclined to agree with us as to the right way to behave, rather than those who are likely to offer such affronts. Further, when taking offence, we directly resist the attribution of lower standing than we perceive ourselves to have within a particular social interaction. Reporting later about experiencing some offensive act, fails to do that.

---

[56] Especially one like Smith's account of blame as a protest, "Moral blame and moral protest". Again, though, to be offended doesn't always involve or require blaming someone as Chapter 4 discussed.

[57] With thanks to Simon Caney for suggesting this line of objection. It might draw support from just war theory or the ethics of self-defence, and such a framework of talk of proportionality is used in Billingham & Parr, "Enforcing social norms"—although, of course, taking offence at a comment in a social interaction is radically unlike going to war or hurting another.

6.4. Burdens on the offended

Before concluding that we ought to cultivate an inclination to take offence, there is one last set of costs that need to be addressed: those to the offended party, either of taking offence itself, or of becoming the kind of person who takes offence. Troublingly, such costs are likely to fall heaviest on the most disadvantaged, given that they are the ones who most frequently experience affronts to their social standing as equals of a kind at which it is appropriate to take offence. An inclination to take offence may even lie amongst what Lisa Tessman defines as "burdened virtues": "traits that while practically necessitated for surviving oppression or morally necessitated for opposing it, are also costly to the selves who bear them".[58] These costs too, might threaten the case for taking offence to be a civic virtue. These costs, such as they are, might be weighed against the broader benefits to society of taking offence and could threaten the instrumental case for a virtue of (apt) offence-taking. In addition, the other civic virtues appear to tend to improve one's life.[59] How much better is a life in a diverse society when one tolerates the views of others, than the one where one finds oneself constantly in conflict with those with differing beliefs. Being open-minded, too, will make living in a liberal society more rewarding. But does being inclined to take offence appear similarly rewarding?[60]

Inculcating a propensity to take offence might seem burdensome simply in that it makes one's life go less well. This is one of Martha Nussbaum's motivations not to care for the ordinary slights of everyday life: they are all around us. Wouldn't it be better for us not to even see such slights? Still more so, one might think, where people are subjected to ongoing degradations, disrespect, and intrusions, on the grounds that they are taken to belong to a group that lack social standing.[61] Could one make one's life worse, then, by inculcating a propensity to be offended? However, to take up Nussbaum's

---

[58] Tessman, *Burdened Virtues*, p. 107. Note, as my concern is with a civic virtue, I am primarily troubled by the burden rather than the detachment of the virtue from an Aristotelian notion of flourishing, although see note 61 in this chapter.

[59] Whether law-abidingness is altogether good for the person who inculcates it, could be less than clear at least for poorly enforced laws.

[60] It might not have to. Galston, for instance, notes that there is a gap between civic virtue and human virtue, "Pluralism and civic virtue", e.g. p. 625. What is good for society may not be what is good for us. On the other hand, James Bernard Murphy points out that in his earlier work, Galston seems more Aristotelian, linking virtues of justice to human happiness. See Murphy, "From Aristotle to Hobbes".

[61] Nussbaum, *Anger and Forgiveness*.

concern in this case requires that one assume, often wrongly, that members of such groups are not already acutely aware of the everyday experiences that 'place' them within the social hierarchy of a society. It would also require holding that that such affronts lack impact if they are not consciously noticed. Against the latter assumption, studies on stereotype threat suggest that people's performance can be affected by being primed to think about their gender or race while taking a test.[62] The burden of noticing or otherwise being affected by affronts to one's standing as a social equal is not created then, by inculcating a disposition to take offence. Rather, it is the product of the background social inequalities of a society.

Taking offence at such affronts may still appear burdensome in its social risks and the energy it requires, even if not in the attention that it involves. To be offended may be emotionally draining, it may put those who take it on the spot, or open them to retaliation from others. The latter social risks of taking offence have appeared throughout this book, from the characterisation of the humourless feminist to the social costs of attempting to enforce norms that others reject. However, these are best understood as practical constraints on action, such that the balance of costs might be such that on this or that occasion one would be better off refraining from expressing that one takes offence, rather than reasons against taking offence altogether.[63] Often, offence does not provoke such backlash; sometimes, taking it can have social benefits.

On the flip side, too, *failing* to resist these affronts is also burdensome, in much the same ways as taking offence. It can also often be emotionally draining to bite one's tongue and act as if another has not said anything offensive. It is sometimes socially costly not to resist another's attribution of lower social standing, as taking offence might. The affront coupled with a lack of resistance may encourage others to also adopt the view that one has lesser standing. To illustrate, that one lets this unwarranted intrusion pass might encourage others to similar. By contrast, resisting some small offensive remark can signal to a group that, in general, one will not put up with such remarks, and so dissuade others from acting that way in the future.

---

[62] For instance, see Spencer et al., "Stereotype threat and women's math performance"; Steele & Aronson, "Stereotype and the intellectual test performance of African Americans". The subtlety of the cues varies, but for a discussion of how even subtle factors of a kind the participants might not realise are having an impact can influence performance, see Stone & McWhinnie, "Evidence that blatant versus subtle stereotype threat".

[63] For an illustration of the costs of protesting microaggressions in particular, which may provide prudential reasons not to, see Rini, "How to take offense", pp. 341–3.

As observed in Chapter 2, when confronted with an offensive act, one faces costs either way: there is no cost-free option now available.

Another worry about inculcating a propensity to take offence considers the cost to a person's moral character. Some object to the kind of person we reveal ourselves to be in taking offence or become in cultivating a propensity towards offence. Robin Barrow offers a particularly vivid characterisation of the resulting flaws:

> By definition, if you take offence at some joke, you are being humourless, self-important and arrogant. Even if you are plainly insulted, to treat it as actionable betrays an unattractive and unvirtuous preoccupation with self-image.[64]

Taking offence over the details of our social interactions also brings to mind Philippa Foot's remark, often cited in works on manners, that none could be devoted to behaving "comme il faut". At least, what kind of person cares deeply about *others* not being so devoted to the right manners?[65] Existing accounts of the importance of manners and civility tend to focus on treating others with respect, rather than what we ought to do where that respect is not shown. Perhaps that is for good reason.[66]

The precise relation between moral and civic virtues is disputed but some, at least, hold that cultivating a civic virtue should be a good thing, and not only for its instrumental benefits for society.[67] Perhaps taking offence fails at this last hurdle. At the best, then, it would be a civic virtue that is in tension with the cultivation of moral virtue. We would be better people if we didn't care about the small stuff—even if we are better citizens, under certain unjust conditions, when we do. Yet social standing has deep significance in how life goes, shaping whether it is characterised by unwarranted intrusions, expressions of disregard and disrespect, experiences of exclusion, and a lack of power over the way one's interactions go. Further, our social standing is not unrelated to the standing of others; rather, our standing is shaped by the groups with which others identify us. By resisting an affront to yourself, you can be resisting an attribution of lesser standing to those like you too.

---

[64] Barrow, "On the duty of not taking offence", pp. 273–4.
[65] Foot, "Morality as a system of hypothetical imperatives", p. 314.
[66] E.g., Buss, "Appearing respectful"; Calhoun, "The virtue of civility".
[67] For discussions, see Galston, "Pluralism and civic virtue"; Murphy, "From Aristotle to Hobbes".

To attend to one's standing as a social equal, then, looks morally justifiable and not just socially desirable.[68]

Once we have in view how the web of manners and ordinary practices constructs unjust social inequalities, Foot's comment on manners looks less compelling. So, too, Barrow's depiction of the person's taking offence strikes home best when we consider those who claim greater than equal standing, or who protest intrusions against their inflated sense of their own standing: take the professor deeply offended by a graduate student who makes a joke with him as its object. But, I'd suggest, it falls flat when we think of resisting affronts to one's standing as a social equal. Indeed, Barrow's own opening example is of a man calling a female colleague a "stupid bitch"—a case he uses to set up his suggestion that we (others) take offence too easily these days, and a case he suggests, where the woman probably shouldn't have taken offence.[69] It does not look so very unattractive to take offence at such comments in one's workplace. And we might ask who gains if women train themselves not to mind such remarks.

It could be proposed that we go one step further still. Perhaps some people have not only a civic duty to take offence but, also, a self-directed moral duty. Someone might owe it to herself to become inclined to take offence at affronts to her equal standing.[70] Doing so would shore up her sense of self-respect and standing within a society. If there can be such self-directed duties, the inclination to take offence or otherwise resist having one's standing lowered below being a social equal could be a contender. I suspect this would be unlikely to result in a defence of a duty to take offence in particular: there are other possible forms of resistance and so other ways in which to shore up one's self-respect. All the same, however, the case for thinking an inclination to take offence is in conflict with living a good life is further weakened by these advantages of taking offence for one's sense of one's standing.

To conclude this chapter's assessment of costs and benefits, an inclination to offence is a civic virtue, rather than the civic vice that it has been depicted

---

[68] For the full defence of the attention to standing demonstrated through taking offence, see Chapters 2 and 3.

[69] Barrow "On the duty of not taking offence", at p. 266.

[70] With thanks to Simon Caney and Hallvard Lillehammer for suggesting this line of thought. Arguments have been made that those who are oppressed have a duty to resist. See, for a critique of a series of grounds for such a duty including that it contributes to other's oppression—as well as a defence of a self-regarding grounds for a duty—Silvermint, "Resistance and well-being".

as being in public discussion. To take offence at the right things contributes towards securing the norms that are needed for a tolerant and civil society and may promote a more socially equal society. Neither the usual costs to the offending party or to the offended party succeed in undermining that defence.

7

A social approach, our lives online, and the social emotions

This book has sought to domesticate taking offence as an ordinary but important part of our social interactions, often conveyed through acts as small as raised eyebrows and awkward silences. To take offence is often justified and can be socially valuable, since it is one way to resist everyday social inequalities: the details of interactions that, together, pattern social hierarchies. Alone, such details might not have seemed worthy of much attention; perhaps they even appear to have little moral or political significance. However, there is a distinctively social dimension to equality—to what it is to live together as equals or not—that is made up out of these details, the norms and social practices that underpin them, and what these express and enact. These are the details that make the experience of social inequality pervasive: the ordinary gestures that express a lack of equal respect and consideration; the ways to mark others out as outsiders or 'other'; the small unwarranted intrusions; and the various frustrations of attempts to present a 'face' or self-image, especially as knowledgeable or as possessing some socially valued role or position. Individually, by themselves, each may appear to have little significance but, combined, they are the stuff out of which social inequality is widely enacted and performed in our daily lives.

To take offence is to resist such everyday acts and so it can be an act of direct insubordination against a social hierarchy. Rather than being best understood as an expression of hurt feelings, to take offence is a way to defend against acts that threaten to undermine your social standing as you perceive it. What provokes offence is an affront to your social standing: where someone acts, or fails to act, in a way that doesn't align with your sense of how others ought to treat or regard you. By taking offence, we reject the other's slight to our standing: after all, if we accepted it, we would not take offence. Often, we also communicate our offence through acts of withdrawal, so expressing our estrangement from the offending party. This estrangement is often minor and short-lived, and the actions expressing withdrawal are

On Taking Offence. Emily McTernan, Oxford University Press. © Oxford University Press 2023.
DOI: 10.1093/oso/9780197613092.003.0008

often small. Still, by taking offence you signal a resistance to the other's attribution of lesser standing than you take yourself to have.

For the most part, and especially for fine-grained acts, it is the underlying social norms and practices, and their social meanings, that make an act into one that, say, expresses respect or disrespect; into one that subtly signals one's acceptance or rejection of another's expertise; or into something that feels like an intrusion. To take offence thus signals a resistance to these underlying social norms or social practices, or to the uneven application of general social norms, such as where we are less careful to follow norms of politeness when interacting with those whom we regard as beneath us.[1] Many members of discriminated against or marginalised groups find that they face a set of commonly experienced affronts. Especially when people take offence at some common affront to those who are like them, to take offence is to resist the general patterning of socially unequal relations. Hence, to take offence at the right things makes a small contribution towards promoting social equality; collectively, doing so can make a substantial difference. Our compliance with the social norms and practices that enact social inequality is what keeps on sustaining the social hierarchies—and resisting these, such as by taking offence, can reshape them.

Even when others reject or misread offence's signal, taking offence can still be a way to resist. At the least, the offended party attributes to herself more standing than others treat her as if she has, and so she still resists another's lowering of her standing. To take offence also reflects a person's underlying commitments.[2] In order to take offence, you must be paying attention to how others treat and regard you, and take it to matter: rightly so, given the significance of social standing and the way in which our standing is constructed through our interactions. Further, to take offence at an affront rooted in some unjust social hierarchy reveals a commitment to a more socially equal society and to a better set of norms of civility. This form of offence-taking has sufficient social value in its promotion of social equality and civility and, as I've argued, sufficiently limited social costs that the inclination to take offence at inegalitarian affronts is a civic virtue.

---

[1] This understanding of the role of politeness norms and practices is influenced by Buss, "Appearing respectful"; Calhoun, "The virtue of civility"; Olberding, *The Wrong of Rudeness*, see Chapters 2 and 3 of this book for discussions. On the latter, see, for instance, Olberding's contrast between her treatment as a professor and as a maid, *The Wrong of Rudeness*, p. 47.

[2] To once more echo Strawson on the reactive attitudes, rather than being mere tools or tactics in our social negotiations, these "really are expressions of our moral attitudes". Strawson, *Freedom and Resentment*, p. 25.

In this last chapter, I turn to a contemporary issue to complete the book's investigation of the moral and political significance of offence. So, in the current moment, when considering offence it might be that what springs to mind is, in particular, people taking offence on social media. Further, our online practices of offence might look different from the offline practices that have been the book's primary focus. First, then, I will address the increasing regulation against offensive content that appears to be especially prevalent on online platforms. I weigh the benefits of preventing offensive content against the potentially greater advantages of leaving the dynamics of offence and repair to play out, in cases that fall short of hate speech. Second, I assess a set of apparent further differences in how our practices of offence function online as compared to offline. I suggest that the increased visibility of having offended, along with the way that offence can spiral beyond the original audience, could threaten the justifiability of taking offence on certain kinds of online platforms, if our practices of taking offence go unmodified. Considering these features of our online practices also reveals the importance of the background of continuing relationships and the norms that usually constrain our expressions and receptions of offence. To bring this book to a close, I situate the defence of offence within a broader case for the significance of social emotions.

7.1. A regulatory turn

I began the book with a contrast to Joel Feinberg's disunified cluster of disliked states that make up what he terms 'offence' when addressing the legal regulation of offensive conduct.[3] The concerns of this book have been very different, since I offer an account and defence of a distinct emotion of offence, and focus on offence's role in negotiating social standing in our interactions and in contesting wider hierarchies. However, an inclination to regulate offensive conduct has crept beyond the law court, and beyond hate speech of the kind that legal bans target. Rather than leaving things to play out through our social interactions in the usual way—we are, after all, familiar with the play of affront, offence, and (often) repair—there is a turn to institutions or organisations to step in and control through nonlegal regulation what

---

[3] Feinberg, *Offense to Others*.

happens in this space. The impulse towards regulation may be most evident on social media, as demonstrated in its content moderation.

My interest here is restricted to the attempts to regulate, outside of the law, speech that falls far short of the usual definitions of hate speech of the kind to be legislated against. A microaggression, for instance is offensive and contributes to reinforcing hierarchy. But it does not deny others' basic humanity or dignity, nor does it count as 'fighting words', and nor is it threatening and abusive.[4] Even if a microaggression were taken to fall into some particular definition of hate speech, still a legal framework would struggle to police utterances of this kind.

To offer one example of the regulation that I have in mind, take the social media site 'Facebook' and its 'Community Standards'. These standards offer a radically broad understanding of what they term "hate speech", including amongst other categories content that counts as "targeting a person or group of people on the basis of their protected characteristic(s) with either: terms expressing dismissal, including . . . don't respect, don't like, don't care for"; "cursing"; or "Terms or phrases calling for engagement in sexual activity, or contact with genitalia, anus, faeces or urine."[5] As defined by Facebook then, such regulated "hate speech" ranges far beyond what legal systems restrict: it would include statements like "men are dicks" or "I don't care for women", statements that, while offensive, carry little risk of anything resembling immediate threat or violence, and are not easily characterised as serious denials of basic humanity or dignity. People can be banned from the platform for such utterances. At the least, one's words will be deleted, such that no one else can come across them. In one case, a woman was barred from Facebook for 30 days for commenting, "men are scum", on a post about the 'MeToo' movement.[6]

---

[4] An exception to note to the above is that Derald Wing Sue, who includes 'micro-assaults' amongst microaggressions, which may include some abusive and threatening acts, e.g., Sue et al., "Racial microaggressions in everyday life". On these definitions of hate speech, Jeffrey Howard comments that "hate speech is a term of art, referring to the particular expressions of hatred against particular (groups of) people in particular contexts", and surveys a set of formulations, in his, "Free speech and hate speech", pp. 95–6. On dignity and hate speech, see Waldron, *The Harm in Hate Speech*. The tolerance for legal regulation against hate speech varies dramatically between countries, with the United States being especially wary and Europe more favourable. Maxime Lepoutre argues, perhaps controversially, that even the United States bans some hateful speech, like targeted threats or fighting words of a certain kind, as he puts it, "the main debate concerns not whether, but which kinds of hate speech should be prohibited"; "Hate speech in public discourse", p. 854.

[5] Available at https://transparency.fb.com/en-gb/policies/community-standards/hate-speech/.

[6] For a discussion of the case see Van Zuylen-Wood, " 'Men are scum' ". This fell under the "dehumanising language" category and so closer, perhaps, to hate speech 'proper'.

Facebook is no outlier in its regulation of speech that offends. Other social media platforms do this too and offline various employers have issued codes of conduct to their employees on what to say. Codes of conduct have also appeared at some comedy clubs and events at universities where comedians perform. These, for instance, ban content that 'punches down' in targeting people who are marginalised or oppressed, and mining that experience for humour.[7] Are these sorts of interventions welcome moves in the negotiations of social norms and practices which have been this book's subject?

Amongst the chief worries about the supposed culture of taking offence is that it might threaten free speech and, especially, the open debate of controversial issues.[8] People won't feel free, the thinking goes, to say what they want where there is such a backlash. But given the domestication of offence in this book, that worry seems most apt and most pressing when considering the turn to regulation, with its institutional penalties for those who offend, such as being banned from venues or facing disciplinary procedures at work.[9] Indeed, simply the removal of offensive speech that happens where, say, Facebook deletes one's post for being offensive, or comedians are forbidden from making jokes on certain topics at comedy nights, might be troubling even without the infliction of penalties. Where such prohibitions become sufficiently widespread, they might seem to amount to a suppression of speech. By contrast, simply taking offence is not the kind of consequence that threatens speech: recall, once again, that offence is not the same as public shaming. To have others offended by what one says doesn't infringe upon one's right to speak: we have no right to a receptive and acquiescent audience.

Here, too, we can appeal to a familiar argument from the literature on free speech that defends countering speech with speech. The thought there is that we should permit wrong (and wrongful) things to be said on the grounds that counter-speech works. The best thing to do, the argument goes, is to convince those with the wrong views, rather than suppressing their speech.

---

[7] For one code, see Quantum Leopard comedy night: "QUANTUM LEOPARD has a 'no kicking down' policy on all material. No chav-bashing, racism, sexism, homophobia or transphobia, ableism, whorephobia etc. QUANTUM LEOPARD is slightly sad that this even needs saying." Available here: https://www.facebook.com/groups/quantumleopardcomedy/. As another example, see BBC Newsbeat, "Comedian refused to sign".

[8] This assumes a broad conception of free speech—beyond simply protecting speech from government interference. On a narrower conception see Schauer *Free Speech*, pp. 7–10. For a broad conception, see Mill, *On Liberty*.

[9] This isn't to say that all things considered these consequences are always objectionable: that depends on the nature of the job or venue, I suspect, and the content of the offensive speech in question.

Otherwise, one may merely drive the expressions of wrongful views underground, where they can no longer be countered.[10] Sometimes, the way that we counter bad speech might be by taking offence. We often express our offence more subtly than simply stating "I'm offended by that". But resistance to offensive speech through taking offence and its associated behaviours of withdrawal, from raising eyebrows or not laughing at jokes, to saying "that's offensive", is all still communicative conduct.[11] To take offence, then, is a contribution to the conversation and negotiation.

Taking offence, admittedly, may not resemble the kind of mannerly interjection into a debate that some seem to prefer when addressing, say, the vigorous way that university students interact with controversial speakers or with disagreeable ideas.[12] However, that doesn't make offence any less an intervention into the marketplace of ideas: here, I side with Eve Wagner and Jeremy Waldron in denying that free speech is only preserved where people follow some orderly and controlled framework for discussion. As Waldron argues, "Ideas come to life in the rough-and-tumble of active and even disruptive opposition".[13] The values underpinning free speech, he argues, are promoted by the "happy cacophony" of less controlled interactions.[14] That includes, I would add, where some take offence in order to express their disagreement.

Taking offence is, in particular, a way to directly counter the ranking in a social hierarchy that is expressed and enacted in an interaction through another's affront. If Facebook removes some piece of offensive speech, then no such countering of that speech is possible, although one instance of the speech that might have contributed to social inequality is removed. Thus there might sometimes be reason to prefer to let the social dynamics play out, over removing or preventing offensive speech falling far short of hate speech of the kind regulated by the law. The process of someone taking offence

---

[10] Rae Langton describes this as the 'more speech doctrine', in her "Blocking as counter-speech". See also J. S. Mill for a defence of hearing even the wrong opinions since we can't be sure and that way have a "livelier impression of truth", *On Liberty*, p. 19. For a recent defence of counter-speech, instead of extensive bans on speech, see Lepoutre, "Hate speech in public discourse".

[11] Offence isn't best understood as having to be expressed through direct verbal statements of one's offence: gestures will do, and it is often subtle. But free speech scholars draw the boundaries of freedom of expression more permissively than restricting it to statements like "I'm offended" anyway. To illustrate, imagine that a state banned raised eyebrows. That looks like it would undermine our freedom of expression. With thanks to Jeff Howard for discussion on this point.

[12] See the comments of UCL's Vice-Chancellor, Michael Spence, as reported in Turner, "Students must learn to disagree."

[13] Waldron, "Heckle", p. 19; see also Wagner, "Heckling".

[14] Waldron, "Heckle", p. 20.

counters the offensive speech in a way that supressing the speech does not: it directly resists an attribution of lesser standing. Where the offensive speech taps into common themes in the socially unequal treatment of one's group, then to be able to resist it, publicly, is to resist the wider social patterning of a social hierarchy.

There is also an advantage of taking offence playing the countering role, over more traditionally conceived of forms of countering speech, such as proposing counterarguments. To be optimistic about the effectiveness of taking offence in challenging offensive speech does not require that we hold that people are readily converted from their (hateful) views through the presentation of the alternative view or through the offer of reasons. A person need not be convinced to believe different things in order to be dissuaded from offending others again. The social costs that follow from causing that offence may suffice.

In resisting some background hierarchy, the balance of arguments as to when it would be tactically better to leave the offending speech up and counter it by taking offence, and when it would be better to delete the offending content, will depend on the details of the case and, in particular, on the stability of the social norms that are in play.[15] On the side of deletion, removing the offensive speech can contribute to shaping our social norms. Our adherence to social norms involves the expectation that others will also comply with these norms.[16] Suppose, to illustrate, that there is a widely held antidiscriminatory norm. To remove speech that breaks that antidiscriminatory norm can contribute to keeping the norm in place, since it supports the belief that others comply with that norm too by removing a counterinstance that could corrode that belief.

On the side of leaving speech up and countering it, realising that people find these sorts of discriminatory statements offensive, through people taking offence, provides a more direct way to intervene on social norms and adherence to these. To take offence is a clear statement that another fails to behave as expected or as is deemed fitting, and it demonstrates a willingness to enforce the relevant norm: taking offence is a form of norm enforcement, as Chapter 2 discussed. Indeed, we are often in situations where the best

---

[15] For the background account of social norms used here, see Chapter 2. I draw on the conception of norms in Anderson, "Beyond homo economicus" and Brennan et al., *Explaining Norms* in particular.

[16] On norms and expectations about other's behaviour, see Bicchieri & Xiao, "Do the right thing"; Brennan et al., *Explaining Norms*.

strategy to improve our norms would be something other than hiding a violation of some desired norm. Take cases in which the norms are contested, where there may not be an underlying expectation of compliance from (all) others in the first place. Leaving offensive speech visible to be countered by offence, then, is likely to be especially useful where an antidiscriminatory norm or practice is still emerging. Still, even for well-embedded norms, the preservation of people's expectations of compliance with the norm that is supported by removing the offensive speech would have to be weighed against the alternative of leaving it up to prompt offence and other forms of contestation. Such active contestation would result in increased awareness that others are willing to enforce the norm, and that they publicly, and actively, endorse it, in a way that deleting the speech does not.[17]

The social approach to offensive speech, of letting these dynamics of offence-taking play out, thus has its advantages when we seek to negotiate our standing, as compared to a turn to regulation. There is a stronger countervailing reason against leaving the offensive speech visible in cases where an antidiscriminatory norm is already well-embedded but even that may not be decisive, given the force of seeing the norm actively enforced. With that rosy picture of how offence might function online in view however, I turn to consider a challenge. Putting aside the prevalence of regulation, there are other more diffuse and potentially more problematic ways in which our offence online may differ from our offline practices. Do these differences undermine the positive picture of offence-taking online that has been presented thus far?

7.2. Taking offence online

Online, people call for, or engage in, behaviours of withdrawal of a sort that is indicative of offence, such as refusing to accept a joke as funny; 'blocking' the offending party on a social media platform; declaring they would not want to be in their company or stating, outright, that they are offended. As I've argued, that ought not be confused with public shaming given the differing motivations and resulting actions. But much of this book has addressed our

---

[17] Institutional punishments—workplace sanctions, say—may also count as enforcing a norm and they can be highly visible. The argument given targets content moderation in particular, but there are other good reasons to be cautious about increasing the control that employers have over their employees and, especially, their employees' lives.

offline practices. So, one might wonder, does the same defence of offence apply to our online practices?

The most important observation to make here is a deflationary one: we ought not take our online lives to be entirely novel or as raising especially philosophically distinctive questions. Online forums and social media are simply one more place in which we negotiate social norms and practices around standing, along with places like our workplaces, universities, pubs, trains, parties, and public spaces, through all manner of daily interactions. Unsurprisingly, then, many instances of taking offence online look much as they do offline, with offence expressed through acts like failing to respond to offensive jokes, leaving a silence by not replying, and the like. A running theme of the book has been the observation that taking offence is an ordinary, everyday, and noncatastrophic part of our interactions. That includes our interactions with friends, relatives, and acquaintances online, as well as offline. However, the way in which certain online platforms are constructed might create a context for offence that functions a little differently to many offline spaces, perhaps producing more exaggerated instances of offence-taking. Surveying three features that could contribute to the exaggerated nature of offence online, however, I will argue that only sometimes—and often only apparently—is this so.

The first apparent difference is that online sometimes we engage with people to whom we have minimal or distant connections, and perhaps more often than we do offline. A more distant set of connections is, after all, one of the things that the internet offers us: the ability to talk to others with whom we otherwise wouldn't, as we share no other space. Such distance has consequences. As Chapter 1 argued, if we are distant, then we are more likely to engage in symbolic forms of withdrawal. Since we have no direct contact, we may need to perform some more dramatic act in order to convey the same degree of offence as a raised eyebrow would to a friend. But, as also argued in Chapter 1, one should be wary of automatically taking grander gestures of offence as having greater social costs or as conveying greater offence. What appears exaggerated is often, in fact, necessary to convey offence across a distance, while we attend more closely to the potential offence of those to whom we are close and so need only small-scale gestures to express the same offence. What distant others think of us also tends to matter less with regards to our social standing than those with whom we have closer, and more frequent, contact.

A second difference, and one with more significance as we consider how to translate our practices online, is that one's offence may be more visible on some online platforms, depending on their design. Given the potential reach of online platforms, the audience that witnesses that you've done something offensive may be larger, and the evidence that you've been offensive can persist, if that is the way the online platform has been constructed. Even smaller gestures of taking offence can, as a result, be more visible, let alone the grander gestures needed to convey offence to those more distant. As a result, the accompanying feelings on the part of the offending party, such as humiliation, shame, awkwardness, or embarrassment, might also be heightened. Given that these emotions concern the way in which we take it that others are perceiving us, if there are more witnesses, or we feel that our mis-stepping, inappropriate, or objectionable actions are more obvious to others, by being more visible, then we may feel these emotions more strongly or deeply. The potential social costs to one's reputation that result from one having been offensive also threaten to be greater. More people will know, or come to know, that you've behaved offensively.

These increased costs might upset the defence of offence for certain online settings. Perhaps these costs exceed the benefits of taking offence, or the costs for particular offending individuals exceeds what could be proportionate, even given the argument in the last chapter for bearing higher costs when one offends on the grounds of a forwards-looking responsibility to tackle injustice. Again, however, it is worth bearing in mind how much of our offence-taking online would still look as it does offline and would still be justified in the same way: the internet is not only a place of public interactions amongst strangers, but also a place for a series of smaller communities and interactions amongst people who do know each other. Further, the social costs of having caused offence vary with distance: one's offensive act being visible to very distant others may matter little for one's self-perception or social reputation as compared to those close knowing about it.

I suspect that, despite these mitigating factors, increased visibility may mean that we ought to be more careful about how we *express* offence in certain online forums. We should do so in order to avoid excessive costs, although this problem will be mitigated by the ways in which distance diminishes the impact of our having taken offence. But perhaps more pressingly, we should also be cautious in our expressions on public platforms in order to avoid conveying greater offence than we actually feel. We want to convey some degree of offence, express a certain amount of estrangement with our withdrawal, and not more than that. The behaviours that do a good job of expressing a certain degree of offence and withdrawal in our offline lives, and so aptly negotiating or reinforcing the norms of civility and the social meanings that underlie them, won't necessarily be read in the same way in online forums with a potentially large audience and where our speech, and others' offence at it, may linger. We should be aware that our offence-taking is more visible online and attenuate it accordingly.

Modifications in our expressions of offence would not be unique to online offence-taking, as noted earlier: we often moderate our displays of offence depending on our environment. Offence might be more vigorously expressed in the pub than the classroom, say, or a raised eyebrow might be used on one's partner where a more overt gesture would be used for a stranger. But online we can be less clear about the adjustments that we should make. It is easy to forget how visible one's online gestures can be, on some platforms—but, on the flipside, it is also easy to exaggerate the visibility of what one says online, taking it to have more lasting reach and significance than it does, as others scroll past one's post. These uncertainties will sometimes upset our calibrations of our gestures of offence.

We may also tend to be more careless in how we express our offence in communities of strangers online, thinking less about how to modify its expression. Often, when we take offence, we do so in the context of an ongoing relationship that will continue beyond the offensive act (unless the offence is too great). This encourages us to be moderate in our expressions of offence, since a continuation of our relations with the other side is expected, as long as the offensive act is not so offensive that we break off relations altogether. And our reception of, and the costs of, another's offence is also moderated by ongoing relations. We know that we have mis-stepped or behaved inappropriately, but we think that repair is possible. The offended party, we may think, cares enough about our continued relations to offer a (non-relationship ending) indication that something we have done offends them. Offence amongst strangers and perhaps especially online, where our connection may feel thin and fleeting, is not constrained in its expression and its experience in these ways.

A third difference between our offline and online lives may further trouble a defence of offence for a subset of social media platforms. On certain social media platforms, an offensive act sometimes becomes more widely known in a way that also creates more offended parties. Suppose, then, that I say something offensive to a small group. Those present and affronted may take offence. Online, the audience is often much larger, such that people far beyond one's ordinary social circles may be offended. Suppose, to illustrate, that instead of saying something offensive offline, I put it on Twitter, so potentially affronting the (perhaps larger) audience that my tweets tend to have. It is then 'quote tweeted' by various others, who add their own reactions, to their own audiences. Can these further audiences also take offence? If they do, then my original offensive comment may mean a great many are estranged from me, express withdrawal, and impose the social costs of offence: offence spirals.

Offline, too, we are sometimes told about an offensive remark that we did not directly witness. But I suspect that in our offline lives, as compared on online, we tend to have much clearer practices in play that shape the reactions we have towards affronts that are directed at us ("you are a terrible person"), compared to ones that we just hear about ("Fred said you are a terrible person"). There is a further important distinction here between reported affronts that are about us as particular individuals ("Fred said you were a terrible person") as compared to those about those who are 'like us' in some socially salient sense, but that are not directed at us qua individuals ("Fred said women are overemotional at work").[18] Affronts directed at you, or reports of affronts about you in particular likely offend: even if you don't hear it directly, still the affront can directly threaten your standing. Hearing about an affront to those who are 'like us' in some socially salient sense, but where the affront is not directed at us, may instead lead to a whole range of other emotions, like anger, indignation, fury, irritation, or despair. But often we won't experience the report of the offensive remark as itself an affront to our standing in *this* social interaction, which is what triggers offence and what makes offence an intervention into our social interactions that resists that attribution of lesser standing. Our understanding as to when we are affronted often excludes mere reports of this kind.

Of course, upon encountering the offending party (Fred), we might be moved to take offence even at such reported indirect affronts. I suspect that is particularly likely if they say something further along similar lines or suggestive of such. We might then come to see Fred's behaviour as an affront to our own standing and in this interaction—and cumulatively so, such that we take offence at the original remarks.

---

[18] There is an in-between case here, say, "Your colleague, Fred, said that women are always overemotional at work", a general insult but one that potentially pertains directly to you, as one female colleague. That would likely offend you even in a report.

So, what happens to these practices of offence-taking online? Two features found on some platforms might be what leads to the spiralling of offence: more people taking an affront to be offensive than we would expect, or than we would see as apt. One is that on some online platforms, and when interacting with strangers, we lack the motivations we often have in our offline lives to patch up our relations after being offended. In online communities that consist of fleeting contact with strangers, we lack the counterbalancing good will from previous encounters, and the need to repair relations for future ones. In our ordinary lives, there are limits to how many others we can get away with withdrawing from, but not so in such a fleeting community of strangers. Perhaps, then, we will be more careless with when to see an affront in these online contexts: what is there to lose, in being offended at something a stranger said to someone else?

The other feature emerges from considering an important exception to the practices above, of cases where a merely reported affront to those like us can, itself, be treated as a fresh affront. So, we can experience a threat to our social standing from the fact that the other person reported this affront, here and now, or from the precise way that they have chosen to report it. That might be what is sometimes happening online. For instance, perhaps sometimes, 'quote tweets', where someone reports another's tweet, do, or look like they do, act as a threat to our social standing, where they report some offensive comment made to one's group or to those like oneself in some socially salient sense. After all, on Twitter, the affront is made highly public. We may find that a (new) threat to our social standing. Here, how the offensive statement or act is put in context will be crucial. There may be ways of repeating an affront that mitigate the chances that it will function as an affront in its reporting, and ways that don't.

There are reasons, then, to be wary about how well our practices of offence will translate onto certain, particularly formulated, online platforms given the visibility of offence and the possibility of its spiralling and excess. Much of our lives online will look much like that offline where we are already in relations with others and have existing social bonds. But there is a way that the internet enables us to interact with strangers that, given the particularities of the design of platforms, throws up some challenges in translating our expressions of offence and in figuring out when we are really the ones affronted. Our online connections sometimes lack the sense of connection, the norms, and perhaps the willingness to work together to repair which we hope for in our social interactions and, often though not always, find offline.

These sorts of difficulties in translation are a problem with our online lives that is far from unique to taking offence: practices of shaming and our epistemic norms, too, face parallel challenges.[19] Still, we should be more cautious about defending offence on certain online social media platforms by contrast to the rest of our lives, just as we should be more cautious about shaming others or about trusting the information we gather from our social networks on these platforms. We may also need better online norms or better designed platforms in order to avoid offence's spiralling and excess. To conclude the book, I'll turn from the detail to the bigger picture once more: from these fine-grained details of offence in action within a particular setting, to the general interest of social emotions.

7.3. The social emotions beyond offence

Often, the social emotions are overlooked, certainly they are yet to receive the sustained philosophical attention of moral emotions like anger and resentment.[20] By social emotions I pick out a category of emotions, including shame, embarrassment, and, of course, offence. These are emotions that are directly concerned with our social interactions and social standing, with the 'face' or self-image that we present and others' reactions to it. I end this book with a brief case for the wider importance of these social emotions.

Macalester Bell suggests one reason for their oversight, observing that moral philosophers have tended to say little about the social concerns that underlie these social emotions, like status and esteem.[21] Perhaps such matters might have appeared to have relatively little moral significance: why would we care much about how others think of us? To care about these matters also requires attending to politeness and social convention, and some might have been disinclined to take these as serious or as significant.

---

[19] To illustrate, on fake news and for an analysis of the unstable norms on social media as compared to offline, regarding what we endorse, see Rini, "Fake news and partisan epistemology". On shaming online see Billingham & Parr, "Online shaming".

[20] Bell's work on contempt is an important exception, e.g., *Hard Feelings*. Other exceptions include Buss, "Appearing respectful"; Calhoun, "The virtue of civility"; Olberding, *The Wrong of Rudeness*; along with mentions largely in passing by some political philosophers, shortly discussed. One might here also consider pride, if somewhat indirectly as a social emotion, in the various attempts to defend a virtue of humility or modesty, see for instance, Statman, "Modesty, pride, and realistic self-assessment"; Bonmarito, "Modesty as a virtue of attention"; Driver, *Uneasy Virtue*.

[21] Bell, *Hard Feelings*, p. 99.

However, as I have argued in Chapters 2 and 3, these social concerns about how others treat and regard us in our interactions tie into injustices in societies marred by social inequalities. Even aside from that, our ability to successfully interact on terms that we find agreeable, to have the way in which we wish to present ourselves accepted by others and to have others collaborate with our self-presentations, or to have others treat us as equals, are all significant in how well our lives go. So, too, then, are the social emotions that are attached to these social matters. Social emotions reflect our attentiveness to our social standing, to our presentations of our self-image or face, and to how this is received. Sometimes, these emotions reveal our concern over our standing and our calibration and recalibration of how we are regarded by others, as where we feel embarrassment, offence, shame or pride. Sometimes, these emotions are the way in which we convey to others that they have misstepped or acted incorrectly or inappropriately, as when we take offence at another's acts, or feel contempt or disdain for others, with the accompanying tendencies towards acts of withdrawal.[22]

Political philosophers of a certain stripe may take less convincing of the importance of certain social emotions. Discussions of pity, envy, and shame in contemporary egalitarianism make this terrain not altogether unfamiliar, although such emotions tend to be treated as signals of unjust hierarchies, rather than as interventions in its negotiation. Elizabeth Anderson describes the pitying attitudes that a state that engages in luck egalitarian distributions embodies: she imagines a series of letters that such a state might write to those worse off through no fault or choice of their own, offering them compensation for lacking talent or being ugly.[23] The envy test is another example, presented as a check on whether distributions are fair: if not, we will envy the other's bundle of resources.[24] The social emotions also appear in the context of the republican 'eyeball test' as discussed by Phillip Pettit, that we must be able to look one another in the eye "without reasons for fear or deference".[25]

The extra step in this book is that such emotions don't just signal a possible injustice or mistake: say, that we've misfired in our distributions, that there is some objectionable inequality to be corrected, or that we have adopted a

---

[22] Offence plays both roles as a response to an attribution of lesser standing (and so a threat to how one presents and construes oneself) but also a rejection of that attribution.

[23] Anderson, "What is the point of equality".

[24] Dworkin, "What is equality".

[25] For an interesting discussion of precisely what the eyeball test does or can do in republican theorising, see Haugaard & Pettit, "A conversation on power and republicanism", for the version of the eyeball test quoted, see p. 27.

flawed conception of equality. Rather, the social emotions are also ways in which we intervene in our social worlds. Such interventions can contribute to injustice, or they can resist it. This book makes this argument in the particular case of offence. But the other social emotions, too, stand in need of more nuanced accounts of their normative significance and social functions. For instance, to pity another, and especially to pity some socially salient group, can be an expression or enactment of social inequality and, likewise, to shame.[26] On the flip side, however, shame and embarrassment can sometimes function to mitigate social inequalities. Take social norms that make it shameful or embarrassing to flash one's wealth about, which can contribute to citizens feeling more equal, since inequalities of wealth are less visible and so to some extent less segregating. Or consider that shaming people for openly racist, sexist, homophobic, or otherwise discriminatory views can strengthen the norms that mark these views as socially unacceptable.

Offence, then, is only one of the social emotions that should receive more attention from philosophers, given the significance of these emotions in navigating and shaping our social norms and social interactions. Social emotions, like offence, contribute to sustaining social inequalities, but they can also contribute to undermining them. Our social hierarchies may sometimes have social remedies: after all, it is we who sustain their underlying social norms and social practices, and their social meanings.

---

[26] A more direct role of social emotions is found in Jonathan Wolff's argument that the state must avoid forcing shaming revelations from citizens when providing welfare, "Fairness, respect, and the egalitarian ethos". See also, on shame's threat to self-respect, McTernan, "The inegalitarian ethos". For a reply to these shame arguments, see Preda & Voigt, "Shameless luck egalitarians".

Bibliography

Adler, Robert S., and Ellen R. Peirce. "The legal, ethical, and social implications of the reasonable woman standard in sexual harassment cases". *Fordham L. Rev.* 61 (1992): 773–827.

Aly, Waleed, and Robert Mark Simpson. "Political correctness gone viral". In *Media Ethics, Free Speech, and the Requirements of Democracy,* edited by Carl Fox & Joe Saunders (Routledge 2019), 125–143.

Anderson, Elizabeth. "What is the point of equality?" *Ethics* 109, no. 2 (1999): 287–337.

Anderson, Elizabeth. "Beyond homo economicus: New developments in theories of social norms". *Philosophy & Public Affairs* 29, no. 2 (2000): 170–200.

Anderson, Elizabeth. "I—Expanding the egalitarian toolbox: Equality and bureaucracy". *Aristotelian Society Supplementary Volume* 82, no. 1 (2008): 139–160.

Anderson, Kristin J., and Campbell Leaper. "Meta-analyses of gender effects on conversational interruption: Who, what, when, where, and how". *Sex Roles* 39, no. 3–4 (1998): 225–252.

Anderson, Luvell. "Racist humor". *Philosophy Compass* 10, no. 8 (2015): 501–509.

Anderson, Luvell., and Lepore, Ernie. "Slurring words". *Noûs* 47, no. 1, (2013): 25–48.

Arneson, Richard. "Shame, stigma, and disgust in the decent society". *The Journal of Ethics* 11, no. 1 (2007): 31–63.

Athanassoulis, Nafsika. "A response to Harman: Virtue ethics and character traits". *Proceedings of the Aristotelian society* 100 (2000): 215–221.

Attardo, Salvatore. "Violation of conversational maxims and cooperation: The case of jokes". *Journal of Pragmatics* 19, no. 6 (1993): 537–558.

Attardo, Salvatore. "Humour in language". *Oxford Research Encyclopedia of Linguistics* (2017), online, DOI: 10.1093/acrefore/9780199384655.013.342.

Axelsen, David V., and Juliana Bidadanure. "Unequally egalitarian? Defending the credentials of social egalitarianism". *Critical Review of International Social and Political Philosophy* 22, no. 3 (2019): 335–351.

Bailey, Alison. "On anger, silence, and epistemic injustice". *Royal Institute of Philosophy Supplements* 84 (2018): 93–115.

Barrow, Robin. "On the duty of not taking offence". *Journal of Moral Education* 34, no. 3 (2005): 265–275.

Bartky, Sandra Lee. "The pedagogy of shame". In *Feminisms and Pedagogies of Everyday Life,* edited by Carmen Luke (SUNY Press, 1996), 225–241.

Bates, Laura. *Everyday Sexism* (Simon & Schuster, 2014).

Bejan, Teresa M. *Mere Civility* (Harvard University Press, 2017).

Bell, Macalester. "A woman's scorn: Toward a feminist defense of contempt as a moral emotion". *Hypatia* 20, no. 4 (2005): 80–93.

Bell, Macalester. "Anger, virtue, and oppression". In *Feminist Ethics and Social and Political Philosophy: Theorizing the Non-Ideal,* edited by Lisa Tessman (Springer Netherlands, 2009), 165–183.

Bell, Macalester. *Hard Feelings: The Moral Psychology of Contempt* (Oxford University Press, 2013).

Ben-Porath, Sigal, and Gideon Dishon. "Taken out of context: Defending civic education from the situationist critique". *Philosophical Inquiry in Education* 23, no. 1 (2015): 22–37.

Benatar, David. "Prejudice in jest: when racial and gender humor harms". *Public Affairs Quarterly* 13, no. 2 (1999): 191–203.

Bergmann, M. "How many feminists does it take to make a joke? Sexist humor and what's wrong with it". *Hypatia* 1, no. 1 (1986): 63–82.

Bicchieri, Cristina. "Norms of cooperation". *Ethics* 100, no. 4 (1990): 838–861.

Bicchieri, Cristina, and Erte Xiao. "Do the right thing: But only if others do so". *Journal of Behavioral Decision Making* 22, no. 2 (2009): 191–208.

Billingham, Paul, and Tom Parr. "Online public shaming: Virtues and vices". *Journal of Social Philosophy* 51, no. 3 (2020): 371–390.

Billingham, Paul, and Tom Parr. "Enforcing social norms: The morality of public shaming". *European Journal of Philosophy* 28, no. 4 (2020): 997–1016.

Brennan, Geoffrey, Lina Eriksson, Robert E. Goodin, and Nicholas Southwood. *Explaining Norms* (Oxford University Press, 2013).

Brennan, S. (2016). "The moral status of micro-inequities: In favor of institutional solutions". In *Implicit Bias and Philosophy, Volume 2: Moral Responsibility, Structural Injustice, and Ethics*, edited by Michael Brownstein & Jennifer Saul (Oxford University Press, 2016), 235–253.

Brown, Penelope and Stephen C. Levinson. *Politeness: Some Universals in Language Usage* (Vol. 4) (Cambridge University Press, 1987).

Bommarito, Nicolas. "Modesty as a virtue of attention". *Philosophical Review* 122, no. 1 (2013): 93–117.

Bommarito, Nicolas. "Virtuous and vicious anger". *Journal of Ethics & Social Philosophy*, 11, no. 3 (2016): 1–27.

Burrow, Sylvia. "The political structure of emotion: From dismissal to dialogue". *Hypatia* 20, no. 4 (2005): 27–43.

Buss, Sarah. "Appearing respectful: The moral significance of manners". *Ethics* 109, no. 4 (1999): 795–826.

Calhoun, Cheshire. "The virtue of civility". *Philosophy & Public Affairs* 29, no. 3 (2000): 251–275.

Callan, Eamonn K. *Creating Citizens: Political Education and Liberal Democracy* (Clarendon Press, 1997).

Callan, Eamonn K. "Debate: Liberal virtues and civic education". *Journal of Political Philosophy* 23, no. 4 (2015): 491–500.

Campbell, Bradley, and Jason Manning. "Microaggression and moral cultures". *Comparative Sociology* 13, no. 6 (2014): 692–726.

Campbell, Bradley, and Jason Manning. "The new millennial 'morality': Highly sensitive and easily offended". *Time Magazine* (2015, November 17). Retrieved from http://time.com/4115439/student-protests-microaggressions/.

Campbell, Bradley, and Jason Manning. *The Rise of Victimhood Culture: Microaggressions, Safe Spaces, and the New Culture Wars* (Springer, 2018).

Campbell, Sue. "Being dismissed: The politics of emotional expression". *Hypatia* 9, no. 3 (1994): 46–65.

Carlin, Diana B., and Kelly L. Winfrey. "Have you come a long way, baby? Hillary Clinton, Sarah Palin, and sexism in 2008 campaign coverage". *Communication Studies* 60, no. 4 (2009): 326–343.

Carroll, Noël. "Humour". In *The Oxford Handbook of Aesthetics*, edited by Jerrold Levinson (Oxford University Press, 2003), 344–365.

Carroll, Noël. "On jokes". *Midwest Studies in Philosophy* 16 (1991): 280–301.

Carpenter, Christopher S., and Samuel T. Eppink. "Does it get better? Recent estimates of sexual orientation and earnings in the United States". *Southern Economic Journal* 84, no. 2 (2017): 426–441.

Cherry, Myisha. "The errors and limitations of our 'anger-evaluating' ways". In *The Moral Psychology of Anger*, edited by Myisha Cherry & Owen Flanagan (Rowman & Littlefield, 2018), 49–65.

Cogley, Zac. "A study of virtuous and vicious anger". In *Virtues and Their Vices*, edited by Kevin Timpe & Craig A. Boyd (Oxford University Press, 2014), 199–224.

Cohen, Gerald Allan. *Rescuing Justice and Equality* (Harvard University Press, 2008).

Cohen, Joshua. "Taking people as they are?" *Philosophy & Public Affairs* 30, no. 4 (2001): 363–386.

Collectif. "Nous défendons une liberté". *Le Monde* (2018, January 9). Retrieved from https://www.lemonde.fr/idees/article/2018/01/09/nous-defendons-une-liberte-d-imp ortuner-indispensable-a-la-liberte-sexuelle_5239134_3232.html.

Collini, Stefan. *That's Offensive!: Criticism, Identity, Respect* (Seagull Books, 2010).

Collins, Patricia Hill. "Learning from the outsider within: The sociological significance of Black feminist thought". *Social Problems* 33, no. 6 (1986): 14–32.

Culpeper, Jonathan. "Reflections on impoliteness, relational work and power". In *Impoliteness in Language: Studies on Its Interplay with Power in Theory and Practice*, edited by Derek Bousfield & Miriam A. Locher (Mouton de Gruyter, 2008), 17–44.

Culpeper, Jonathan. *Impoliteness: Using Language To Cause Offence* (Vol. 28) (Cambridge University Press, 2011).

Cunningham, Stewart, Teela Sanders, Lucy Platt, Pippa Grenfell, and P. G. Macioti. "Sex work and occupational homicide: Analysis of a UK murder database". *Homicide Studies* 22, no. 3 (2018): 321–338.

Cuomo, Chris J. "Climate change, vulnerability, and responsibility". *Hypatia* 26, no. 4 (2011): 690–714.

Cureton, Adam. "Offensive beneficence". *Journal of the American Philosophical Association* 2, no. 1 (2016): 74–90.

Cureton, Adam. "The limiting role of respect". In *The Oxford Handbook of Philosophy and Disability*, edited by Adam Cureton & David Wasserman (Oxford University Press, 2020), ch. 22, 390–398.

D'Arms, Justin, and Daniel Jacobson. "The moralistic fallacy: On the 'appropriateness' of emotions". *Philosophy and Phenomenological Research* 61, no. 1 (2000): 65–90.

Dawkins, R. [@RichardDawkins] (2013, August 8). "All the world's Muslims have fewer Nobel Prizes than Trinity College, Cambridge. They did great things in the Middle Ages, though." [Tweet]. Retrieved from https://twitter.com/richarddawkins/status/365 473573768400896?lang=en.

D'Errico, Francesca, and Isabella Poggi. "The lexicon of feeling offended". In *Symposium on Emotion Modelling and Detection in Social Media and Online Interaction*, (2018): 9–15. Retrieved from https://www.researchgate.net/publication/326096901_ The_lexicon_of_feeling_offended.

Desmond, Matthew, Andrew V. Papachristos, and David S. Kirk. "Police violence and citizen crime reporting in the black community". *American Sociological Review* 81, no. 5 (2016): 857–876.

De Sousa, Ronald. *The Rationality of Emotion* (MIT Press, 1990).

Devereaux, Mary. "Beauty and evil: The case of Leni Riefenstahl". In *Aesthetics*, edited by *David Goldblatt, Lee B. Brown & Stephanie Patridge* (Routledge, 2017), 125–129.

Doris, John M. *Lack of Character: Personality and Moral Behavior* (Cambridge University Press, 2002).

Dotson, Kristie. "Tracking epistemic violence, tracking practices of silencing". *Hypatia* 26, no. 2 (2011): 236–257.

Driver, Julia. *Uneasy Virtue* (Cambridge University Press, 2001).

Drucker, Ari, Ofer Fein, Dafna Bergerbest, and Rachel Giora. "On sarcasm, social awareness, and gender". *Humor* 27, no. 4 (2014): 551–573.

Dubreuil, Benoît. "Punitive emotions and norm violations". *Philosophical Explorations* 13, no. 1 (2010): 35–50.

Duff, R. Antony. "Penal communications: recent work in the philosophy of punishment". *Crime and Justice* 20 (1996): 1–97.

Dworkin, Ronald. "What is equality? Part 2: Equality of resources". *Philosophy & Public Affairs*, 10, no. 4, (1981): 283–345.

Dynel, Marta. "No aggression, only teasing: The pragmatics of teasing and banter". *Lodz papers in pragmatics* 4, no. 2 (2008): 241–261.

Elford, Gideon. "Equality of status and distributive equality". *The Journal of Value Inquiry* 46, no. 3 (2012): 353–367.

Elford, Gideon. "Survey article: relational equality and distribution". *Journal of Political Philosophy* 25, no. 4 (2017): 80–99.

Fatima, Saba. "On the edge of knowing: Microaggression and epistemic uncertainty as a woman of color". In *Surviving Sexism in Academia*, edited by Kirsti Cole & Holly Hassel (Routledge, 2017), 147–154.

Fehr, Ernst, and Urs Fischbacher. "Third-party punishment and social norms". *Evolution and Human Behavior* 25, no. 2 (2004): 63–87.

Fehr, Ernst, and Urs Fischbacher. "Social norms and human cooperation". *Trends in Cognitive Sciences* 8, no. 4 (2004): 185–190.

Feinberg, Joel. *The Moral Limits of the Criminal Law. Vol. 2, Offense to Others* (Oxford University Press, 1985).

Fernandez, Colin. "Female academic whose accusation of sexism cost Nobel laureate Sir Tim Hunt his job claims she has been 'bundled out' of her university post". *Daily Mail.* (2016, December 6). Retrieved from https://www.dailymail.co.uk/news/article-4003 774/Academic-accusation-sexism-cost-Nobel-knight-job-claims-bundled-leaving-university-post.html.

Files, Julia A., Anita P. Mayer, Marcia G. Ko, Patricia Friedrich, Marjorie Jenkins, Michael J. Bryan, Suneela Vegunta, et al. "Speaker introductions at internal medicine grand rounds: forms of address reveal gender bias". *Journal of Women's Health* 26, no. 5 (2017): 413–419.

Filipovic, Jill. "Sexism in the workplace is alive and well: Adria Richards is its latest victim". *The Guardian* (2013, March 26). Retrieved from https://www.theguardian.com/commentisfree/2013/mar/26/adria-richards-gets-rape-threats-for-speaking-out-about-workplace-sexism.

Fischer, Clara. "Feminist philosophy, pragmatism, and the "turn to affect": A genealogical critique". *Hypatia* 31, no. 4 (2016): 810–826.

Foot, Philippa. "Morality as a system of hypothetical imperatives". *The Philosophical Review* 81, no. 3 (1972): 305–316.

Foot, Philippa. *Virtues and Vices and Other Essays in Moral Philosophy* (Oxford University Press, 2002 [1978]).

Ford, Thomas E., and Mark A. Ferguson. "Social consequences of disparagement humor: A prejudiced norm theory". *Personality and Social Psychology Review* 8, no. 1 (2004): 79–94.

Fourie, Carina. "What is social equality? An analysis of status equality as a strongly egalitarian ideal". *Res Publica* 18, no. 2 (2012): 107–126.

Fourie, Carina, Fabian Schuppert, & Ivo Wallimann-Helmer. "The nature and distinctiveness of social equality: An introduction". In *Social Equality: On What it Means to Be Equals*, edited by Carina Fourie, Fabian Schuppert, & Ivo Wallimann-Helmer (Oxford University Press 2015), 1–17.

Fox, Claire. "Generation Snowflake: How we train our kids to be censorious cry-babies". *The Spectator* (2016, June 4). Retrieved from https://www.spectator.co.uk/2016/06/generation-snowflake-how-we-train-our-kids-to-be-censorious-cry-babies/.

Fox, Claire. *'I Find That Offensive!'* (Biteback Publishing, 2016).

Freud, Sigmund. *Jokes and their Relation to the Unconscious (Der Witz und seine Beziehung zum Unbewußten)*. Translated by James Strachey (Penguin [1905] 1974).

Friedlaender, Christina. "On microaggressions: Cumulative harm and individual responsibility". *Hypatia* 33, no. 1 (2018): 5–21.

Fricker, Miranda. "Reason and emotion". *Radical Philosophy* 57 (Spring) (1991): 14–19.

Fricker, Miranda. *Epistemic Injustice: Power and the Ethics of Knowing* (Oxford University Press, 2007).

Frye, Marilyn. *The Politics of Reality: Essays in Feminist Theory* (Crossing Press 1983).

Gadsby, Hannah. *Hannah Gadsby: Nanette.* Recording of the Sydney Opera House performance. Available on Netflix (11 June 2018) https://www.netflix.com/title/80233611.

Galeotti, Anna Elisabetta. *Toleration as Recognition* (Cambridge University Press, 2002).

Galston, William A. *Liberal Purposes: Goods, Virtues, and Diversity in the Liberal State.* (Cambridge University Press, 1991).

Galston, William A. "Pluralism and civic virtue". *Social Theory and Practice*, 33, no. 4, (2007): 625–635.

Gaut, Berys Nigel. "Just joking: The ethics and aesthetics of humor". *Philosophy and Literature* 22, no. 1 (1998): 51–68.

Gervais, Ricky. [@rickygervais] (2017, March 30). "Offence often occurs when people mistake the subject of a joke with the actual target. They're not always the same." [Tweet]. Retrieved from https://twitter.com/rickygervais/status/847398023680245760.

Goffman, Erving. *International Ritual: Essays on Face-to-face Behavior* (New York: Double Day Anchor Books, 1967).

Goldie, Peter. "Emotion". *Philosophy Compass* 2, no. 6 (2007): 928–938.

Grice, Herbert P. "Logic and conversation". In *Speech Acts* (Brill, 1975), 41–58.

Haidt, Jonathan. "The moral emotions". In *Handbook of Affective Sciences*, edited by Richard J. Davidson, Klaus R. Scherer, & H. Hill Goldsmith (Oxford University Press, 2003), 852–870.

Haidt, Jonathan. "The unwisest idea on campus: Commentary on Lilienfeld". *Perspectives on Psychological Science* 12, no. 1 (2017): 176–177.

Harman, Gilbert. "Moral philosophy meets social psychology: Virtue ethics and the fundamental attribution error". *Proceedings of the Aristotelian Society* 99 (1999): 315–331.

Hart, Herbert L. "The presidential address: Prolegomenon to the principles of punishment". *Proceedings of the Aristotelian Society* 60 (1959): 1–26.

Haugaard, Mark, and Philip Pettit. "A conversation on power and republicanism: An exchange between Mark Haugaard and Philip Pettit". *Journal of Political Power* 10, no. 1 (2017): 25–39.

Haugh, Michael. "Impoliteness and taking offence in initial interactions". *Journal of Pragmatics* 86 (2015): 36–42.

Hechter, Michael, and Karl-Dieter Opp. *Social Norms* (Russell Sage Foundation, 2001).

Hickey, Kate. "Australian bricklayer employment ad says "No Irish" need apply". *Irish Central* (2012, March 13). Retrieved from https://www.irishcentral.com/news/austral ian-bricklayer-employment-ad-says-no-irish-need-apply-142442405-237434871.

Holroyd, Jules. "Responsibility for implicit bias". *Journal of Social Philosophy* 43 (2012): 274–306.

Hom, Christopher. "Pejoratives". *Philosophy Compass* 5, no. 2, (2010): 164–185.

Hom, Christopher. "A puzzle about pejoratives". *Philosophical Studies* 159 (2012): 383–405.

Hopfensitz, Astrid, and Ernesto Reuben. "The importance of emotions for the effectiveness of social punishment". *The Economic Journal* 119, no. 540 (2009): 1534–1559.

Howard, Jeffrey W. "Free speech and hate speech". *Annual Review of Political Science* 22, (2019): 93–109.

Hume, David. *A Dissertation on the Passions* (Oxford University Press, 1978 [1740]).

Jacobson, Daniel. "In praise of immoral art". *Philosophical Topics* 25, no. 1 (1997): 155–199.

Jaggar, Alison M. 2004 [1983]. "Feminist politics and epistemology: The standpoint of women". In *The Feminist Standpoint Theory Reader: Intellectual and political controversies*, edited by Sandra G. Harding (Psychology Press, 2004), 55–66.

Jeffries, Stuart. "Is standup comedy doomed? The future of funny post-Kevin Hard, Louis CK and Nanette". *The Guardian* (2019, January 19). Retrieved from https://www.theg uardian.com/culture/2019/jan/19/is-standup-comedy-doomed-future-of-funny-kevin-hart-louis-ck-nanette.

Jewkes, Rachel. "Intimate partner violence: Causes and prevention". *The Lancet* 359, no. 9315 (2002): 1423–1429.

Jillette, Penn & Provenza, Paul (Directors). *The Aristocrats* [Motion Picture]. Mighty Cheese Productions, Think Film Inc (2005).

"Jon Snow: Ofcom investigates 'white people' remark at Brexit rally". *BBC News* (2019, April 8). Retrieved from https://www.bbc.co.uk/news/uk-47856058.

Johnson, A. Michael. "The 'only joking' defense: Attribution bias or impression management?" *Psychological Reports* 67, no. 3 (1990): 1051–1056

Jones, Peter. "Toleration, recognition and identity". *Journal of Political Philosophy* 14, no.2, (2006): 123–143.

Jones, Trina, and Kimberly Jade Norwood. "Aggressive encounters & white fragility: Deconstructing the trope of the angry black woman". *Iowa L. Rev.* 102 (2016): 2017–2070.

Jost, John T., Laurie A. Rudman, Irene V. Blair, Dana R. Carney, Nilanjana Dasgupta, Jack Glaser, and Curtis D. Hardin. "The existence of implicit bias is beyond reasonable doubt: A refutation of ideological and methodological objections and executive summary of ten studies that no manager should ignore". *Research in Organizational Behavior* 29 (2009): 39–69.

Kahan, Dan M. "What's really wrong with shaming sanctions". *Texas Law Review* 84, no. 7 (2006): 2075–2096.

Kant, Immanuel. *Observations on the Feeling of the Beautiful and the Sublime*. Trans. John T. Goldthwait (University of California Press, 1960 [1764]).

Kasper, Gabriele. "Linguistic politeness: Current research issues". *Journal of Pragmatics* 14, no. 2 (1990): 193–218.

Kenny, Kevin. "Race, violence, and anti-Irish sentiment in the nineteenth century". In *Making the Irish American: History and heritage of the Irish in the United States*, edited by J.J. Lee & Marion Casey (NYU Press, 2007): 364–378.

Kristjansson, Kristjan. "Can we teach justified anger?" *Journal of Philosophy of Education* 39, no. 4 (2005): 671–689.

Kymlicka, Will, and Wayne Norman. "Return of the citizen: A survey of recent work on citizenship theory". *Ethics* 104, no. 2 (1994): 352–381.

Langton, Rae. "Blocking as counter-speech". In *New Work on Speech Acts*, edited by Daniel Fogal, Daniel W. Harris, Matt Moss (Oxford University Press, 2018), pp.144–164.

Lederman, Leandra. "The interplay between norms and enforcement in tax compliance". *Ohio St. LJ* 64 (2003): 1453–1514.

Lee, Cynthia. *Murder and the Reasonable Man: Passion and Fear in the Criminal Courtroom* (NYU Press, 2003).

Lepoutre, Maxime. "Hate speech in public discourse: A pessimistic defense of counterspeech". *Social Theory and Practice* 43, no. 4 (2017): 851–883.

Lessig, Lawrence. "Social meaning and social norms". *University of Pennsylvania Law Review* 144, no.5 (1996): 2181–2189.

Lewis, Michael. "The self in self-conscious emotions". In *Annals of the New York Academy of Sciences: Vol. 818. The Self Across Psychology: Self-Recognition, Self-Awareness, and the Self Concept*, edited by Joan Gay Snodgrass and Robert L. Thompson (New York Academy of Sciences, 1997), 119–142.

Lillehammer, Hallvard. "Who is my neighbour? Understanding indifference as a vice". *Philosophy* 89, no.4, (2014): 559–579.

Lippert-Rasmussen, Kasper. *Luck Egalitarianism* (Bloomsbury Publishing, 2015).

Lippert-Rasmussen, Kasper. *Relational Egalitarianism: Living as Equals* (Cambridge University Press, 2018).

Locher, Miriam A., and Richard J. Watts. "Politeness theory and relational work". *Journal of Politeness Research. Language, Behaviour, Culture* 11, no. 1 (2005): 9–33.

Locher, Miriam A., and Richard J. Watts. "Relational work and impoliteness: Negotiating norms of linguistic behavior". In *Impoliteness in Language. Studies on its Interplay with Power in Theory and Practice*, edited by D. Bousfield & Miriam A. Locher (Berlin: Mouton de Gruyter, 2008), 77–99.

Locher, Miriam. A. (2011). "Situated impoliteness: The interface between relational work and identity construction". In *Situated Politeness* edited by Bethan L. Davies, Michael Haugh, and Andrew John Merrison (Bloomsbury, 2011), 187–208.

Lockyer, Sharon, and Michael Pickering. "You must be joking: The sociological critique of humour and comic media". *Sociology Compass* 2, no. 3 (2008): 808–820.

"London Bus Attack: Teens admit to threatening women who refused to kiss". *BBC News*. (2019, November 28). Retrieved from https://www.bbc.co.uk/news/uk-england-london-50586498.

Lorde, Audre. "The uses of anger". *Women's Studies Quarterly* 25, no. 1/2 (1997 [1981]): 278–285.

Lukianoff, Greg, and Jonathan Haidt. "The coddling of the American mind". *The Atlantic*, September Issue 2015. Retrieved from http://www.theatlantic.com/magazine/archive/2015/09/the-coddling-of-the-american-mind/399356/.

Lukianoff, Greg, and Jonathan Haidt. *The Coddling of the American Mind: How Good Intentions and Bad Ideas Are Setting Up a Generation for Failure* (Penguin Books, 2019).

Marmot, Michael, and Richard Wilkinson (Eds.). *Social Determinants of Health* (Oxford University Press, 2005).

Manne, Kate. *Down Girl: The Logic of Misogyny* (Oxford University Press, 2017).

McGraw, A. Peter, and Caleb Warren. "Benign violations: Making immoral behavior funny". *Psychological science* 21, no. 8 (2010): 1141–1149.

McGraw, A. Peter, Caleb Warren, Lawrence E. Williams, and Bridget Leonard. "Too close for comfort, or too far to care? Finding humor in distant tragedies and close mishaps". *Psychological Science* 23, no. 10 (2012): 1215–1223.

McKie, Robin. "Tim Hunt and Mary Collins: 'We're not being chased out of the country. Our new life's an adventure.'" *The Guardian* (2015, December 19). Retrieved from https://www.theguardian.com/uk-news/2015/dec/19/tim-hunt-mary-collins-weve-not-been-chased-out-of-the-country.

McTernan, Emily. "The inegalitarian ethos: Incentives, respect, and self-respect". *Politics, Philosophy & Economics* 12, no. 1 (2013): 93–111.

McTernan, Emily. "How to make citizens behave: Social psychology, liberal virtues, and social norms". *Journal of Political Philosophy* 22, no.1 (2014): 84–104.

McTernan, Emily. "Microaggressions, equality, and social practices". *Journal of Political Philosophy* 26, no. 3 (2018): 261–281.

McTernan, Emily. "Moral character, liberal states and civic education". In *The Oxford Handbook of Moral Psychology*, edited by John Doris & Manuel Vargas (Oxford University Press, 2022), 863–876.

McWhorter, John. "Our oppressive moment". *Quilette*. (2020, July 29). Retrieved from https://quillette.com/2020/07/29/our-oppressive-moment/.

Medina, José. *The Epistemology of Resistance: Gender and Racial Oppression, Epistemic Injustice, and the Social Imagination* (Oxford University Press, 2013).

Meikle, James. "Richard Dawkins criticised for Twitter comment about Muslims". *The Guardian* (2013, August 8). Retrieved from https://www.theguardian.com/science/2013/aug/08/richard-dawkins-twitter-row-muslims-cambridge.

Mill, John Stuart. *On Liberty and Utilitarianism* (Penguin Classics 2006 [1859]).

Miller, Christian. "Social psychology and virtue ethics". *The Journal of Ethics* 7, no.4, (2003): 365–392.

Miller, David. "Complex equality". In *Pluralism, Justice, and Equality*, edited by David Miller & Michael Walzer (Oxford University Press 1995), 197–225.

Miller, David. "Equality and justice". *Ratio* 10, no. 3 (1997): 222–237.

Mills, Charles. "White ignorance". In *Race and Epistemologies of Ignorance*, edited by Shannon Sullivan & Nancy Tuana (SUNY Press, 2007), 11–38.

Morreall, J. "Philosophy of Humor". In *The Stanford Encyclopedia of Philosophy* (Winter 2016 Edition). Retrieved from https://plato.stanford.edu/archives/win2016/entries/humor.

Murphy, James Bernard. "From Aristotle to Hobbes: William Galston on civic virtue". *Social Theory and Practice* 33, no. 4 (2007): 637–644.

Murphy, Jeffrie G. "Forgiveness and resentment". *Midwest Studies in Philosophy* 7 (1982): 503–516

Nadal, Kevin L., Marie-Anne Issa, Jayleen Leon, Vanessa Meterko, Michelle Wideman, and Yinglee Wong. "Sexual orientation microaggressions: 'Death by a thousand cuts' for lesbian, gay, and bisexual youth". *Journal of LGBT Youth* 8, no. 3 (2011): 234–259.

Nadal, Kevin L., Katie E. Griffin, Yinglee Wong, Sahran Hamit, and Morgan Rasmus. "The impact of racial microaggressions on mental health: Counseling implications for clients of color". *Journal of Counseling & Development* 92, no. 1 (2014): 57–66.

Newsbeat. "Comedian refused to sign 'behavioural agreement' before gig". *BBC News*. (2018, December 12). Available at https://www.bbc.co.uk/news/newsbeat-46541002.

Niker, Fay. "Policy-led virtue cultivation: Can we nudge citizens towards developing virtues?" In *The Theory and Practice of Virtue Education*, edited by Tom Harrison & David Ian Walker (Routledge, 2018), 153–167.

Nordmarken, Sonny. "Microaggressions". *TSQ: Transgender Studies Quarterly* 1, no. 1–2 (2014): 129–134.

Nussbaum, Martha C., *Anger and Forgiveness: Resentment, Generosity, Justice* (Oxford University Press, 2016).

Nussbaum, Martha C. *Hiding from Humanity: Disgust, Shame, and the Law* (Princeton University Press, 2009).

Olberding, Amy. "Subclinical bias, manners, and moral harm". *Hypatia* 29, no. 2 (2014): 287–302.

Olberding, Amy. "Etiquette: A Confucian contribution to moral philosophy". *Ethics* 126, no. 2 (2016): 422–446.

Olberding, Amy. "The moral gravity of mere trifles". In *The Forum*, London School of Economics and Political Science (2017). Available at http://eprints.lse.ac.uk/80914/.

Olberding, Amy. *The Wrong of Rudeness: Learning Modern Civility from Ancient Chinese Philosophy* (Oxford University Press, 2019).

Olin, Lauren. "Questions for a theory of humor". *Philosophy Compass* 11, no. 6 (2016): 338–350.

Oliver, Melvin, and Thomas Shapiro. *Black Wealth/White Wealth: A new perspective on racial inequality* (Routledge, 2013).

O'Neill, Martin. "Liberty, equality and property-owning democracy". *Journal of Social Philosophy* 40, (2009): 379–396.

Pansardi, Pamela. "Power to and power over: Two distinct concepts of power?" *Journal of Political Power* 5, no. 1 (2012): 73–89.

Pérez Huber, Lindsay, and Daniel G. Solorzano. "Visualizing everyday racism: Critical race theory, visual microaggressions, and the historical image of Mexican banditry". *Qualitative Inquiry* 21, no. 3 (2015): 223–238.

Pérez Huber, Lindsay, and Daniel G. Solorzano. "Racial microaggressions as a tool for critical race research". *Race Ethnicity and Education* 18, no. 3 (2015): 297–320.

Pettigrove, Glen. "Meekness and 'moral' anger". *Ethics* 122, no. 2 (2012): 341–370.

Pettit, Philip. *Republicanism: A Theory of Freedom and Government* (Oxford University Press, 1997).

Pickett, Kate E., and Richard G. Wilkinson. "Income inequality and health: a causal review". *Social Science & Medicine* 128 (2015): 316–326.

Pierce, Chester. "Stress analogs of racism and sexism: Terrorism, torture, and disaster". In *Mental Health, Racism and Sexism* edited by Charles V. Willie, Patricia Perri Rieker, Bernard M. Kramer, Bertram S. Brown (University of Pittsburgh Press, 1995), 277–293.

Poggi, Isabella, and Francesca D'Errico. "Feeling offended: A blow to our image and our social relationships". *Frontiers in Psychology* 8 (2018): 1–16.

Popa-Wyatt, Mihaela, and Jeremy L. Wyatt. "Slurs, roles and power". *Philosophical Studies* 175, no. 11 (2018): 2879–2906.

Preda, Adina, & Voigt, Kristin. "Shameless luck egalitarians". *Journal of Social Philosophy* (2022): 1–18.

Prinz, Jesse J., and Shaun Nichols. "Moral emotions". In *The Moral Psychology Handbook* edited by John Doris & the Moral Psychology Research Group (Oxford University Press, 2010), 111–146.

Qi, Xiaoying. "Face: A Chinese concept in a global sociology". *Journal of Sociology* 47, no. 3 (2011): 279–295.

Rawls, John. *A Theory of Justice* (Harvard University Press, 1971).

Rawls, John. "The idea of public reason revisited". *The University of Chicago Law Review* 64, no. 3 (1997): 765–807.

Richard, Mark. *When Truth Gives Out* (Oxford University Press, 2008).

Rini, Regina. "Fake news and partisan epistemology". *Kennedy Institute of Ethics Journal* 27, no. 2 (2017): 43–64.

Rini, Regina. "How to take offense: Responding to microaggression". *Journal of the American Philosophical Association* 4, no. 3 (2018): 332–351.

Rini, Regina. *The Ethics of Microaggression* (Routledge, 2020).

Ronson, Jon. *So You've Been Publicly Shamed* (Riverhead Books, 2016).

Royzman, Edward, Pavel Atanasov, Justin F. Landy, Amanda Parks, and Andrew Gepty. "CAD or MAD? Anger (not disgust) as the predominant response to pathogen-free violations of the divinity code". *Emotion* 14, no. 5 (2014): 892–907.

Rozin, Paul, Laura Lowery, Sumio Imada, and Jonathan Haidt. "The CAD triad hypothesis: a mapping between three moral emotions (contempt, anger, disgust) and three moral codes (community, autonomy, divinity)". *Journal of Personality and Social Psychology* 76, no. 4 (1999): 574–586.

Runciman, Walter Garrison. "'Social' equality". *The Philosophical Quarterly* 17, no. 68 (1967): 221–230.

Saul, Jennifer. "Ranking exercises in philosophy and implicit bias". *Journal of Social Philosophy* 43, no. 3 (2012): 256–273.

Scanlon, Thomas M. *Moral Dimensions: Permissibility, Meaning, Blame* (Harvard University Press, 2008).

Schauer, Frederick F. *Free Speech: A Philosophical Inquiry* (Cambridge University Press, 1982).

Scheffler, Samuel. "What is egalitarianism?" *Philosophy & Public Affairs* 31, no. 1 (2003): 5–39.

Scheffler, Samuel. "The practice of equality". In *Social Equality: On What it Means to Be Equals*, edited by Carina Fourie, Fabian Schuppert, & Ivo Wallimann-Helmer, (Oxford University Press, 2015), 21–44.

Schemmel, Christian. "Why relational egalitarians should care about distributions". *Social Theory and Practice* 37, no. 3 (2011): 365–390.

Schlenker, Philippe. "Expressive presuppositions". *Theoretical Linguistics* 33, no. 2 (2007): 237–245.

Schuppert, Fabian. "Non-domination, non-alienation and social equality: towards a republican understanding of equality". *Critical Review of International Social and Political Philosophy* 18, no. 4 (2015): 440–455.

Schuppert, Fabian. "On the range of social egalitarian justice". (Unpublished, 2017).

Scruton, Roger, and Peter Jones. "Laughter". *Proceedings of the Aristotelian Society, Supplementary Volumes* 56 (1982): 197–228.

Shand, John. "Taking offence". *Analysis* 70, no. 4 (2010): 703–706.

Sharpe, Robert A. "Seven reasons why amusement is an emotion". *Journal of Value Inquiry* 9, no. 3 (1975): 201–203.

Shoemaker, David, and Manuel Vargas. "Moral torch fishing: A signaling theory of blame". *Noûs* 55, no. 3 (2021): 581–602.

Sher, George. "Debate: Taking offense". *Journal of Political Philosophy* 28, no. 3 (2020): 332–342.

Silvermint, Daniel. "Resistance and well-being". *Journal of Political Philosophy* 21, no. 4 (2013): 405–425.

Simpson, Robert. "Regulating offense, nurturing offense". *Politics, Philosophy & Economics* 17, no. 3 (2018): 235–256.

Smith, Angela. (2013). "Moral blame and moral protest". In *Blame: Its Nature and Norms* edited by Justin D. Coates and Neal A. Tognazzini (Oxford University Press, 2013), 27–48.

Smuts, Aaron. "The ethics of humor: Can your sense of humor be wrong?" *Ethical Theory and Moral Practice* 13, no. 3 (2010): 333–347.

Solnit, Rebecca. *Men Explain Things to Me* (Haymarket Books, 2014).

Spelman, Elizabeth V. "Anger and insubordination". In *Women, Knowledge, and Reality: Explorations in Feminist Philosophy,* edited by Ann Garry and Marilyn Pearsal (Unwin Hyman, 1989), 263–273.

Spencer, Steven J., Claude M. Steele, and Diane M. Quinn. "Stereotype threat and women's math performance". *Journal of Experimental Social Psychology* 35, no. 1 (1999): 4–28.

Srinivasan, Amia. "The aptness of anger". *Journal of Political Philosophy* 26, no. 2 (2018): 123–144.

Stalnaker, Robert. "Common ground". *Linguistics and Philosophy* 25, no. 5/6 (2002): 701–721.

Statman, Daniel. "Modesty, pride and realistic self-assessment". *The Philosophical Quarterly* 42, no. 169 (1992): 420–438.

Staufenberg, Jess. "US university accused of cultural appropriation over 'undercooked' sushi rice". *The Independent* (2015, December 21). Retrieved from https://www.inde pendent.co.uk/news/world/americas/us-university-accused-of-cultural-appropriat ion-over-undercooked-sushi-a6781821.html.

Steele, Claude M., and Joshua Aronson. "Stereotype threat and the intellectual test performance of African Americans". *Journal of Personality and Social Psychology* 69, no. 5 (1995): 797–811.

Steinpreis, Rhea E., Katie A. Anders, and Dawn Ritzke. "The impact of gender on the review of the curricula vitae of job applicants and tenure candidates: A national empirical study". *Sex Roles* 41, no. 7 (1999): 509–528.

Stone, Jeff, and Chad McWhinnie. "Evidence that blatant versus subtle stereotype threat cues impact performance through dual processes". *Journal of Experimental Social Psychology* 44, no. 2 (2008): 445–452.

Strawson, Peter Frederick. *Freedom and Resentment, and Other Essays* (Routledge, 2008).

St Louis, Connie. [@connie_stlouis] (2015, June 8). "Nobel scientist Tim Hunt FRS @ royalsociety says at Korean women lunch 'I'm a chauvinist and keep "girls" single lab' ". [Tweet]. https://twitter.com/connie_stlouis/status/607813783075954688.

Sue, Derald Wing, Christina M. Capodilupo, Gina C. Torino, Jennifer M. Bucceri, Aisha Holder, Kevin L. Nadal, and Marta Esquilin. "Racial microaggressions in everyday life: Implications for clinical practice". *American Psychologist* 62, no. 4 (2007): 271–286.

Sue, Derald Wing. *Microaggressions in Everyday Life: Race, Gender, and Sexual Orientation* (John Wiley & Sons, 2010).

Sue, Derald Wing. "Microaggressions and 'evidence' empirical or experiential reality?" *Perspectives on Psychological Science* 12, no. 1 (2017): 170–172.

Sunstein, Cass R. "Social norms and social roles". *Columbia Law Review* 96, no. 4 (1996): 903–968.

Tagg, Caroline, Philip Seargent, and Amy Aisha Brown. *Taking Offence on Social Media* (Palgrave Macmillan, 2017).

Tayebi, Tahmineh. "Why do people take offence? Exploring the underlying expectations". *Journal of Pragmatics* 101 (2016): 1–17.

Taylor, Gabriele. *Pride, Shame, and Guilt: Emotions of Self-Assessment* (Oxford University Press, 1985).

Terry, Deborah J., and Michael A. Hogg. "Group norms and the attitude-behavior relationship: A role for group identification". *Personality and Social Psychology Bulletin* 22, no. 8 (1996): 776–793.

Tessman, Lisa. *Burdened Virtues: Virtue Ethics for Liberatory Struggles* (Oxford University Press, 2005).

Tosi, Justin, and Brandon Warmke. "Moral grandstanding". *Philosophy & Public Affairs* 44, no. 3 (2016): 197–217.

Tschaepe, Mark. "Addressing microaggressions and epistemic injustice: Flourishing from the work of Audre Lorde". *Essays in the Philosophy of Humanism*, 24, no. 1 (2016): 87–101.

Turner, Camilla, "Students must learn to disagree in order to beat 'cancel culture', says Vice-Chancellor". *The Telegraph* (2021, 25 April). Retrieved from https://www.telegr aph.co.uk/news/2021/04/25/students-must-learn-disagree-beat-cancel-culture-saysv ice-chancellor/.

Van Zuylen-Wood, S. " 'Men are scum': Inside Facebook's war on hate speech". *Vanity Fair* (2019, February 26). Retrieved from https://www.vanityfair.com/news/2019/02/men-are-scum-inside-facebook-war-on-hate-speech

Veatch, Thomas C. "A theory of humor". *Humor: International Journal of Humor Research* 11, no. 2 (1998): 161–215.

Viki, G. Tendayi, Manuela Thomae, Amy Cullen, and Hannah Fernandez. "The effect of sexist humor and type of rape on men's self-reported rape proclivity and victim blame". *Current Research in Social Psychology* 13, no. 10 (2007): 122–132.

Wagner, Eve H. Lewin. "Heckling: A protected right or disorderly conduct?" *Southern California Law Review* 60, no. 1 (1986): 215–238.

Waldron, Jeremy. *The Harm in Hate Speech* (Harvard University Press, 2012).

Waldron, Jeremy. "Heckle: To disconcert with questions, challenges, or gibes". *The Supreme Court Review* 2017, no. 1 (2018): 1–31.

Waldron, Jeremy. "Debate: Taking Offense: A Reply". *Journal of Political Philosophy* 28, no. 3, (2020): 343–352.

Walker, Margaret Urban. *Moral Repair: Reconstructing Moral Relations after Wrongdoing* (Cambridge University Press, 2006).

Walle, Alf H. "Getting picked up without being put down: Jokes and the bar rush". *Journal of the Folklore Institute* 13, no. 2 (1976): 201–217.

Warren, Caleb, and A. Peter McGraw. "Differentiating what is humorous from what is not". *Journal of Personality and Social Psychology* 110, no. 3 (2016): 407–430.

White, Patricia. "Making political anger possible: A task for civic education". *Journal of Philosophy of Education* 46, no. 1 (2012): 1–13.

Whitman, James Q. "What is wrong with inflicting shame sanctions". *Yale Law Journal* 107 (1998): 1055–1092.

Wilkinson, T.M. "Mill's *On Liberty* and social pressure". *Utilitas* 32 (2020): 219–235.

Williams, Patricia J. *Seeing a Color-Blind Future: The paradox of race* (Farrar, Straus and Giroux, 1998).

Wolf, Susan. "Blame, Italian Style". In *Reasons and Recognition: Essays on the Philosophy of T.M. Scanlon*, edited by R. Jay Wallace, Rahul Kumar, and Samuel Freeman (Oxford University Press, 2011), 332–347.

Wolff, Jonathan. "Fairness, respect, and the egalitarian ethos". *Philosophy and Public Affairs* 27 (1998): 97–122.

Wolff, Jonathan. "Fairness, respect and the egalitarian ethos revisited". *The Journal of Ethics* 14, no. 3 (2010): 335–350.

Wolff, Jonathan. (2015). "Social equality and social inequality". In *Social Equality: On What it Means to be Equals*, edited by Carina Fourie, Fabian Schuppert, and Ivo Wallimann-Helmer (Oxford University Press, 2015), 209–226.

Young, Iris Marion. *Justice and the Politics of Difference* (Princeton University Press, 1990).

Young, Iris Marion. *Responsibility for Justice* (Oxford University Press, 2011).

Index

For the benefit of digital users, indexed terms that span two pages (e.g., 52–53) may, on occasion, appear on only one of those pages.

acceptance requirement, 108–9
Anderson, Elizabeth, 22–23
anger
  introduction to, 4–7
  justified offences and, 87–92
  social norms and, 43–45, 49–51
  social standing and, 66–67, 84–85
  taking offence and, 9–10, 11–12, 19, 20–25, 26, 29–30, 34–35
antidiscriminatory norm, 164–65
Attardo, Salvatore, 124

Barrow, Robin, 132, 155, 156
Bell, Macalester, 21–22, 65, 171
belonging, 13–14, 51, 54, 66, 71, 96, 103–4, 153–54
Bergmann, Merrie, 84–85, 89–90, 117–18, 119, 128–29
blame/blaming
  civic virtue and, 149, 151–52
  humorous remarks and, 127
  introduction to, 4–5, 6–7
  justified offence, 95–100
  social standing and, 71–72
Bommarito, Nicolas, 64–65
Brennan, Geoffrey, 42–43
burdened virtues, 153
burdens on offended, 153–57
Burke, Tarana, 3
Buss, Sarah, 39–40, 41–42, 68–69, 120–21

Calhoun, Cheshire, 39–41, 68–69, 120–21
Campbell, Sue, 110–11
Carroll, Noel, 89–90, 118
causing offence, 9, 38, 94, 98, 130, 142, 143–44, 147–48
civic vice, 1, 132, 146, 156–57

civic virtue
  burdens on offended, 153–57
  civility and, 133, 134–39, 155
  cost of offence, 140–52, 159
  introduction to, 132–33
  microaggressions and, 139, 148–52
  offence as, 134–39
  punishment and, 140–41, 146–48
  social equality and, 134–39
  social inequality and, 133, 134–39, 148–49
  social standing and, 132–33, 135, 136–39, 141, 142–43, 148–49, 153–54, 155–56
  victims/victimhood and, 146
civility and civic virtue, 133, 134–39, 155
Cohen, Joshua, 136
contesting offence, 93–95
correctness requirement, 100–7
cost of offence, 56–58, 140–52, 159
Culpeper, Jonathan, 76
culture of taking offence, 3, 11, 26, 29–30, 34, 36, 37, 46–47, 48–49, 52, 53–54, 138–39, 140, 162
Cureton, Adam, 69, 102–3

Dawkins, Richard, 93
degradations, 3, 47–48, 80–81, 82–83, 90, 94, 97, 149, 153–54
deliberate slurs, 93–95, 96–98, 108
D'Errico, Francesca, 24
disagreement over offence, 46, 100–7
disrespect
  civic virtue and, 153–54, 155–56
  emotion of, 17, 18, 22–23
  introduction to, 2
  justified offence and, 97, 100–1, 102–3, 105

disrespect (*cont.*)
  online offence, 159
  social norms and, 39–40, 43–44, 51,
    53–54, 55–56
  social standing and, 68–69, 70–71, 72,
    74–75, 78
distinguishing offence, 20–25
Dotson, Kristie, 72–73

emotion of offence
  analysis of, 12–20
  distinguishing offence, 20–25
  estrangement and, 15–16, 22–23, 28–
    31, 33
  humorous remarks and, 122
  introduction to, 1–2, 5, 9–10
  limits to, 27–32
  in online offence, 160–61, 171–73
  philosophers on, 10–12
  rethinking offence, 25–26
  social interactions and, 12, 13–
    14, 18–19
  social standing and, 10–12, 22–24, 27–
    28, 29, 32–35
  victimhood and, 32–35
epistemic injustice, 66, 72–73
estrangement
  civic virtue and, 143–44, 146–48
  emotion of offence and, 15–16, 22–23,
    28–31, 33
  introduction to, 5
  justified offence and, 92
  online offence and, 158–59, 167–68
  proxy estrangement, 31
  social norms and, 38, 45
ethic of community, 22–23
everyday sexism, 46–47, 54–55, 119

face, 14–15, 17, 24–25, 73–74, 78–79, 97
Fatima, Saba, 91
Feinberg, Joel, 1–2, 5, 11, 160–61
feminism/feminist philosophy, 4–5, 6,
    34–35, 66, 82, 84–85, 107, 111, 145–
    46, 154
Foot, Philippa, 134–35, 155, 156
freedom to pester, 106–7
free speech, 142–43, 146, 162–63
Fricker, Miranda, 72–73

Friedlaender, Christina, 91, 149–50
Frye, Marilyn, 69, 109–10

gendered pronouns, 38, 41
gender jokes, 93, 94, 95, 96–98, 108
generation snowflake, 9, 62–64
Goffman, Erving, 14, 73
good faith limit, 96
group-based hierarchies, 78, 94

Haidt, Jonathan, 21–22
harassment, 52, 71–72, 82. *See also* sexual
    harassment
hate speech, 8, 160–61, 163–64
Hechter, Michael, 54
homophobia, 82, 115, 172–73
humorous remarks. *See also* jokes
  incongruity theory, 117, 122–23, 127
  introduction to, 7, 114–17
  linguistics of jokes, 123–26
  offensive jokes, 126–29
  riskiness of, 129–31
  sarcasm, 117, 118
  sexist humour, 117–18, 128–29
  taking offence, 117–23
  victims/victimhood of, 118, 127
Hunt, Tim, 114–15, 125–26

implicit bias, 96, 135–36, 149–50
incongruity theory, 117, 122–23, 127
Irish jokes, 136–37

Jim Crow laws, 90
jokes. *See also* humorous remarks
  gender jokes, 93, 94, 95, 96–98, 108
  introduction to, 7
  Irish jokes, 136–37
  Jewish jokes, 102
  as justified offence, 114–23
  linguistics of, 123–26
  offensive jokes, 126–29
  rape jokes, 90, 115, 116–17, 119, 127
  sexist jokes, 1–2, 11–12, 16–17, 26, 33,
    47, 49–50, 84–85, 89–90, 122, 128–
    29, 141–42, 144–46
justified offence
  acceptance requirement, 108–9
  anger and, 87–92

blame/blaming, 95–100
contesting offence, 93–95
deliberate slurs, 93–95, 96–98, 108
disagreement over offence, 100–7
facts *vs.* opinion, 93, 94–95,
    96–98, 108
gender jokes, 93, 94, 95, 96–98, 108
intention and, 95–100
introduction to, 6–7, 86–87
microaggressions and, 87–88, 89, 90, 91,
    94–95, 103–4, 110–13
social equality in, 105–6
social inequality in, 86, 89, 112
uptake requirement, 108–13
victims/victimhood of, 111

Kant, Immanuel, 117–18
knower status, 72–73

linguistics of jokes, 123–26
Locher, Miriam, 14, 76, 78–79
Lorde, Audre, 88

mansplaining, 13, 15–16, 22, 47–48
marginalised persons, 34–35, 73,
    79–80, 84, 87, 91, 93–94, 103–5, 110–
    13, 130, 135, 137, 159, 162
McGraw, A. Peter, 120
mental health, 3, 37
MeToo movement, 3, 46–47, 70–71
microaggressions
    civic virtues and, 139, 148–52
    justified offence and, 87–88, 89, 90, 91,
        94–95, 103–4, 110–13
    online offence and, 161
    social norms and, 36, 37, 46–48, 49–
        50, 54–55
    social standing and, 66–67, 70–71,
        80–81, 84
    target campaigns against, 3
micro-defences, 142–43, 146–47
moral commitments, 19–20
moral grandstanding, 56–57, 144–46
moral mistake, 28–29
moral violations, 22–23, 24

negative emotions, 20–21
Nussbaum, Martha, 24, 63–64, 153–54

offensive behaviour, 1, 109, 140–41, 152
offensive jokes, 3, 10n.5, 81–82, 114–15,
    126–29, 130, 166
Olberding, Amy, 39–40, 76–77
online offence
    impact of, 165–71
    introduction to, 8, 158–60
    microaggressions and, 161
    public shaming and, 162, 165–66
    regulation of, 160–65
    social emotions of, 171–73
    social equality and, 159
    social standing and, 158–61, 166,
        170, 171
Opp, Karl-Dieter, 54
ordinary slights, 1, 153–54
oversensitivity, 3, 6–7, 9, 34, 62–64, 65–66,
    82–83, 86–87, 94–95, 108, 110–11

Pierce, Chester, 47–48, 90
Poggi, Isabella, 24
political correctness, 3, 46–47, 50–51
popular opinion, 5–6, 36, 101
proxy estrangement, 31
public criticism, 1
public shaming
    civic virtue and, 140–46, 152
    emotion of offense, 29–30
    introduction to, 1–2
    online offence and, 162, 165–66
    social norms and, 43–44, 45, 51, 56–57
punishment, 140–41, 146–48
put-downs, 3

rape jokes, 90, 115, 116–17, 119, 127
relational egalitarianism. Seem also
    social equality. 5, 14n.21, 63n.4, 66–
    79, 172
religious offence, 19–20, 93, 106
rethinking offence, 25–26

sarcasm, 117, 118
Scruton, Robert, 117, 118
self-assessment, 5, 20–21, 24–25, 44
sexist/sexism
    everyday sexism, 46–47, 54–55, 119
    freedom to pester and, 107
    in humour, 117–18, 128–29

sexist/sexism (*cont.*)
  jokes, 1–2, 11–12, 16–17, 26, 33, 47, 49–50, 84–85, 89–90, 122, 128–29, 141–42, 144–46
  social standing and, 63, 80, 85
sexual assault, 64, 89–90
sexual harassment, 64, 70–71, 72–73, 106–7, 135–36
shame/shaming. *See* public shaming
shunned/shunning, 25–26, 38–39, 51, 71
slur/slurs
  deliberate slurs, 93–95, 96–98, 108
  emotion of offence, 9
  as humorous remarks, 126–27, 128
  philosophy of language on, 5, 10–12
  sexist slur, 79–80
  social norms and, 40–41
  social standing and, 79–80
Snow, Jon, 103
social equality
  civic virtue and, 133, 134–39
  in justified offence, 105–6
  online offence and, 159
  social interactions and, 3, 6
  social standing and, 65, 66–74, 77, 78–79, 83–84
social groups, 40–41, 48, 49–50, 72–73, 78, 83, 94
social inequality
  civic virtue and, 133, 134–39, 148–49
  in justified offence, 86, 89, 112
  social interactions and, 6, 7
  social norms and, 36, 45–46, 47–48, 52
  social standing and, 62–63, 77, 78, 80–81, 84–85
social interactions
  emotion of offence and, 12, 13–14, 18–19
  introduction to, 4–6
  social equality and, 3, 6
  social inequality and, 6, 7
  social standing and, 39, 42, 48–50, 53–56, 62, 65–67, 68, 75–77, 78, 79–80, 81–82
social justice, 3–4, 28–29, 48–49
social meanings, 36–37, 48, 50–51, 53, 55–56, 57, 65–66, 68, 74–75, 83, 102, 104–5, 106, 159, 167–68, 173

social norms
  anger and, 43–45, 49–51
  disrespect and, 39–40, 43–44, 51, 53–54, 55–56
  emotions and, 43–44, 49–50, 59–60
  microaggressions and, 36, 37, 46–48, 49–50, 54–55
  negotiation of, 55–61
  political correctness, 3, 46–47, 50–51
  reinforcement of, 42–46
  renegotiation of, 46–55
  social inequality and, 36, 45–46, 47–48, 52
  social standing and, 37–42
  victims/victimhood and, 36, 44
social role of offence, 6–7, 13–14, 15, 36–37, 60–61, 71, 77, 84
social sanctions, 40, 44, 108, 147–48
social standing
  anger and, 66–67, 84–85
  civic virtue and, 132–33, 135, 136–39, 141, 142–43, 148–49, 153–54, 155–56
  emotion of offence, 10–12, 22–24, 27–28, 29, 32–35
  excess and deficiency in, 63–66
  generation snowflake, 9, 62–64
  introduction to, 5–6, 36–37, 62–63
  microaggressions and, 66–67, 70–71, 80–81, 84
  online offence and, 158–61, 166, 170, 171
  respect and consideration, 44–45, 64, 67–68, 69, 77–78, 83, 137–38, 158
  significance of affronts, 79–83
  social equality and, 65, 66–74, 77, 78–79, 83–84
  social inequality and, 62–63, 77, 78, 80–81, 84–85
  social interactions and, 39, 42, 48–50, 53–56, 62, 65–67, 68, 75–77, 78, 79–80, 81–82
  social norms and, 37–52
  taking offence and, 83–85
  terms of, 74–79
social understandings, 51–52, 96, 102–4
Stone, Lindsay, 114–15, 141
Sue, Derald Wing, 90, 103–4

Taylor, Gabriele, 20–21
Tessman, Lisa, 153
testimonial smothering, 72–73
tolerance, 40, 47, 134, 137–38, 139
Tosi, Justin, 144
Trump, Donald, 31

unequal social standing, 1, 7, 37, 68, 70–
    71, 73, 80, 88, 103–4
unwarranted intrusions, 66, 70–72, 76,
    77–78, 87–88, 91, 101, 154, 155–
    56, 158
uptake requirement, 108–13

victims/victimhood
    civic virtue and, 146

emotion of offence, 32–35, 36
    of humorous remarks, 118, 127
    introduction to, 3, 4, 5–6
    of justified offence, 111
    social norms and, 36, 44

Wagner, Eve, 163
Waldron, Jeremy, 163
Walker, Margaret Urban, 54
Warmke, Brandon, 144
Warren, Caleb, 120
Watts, Richard J., 78–79
Wood, Carmita, 73
wrongful conduct, 11

Young, Iris Marion, 73, 148–49, 150–52